SUSTAINABLE DEVELOPMENT THE SPIRITUAL DIMENSION

SUSTAINABLE DEVELOPMENT
The Spiritual Dimension

KRISHAN SAIGAL

PUBLICATIONS

KALPAZ PUBLICATIONS

DELHI-110052

Sustainable Development : The Spiritual Dimension

Rs. 720

ISBN: 81-7835-672-4

Published in 2008 in India by
Kalpaz Publications
C-30, Satyawati Nagar,
Delhi-110052
E-mail: kalpaz@hotmail.com
Phone : 9212729499

Lasser Type Setting by: Rudra Computer Graphics, Delhi
Printed at : Singhal Print Media, Delhi

Contents

Preface 7

1. **Introduction** 11

2. **Sustainable Development** 25
• Growing International Disparity • Sustainable Development • Ecology, Technology and Sustainable Development • Values and Models of Sustainable Development • Conclusion

3. **The Western Paradigm** 49
• Integrating Economics and Ecology • "New" Economics: the Scientific Dimension • The Factor of Technology • The human welfare approach • Values in Economics • Conclusions

4. **Hinduism: Nature, Society and Economics** 85
• Hinduism • Hinduism and Nature • The Hindu Societal System •The Hindu Socio-economic System • Role of the State • Hindu Economics • Conclusions

5. **Buddhist Teaching, Economics and Ecology** 131
• Buddhist Teachings • Buddhism and Sustainable Development • Critique of the Buddhist Model • Conclusions

6. **Islam and Sustainable Development** **167**
• Islamic Ethics • The Quran and Ecology • Viceregency, Trusteeship, and Socio-economic • Implications

7. **Gandhi: Environment, Economics, Sustainable Development** **205**
• Gandhi and his Principles • Gandhi's Conceptual Framework • Gandhian Socio-economics • The Foundations of Gandhian Economics • Gandhian and Neoclassical Economic thought • Gandhi's Relevance Today • Policy Implications of Gandhian Thought • Critique of the Gandhian Model

8. **The Oceans, Seas and Coasts** **247**
• The Oceanic Ecosystem: the Western Perspective • Oceans: An Eastern Perspective • Ocean: Economics and Wealth • Conclusion

9. **Concluding Remarks** **271**

Bibliography **283**

Index **299**

Preface

The state of the environment has been causing international concern since the 1960s. A number of Committees were set up to suggest means of tackling the issue of environmental stress. But is was only in 1987 that the World Commission on Environment came up with the definition of sustainable development as a means of tackling the environmental problem. The definition that sustainable development meant "the ability of the present generation to meet its needs without compromising the ability of future generations to meet their needs" was vague and ambiguous enough for the international community to endorse it at the United Nations Conference on Environment and Development held in Rio de Janerio in 1992.

The decade following the articulation of the concept of sustainable development was spent in trying to concretize the concept so that it could be used in policy and decision making. While perceptions varied in the different formulations they all had at the core the need for economic development to be based on science and technology. These are discussed in Chapter 2 and the so called Western paradigm in seen to be the rubric in which all discussions take place.

The Western paradigm based on scientific, technological and economic perspectives is explored in Chapter 3. It is noted that economics is still based on the Newtonian concept of linearity and predictability and has ignored the later development of the uncertainty of Heisenberg, the fluctuations from chaos to order of Prigogine and the self-organisation of Jantsch. The latest developments in science has led to Nature being looked at in three ways: as the biosphere being in a state of steady equilibrium; as the biosphere being in constant change through fluctuations from chaos to order; and to the biosphere being an evolutionary self-regulating entity. There is thus a disconnect between economics and the post-Newtonian developments in science.

The Western paradign aspires to be objective, value-free and based on science, technology and economics. The Eastern paradigm is, in contrast, value-loaded in many ways. It also postulates that a change in human will is necessary. In Chapters 4, 5 and 6 we consider the major eastern religions of Hinduism, Buddhism and Islam and the value premises underlying them. Though there are some differences between the three religions there are many commonalities : they all stress the holistic and evolutionary nature of life; all give primacy to human beings and place them in harmonized relations with their environment, social and natural; they stress that everything on earth belongs to God; that man is a trustee and has to act according to God's will; that man has to harmonise his individual needs with that of the community; that equity has to be attained through a voluntary restraint on consumption. The communitarian aspect is obviously in complete contrast to the highly individualized concept of the west. It also needs to be noted that aspects of the eastern or spiritual paradigm are compatible with post-Newtonian science.

It is in the above context that the views of Gandhi are explored in Chapter 7. Gandhi viewed the problems of alienation and poverty, alienation in the advanced world and poverty in the non-industrialised world, as being likely to lead to violence. He developed an alternative socio-economic model based on which there would be full employment and an environment where man could attain his full potential materially, socially and spiritually. It is noted that the essence of the Gandhian system is the centrality of man both as an individual and a social being. It is his will and values that lead to harmony with Nature.

There are three planetary ecosystems: the geosphere, the atmosphere and the oceans. The oceans have been selected to see how the two paradigms. Eastern and Western, would look at them. The reason for selecting the oceans is that they are one of the last frontiers to be exploited and explored and there has in the last few decades been on intensification and diversification of the uses of the oceans. It is seen that in the Western paradigm, broadly speaking, it is the wealth of the oceans and what humanity can get from them: resources, food, energy, space that would matter. The Eastern paradigm would not only look at what can be got from the oceans but also its value-in-existence, that is, its life-giving properties. Also the Eastern paradigm would recall the injunctions in its culture of not fatally injuring the oceans.

In conclusion, it is necessary if a truly global ethic of sustainability to is to emerge for the two paradigms, Eastern and Western, to harmonise. Both are necessary as is the case with Newtonian and post-Newtonian science. The areas where both can contribute need to be delineated through a dialogue of cultures. Only thus can Huntingtons " Clash of Civilizations" be averted.

Krishan Saigal

1

Introduction

The concept of sustainable development was endorsed by all the world's leaders in the U.N. Conference on Environment and Development (UNCED) held at Rio de Janerio in Brazil in 1992. The concept as endorsed in Rio de Janerio represents the dominant paradigm as accepted by Western societies and the westernised elites of the non-Western ones. This book analyses other value systems, and how they look at Nature and sustainability, to see how they could contribute to a "truly" global ethic of sustainability.

After analysing the historical developments between 1967 and the present as figuring in the reports of Pearson, Brandt and Brundtland, and as elaborated in Agenda 21, the global workplan emerging out of UNCED, the various ways in which leaders, scholars and others have perceived sustainable development are explored in the sècond chapter. It is noted that a recurring theme in all perceptions has been the growing economic disparity between nations of the North and South and, inspite of three decades of "development", growing poverty and consequent stress on the environment.

The concepts of sustainable development are seen to vary from the simple one developed by the Brundtland Commission of 'meeting the needs of the present without compromising the future' to more complex formulations in which concepts like irreplaceability, biodiversity, carrying capacity, socioeconomic and eclogical system resilience are included. All formulations, however, have at their core the need for economic growth based on science and technology with culture, and its values, added on. Perhaps Ignacy Sachs has best captured the essence of the various formulations in a technological and economic growth, or Western, paradigm as eco-development which leads to social, economic, ecological, spatial and cultural sustainability.

The stress on technology which is perhaps, uncritically accepted in the developed countries and many in the developing ones, as the answer to the ecological problem has been sharply criticised by many. One set of critics, who believe in limits to growth, consider that the stress on technology, whether environmentally friendly or not, and to the extent that it has connotations of continuous and unlimited growth, is sending out all the wrong signals. Another set of critics see in this emphasis on technology an ostrich-like attitude which pushes the real problems of society and the environment under the carpet so that "business as usual" can be carried on.

A totally different kind of criticism of the techno-economic basis of sustainable development is that it has no globally acceptable set of values. The role of values in human activity has long been stressed by social scientists. According to them, spiritual, moral and cognitive beliefs of a culture play a crucial role in how well human societies adapt to the natural environment. Spiritual and moral ideas also motivate persons to care for the world around them. Besides ethics is necessary to define a new social paradigm which can promote sustainable development in each culture and region of the world. Only then can a new concept develop which can work out solutions on the basis of human cooperation on a global basis.

The introduction of values into the sustainable development paradigm has introduced the dimensions of identity, self-worth and ultimate meanings. This has led Kothari to stress the *holistic* nature of sustainable development, *equity* based on self-reliance, universality of *participation* in decision making - international, national, local - and placing of *value on diversity* whether of economies, cultures or societies.[1] Kothari's formulation captures the essence of what may be called the Eastern paradigm.

The Western paradigm based on scientific, technological and economic perspectives is explored in the third chapter. Three scientific schools of thought regarding Nature are delineated, namely, that which views the biosphere to be in a steady equilibrium state; that which looks at the biosphere as in perpetual change through fluctuations from chaos to order; and that which considers the biosphere as a evolutionary self-regulating entity.

The so-called "paradigm shift" in science - a profound change in the thoughts, perceptions and values that form a particular vision of reality -from the mechanistic to the relativistic, uncertain one is noted. The paradigm from which the shift is taking place has been the dominant one for several hundred years. It includes belief in the scientific method as the only valid approach to knowledge: a view of the universe as a mechanical and deterministic system; a view of life as a competitive struggle for existence; and the view that unlimited material progress can be achieved through economic and technological growth.

To those viewing the world from the perspective of the emerging relativistic-uncertainty paradigm in science, a systems view is necessary to encompass the complex reality that is the world. This being especially true when dealing with planetary ecosystems, sustainable development has to be concieved in a holistic paradigm with economics and technology being considered as one subset of the total system with values being another subset. Other subsets, inter alia, would be the diversity inherent in the different socio-cultures and religions.

The use of systems analysis has profound impacts on technology and economics. One of the outstanding characteristics of today's economies, whether underdeveloped, capitalist or communist, is an obsession with growth. To an extent this is justified because growth is an essential feature of life. But to regard all growth as good without recognizing that, in a finite environment, there has to be a dynamic balance between growth and decline is to make a mistake which has grave ecological implications. Besides growth needs to be differentiated into the necessary and that which can be obstructive, unhealthy or pathological. This would mean that the remapping of an economy is not merely an intellectual task but also involves profound changes in the value system. The idea of wealth itself, which is central to economics, is inextricably linked to human expectations, values and life styles. To define wealth within an ecological framework will mean to transcend its present connotations of material accumulation and give it the broader sense of human enrichment.

The ethic of sustainable development also requires a shared moral language in which to think and deliberate about the meaning of world order - which is itself a necessary precondition for achieving equitable and sustainable development. Each culture and religion of the world can contribute to the needed sense of global solidarity, and to the creation of the moral vocabulary required to hammer out a new concept of world order. This is explored in chapters four through seven.

Religious philosophers and ethicists have a different analysis of the moral plight of human beings from that offered by other thinkers. For the religions of the world, the moral failure of human beings to live in peace and justice with one another and the rest of creation is rooted in a deep, *spiritual failure*. The human will is alienated from the true ground of its being by the greed, lust, selfishness, and craving for pleasure and power that are the motivating powers behind the dominant materialistic world view. No amount of attention to new moral ideas of sustainable development can put the world on a sustainable development path. For the religions of the world, a change in the human will itself is necessary, a deliverance from the bondage of the human spirit. This can only be done with the help of spiritual disciplines that restore the proper relationship of human beings to the ground of being, disciplines that depend upon religious insight and faith.

It is in the above context that a study has been made of three major non-Western religions - Hinduism, Buddhism, and Islam. All the religions emphasise the holistic and evolutionary nature of life. They do not look at life through subdisciplines - economics, ecology, science, politics, management - for they consider that religion is a matter for the whole man and the full man, not for a specialised part of him. All the religions while giving primacy to human beings, place them in harmonised relationships with their environment, social and natural.

All the great scriptures of the world, the Dhammapada, the Vedas, the Quran, were written in poetic, that is a symbolic, language and it is by that alone that any real knowledge, of ultimate truth can be obtained. The language of myth and poetry, of the concrete imagination, engages the senses, the feelings, the affections and the will as well as the reason, and so leads to the transformation of the whole man.

A myth has always a threefold meaning. It has first of all a basis either in nature or in history, that is, in the phenomenal world. It has secondly a psychological meaning, an application to human experience both individual and social. Thirdly, it has a spiritual meaning, reflecting some aspect of ultimate truth or reality.

It is as a work of imaginative genius that we have approached the vedic, quranic and buddhist revelations, or in other words as a mythology. The word 'myth' today has lost its pejorative sense, and it is universally recognized that myth is the language of imaginative insight into ultimate reality, which not only reveals the truth under a symbol, but also enables those who receive the myth to participate in the experience of the poet or prophet who communicates it.

The Hindu and Buddhist myths are essentially cosmic myths and belong to the cosmic revelation. They are based on the cyclic view of time. As in nature everything goes in cycles, the sun rises and sets, the moon waxes and wanes, spring is followed by summer and autumn and winter and then returns again, so in these myths man is born and dies and is born again; 'when the righteousness declines and unrighteousness prevails' God intervenes to restore righteousness even if necessary, through destruction of society; the world comes forth from the One and returns at the dissolution only to come forth again. In contrast, the Quran deals with linear and historical time. In the quranic concept, when injustice and inequity prevail, God punishes even to the extent of wiping out communities which do not obey Divine Will and replacing them by others. Equity and justice are the essence of the Quranic message and any imbalance as between man and man and man and nature has to be corrected: by man, if he repents and realises, or by God if man takes no steps to do the right thing. Thus its prescriptions in essential matters are complementary to the Buddhist - Hindu ones, so that the three form one Asian or Eastern paradigm.

The view of the universe on which classical Western science has been built, that of matter as a solid substance extended in space and time, and of the human mind as a detached observer capable of examining and describing the universe and so gaining control over it, has now been demolished by science itself. The Newtonian model of a world of solid bodies moving in space and time has been replaced by the model of relativity and quantum physics, in which matter is seen as a form of energy and the universe as a field of energies, organized in space-time, so as to form a unified and interdependent whole.

This comes very close to the Buddhist and Hindu view of the 'insubstantiality' (*anatman, maya)* of the universe and of the dynamic character of the elements (*dharmas*) as constantly changing parts of an organized whole. But Western science has been compelled to go even beyond this and to recognize that the human mind as observer is not reality itself, but reality as conditioned by the human mind and senses and the various instruments which it uses to extend the senses. What we observe, as Heisenberg said, is not nature itself but nature exposed to our method of questioning. The old understanding of science is gradually giving way to the view that 'consciousness and physical reality (or empirical reality) should be considered as complementary aspects of reality'[2]. The correspondence of this conclusion to the Hindu-Buddhist view are obvious.

The religions studied - Buddhism, Hinduism, Islam -have many fundamentals in common. They all stress that everything on earth belongs to God; that man is a trustee and has to act according to God's will; that man has to harmonise his individual needs with those of society; that equity has to be attained through voluntary restraint in consumption. But they are also diverse. One - Islam - is a religion of the "book" (Quran) while two - Buddhism, and Islam - have a founder who is a historical person. Only Hinduism is neither historically based nor does it have a founder, thereby making it very difficult for persons brought up in other traditions to understand it. Yet in the diversity of the three religions lies their strength and there is much in them that modern humanity can draw upon in its quest for sustainability.

It is in this context that we examine the views of Gandhi in the seventh chapter. Gandhi developed a philosophy, largely drawn from the mainstream of Indian philosophic tradition, but also significantly influenced by other religious philosophies, particularly Christianity and Islam, to tackle the problems of alienation and poverty. While poverty is the most visible problem of the developing countries, alienation is the most visible problem of the developed countries. While in the Eastern religions economics was not specifically dealt with, Gandhi devoted a lot of attention to economics.

Gandhi's approach to the problems of poverty and alienation rested in his philosophy which centered around six major concepts: Truth, Nonviolence, Bread Labour, *Swadeshi*, (local production), Non-possession and *Satyagraha* (noncooperation with wrong doing). Gandhi made it very clear that none of these concepts was absolute, though man through his unceasing struggle continued to reach what he called a series of Euclidean[3] points each corresponding to these concepts. Like the Euclidean point, to Gandhi his six concepts were not attainable in the absolute sense: but they were to him the final reference points for his theory of social transformation, including the removal of poverty and alienation.

The essence of the Gandhian approach, flowing from his six "points" is the centrality of man, both as an individual and as a social being. In his system man is not alienated because of the variety of approaches that emerge from his conceptual system.

Starting with the simple imperative that economics must remain inseparable from ethics, Gandhi concentrated on man as an uncompartmentalized and integral whole. One may even say that like Marx, Gandhi believed in the total man, through Marx did not pursue his idea to its logical end. Gandhi's solutions were the following:

- centrality of productive work: Gandhi sharply differed from all economists, Marxian or non-Marxian, in respect of the theory of labour. To him, labour was not disutility as economists define it. Labour had four components: (a) as a kind of minimum physical labour which must be performed by everybody from the philosopher to the ordinary workers (and termed by him as bread labour); (b) for earning a living as is normally understood in economics; (c) as an instrument for self-actualization; and (d) as a method of service to others. Once this fourfold view of labour is accepted, no degree of division of labour can really dehumanize man;

localisation of production: to Gandhi localisation did not mean small-scale production only. Gandhi's views on the scale factor are the most misunderstood or misinterpreted. "Small is Beautiful" is a phrase coined by Westerners in the name of Gandhi. There is no such absolute hypothesis in Gandhi. But when other things are equal, small is better than big;

principle of trusteeship: Gandhi refused to accept any of the prevailing economic systems, which may be summarized as capitalist, communist, and mixed economy, since all of them produced alienation of one kind or another. He suggested in turn what he called the system of trusteeship.

Trusteeship has two aspects; its basic principles and structure; and, secondly, the method to achieve a society based upon the principle of trusteeship. Gandhi did not leave behind a model of trusteeship; he only stated the basic principles of its organization. These principles are: (a) no one has any right over property which is a social phenomenon; (b) State ownership of property leads to concentration of economic and political power in the hands of a small bureaucracy which has the monopoly of violence and hence is an antithesis of trusteeship; (c) trusteeship is by definition a communitarian system, a kind of general cooperation of efforts and resources; (d) trusteeship is a system of social self-management and a kind of socialist democracy from below; and (e) trusteeship is based on the Gandhian fourfold view of labour.

Gandhi was not a religious reformer. Nor was he a recluse or hermit living in the forest. He was deeply involved in politics, in the Indian independence struggle for freedom from British rule. Deeply religious, he applied ethical and moral principles to his concept of man and society. He was conscious of the fact that all ancient urban civilizations - Egyptian, Babylonian, Indus Valley - had ended in desertifying the area covered by them. Though he did not use the word sustainability, the future welfare of humanity, in his concept, lay in: taking from the earth enough for one's need (and not for satisfying one's "greed"); simple living and voluntary poverty; living in harmony with nature in a "village-type" of economy.

In chapter eight we look at the oceans. The ocean is one of the three planetary ecosystems, the others being the atmosphere and the geosphere. The oceans have been selected because in the past two decades there has been a "marine revolution" and a diversification and intensification of the uses of the oceans leading to the oceans playing an increasingly important role in the world.[4]

Incredibly little is known about the oceans though they are an integral, and critical, part of the planetary life processes and provide most of the species at present known to man (if we exclude insects then 65% of the presently known animal species are to be found in the oceans). When we add to that percentage the species not so far discovered, and likely to be found in the oceans in the future, the figure goes up considerably. Biological biodiversity, biological productivity, climate and radiation regulation, microbial decomposition and waste recycling are some of the important ecological services provided by the oceans.

The oceans are dynamic systems constantly stirred by vigorous geological activity, driven by the energy from the sun and from nuclear reactions taking place deep within the earth's core. This dynamism, and consideration of the Gaia thesis (according to which life drives the self-regulating mechanism on earth), requires important changes to be made to the way the oceans are viewed.

In the first place a Gaian perspective puts life at the centre of our concerns. It suggests that life has had a formative influence on the environment and that biological processes play an active, central role in ensuring that the planet remains habitable. The preservation of biodiversity, thus, assumes importance.

The second change in perspective demanded by the Gaia hypothesis is that we must consider everything on earth whether living or nonliving to be intimately interlinked with each other. It is not sufficient to consider ecosystems such as the rich salt-marsh zones, or the coral reefs and mangroves, or the open ocean as separate entities. The Gaia hypothesis makes the interconnections between these key ecosystems as important as the ecosystems themselves.

A third major shift necessary is to consider the planet as a whole and not as a mosaic of independent entities defined by human political systems.

The Gaian thesis, it is clear, is very much compatiable with the Eastern paradigm. The self-regulating system is also in line with the theory of the Hindu-Buddhist theory of *karma* and the Islamic concept of Divine punishment for deviating from the right path: pollution of the oceans in this sense does not extinguish all life in the oceans but could lead to unpleasant consequences for humanity. So it would be necessary for humanity to correct itself and take the "right" actions if they are not to get *karmic* or divine retribution.

The oceans, form a unique laboratory for testing out the concepts of sustainable development. There are a number of reasons for this. Dramatic advances in the marine sciences are changing our concept of the oceans and man's place in it. They are also bringing out the need for looking at the oceanic ecosystem in a holistic and integrated manner. Marine technology is available to generate and utilize new living, nonliving, and energy resources which could make a significant contribution toward solving the world's food and energy problems, among others, thereby generating wealth.

The wealth of the oceans looks different depending on the paradigmatic glasses through which you view it. In the Western paradigm, the wealth of the oceans is what humanity can get from it: as resources, food, energy, space. And looked at from the concept of Gross National Product (GNP) it looks small - maybe some 4 per cent of global GNP.

The Eastern paradigm looks at ocean wealth as "value-in-existence", that is, what is the life-giving value of the oceans - and this is something which cannot be mathematically or statistically determined. The national system of accounts (which is what GNP flows from) can neither capture the global, planetary dimension of the oceans nor of its inestimable value to humanity as the sustainer of life. So while in the Western paradigm what would be of importance to humanity is what it can *get* from the oceans, in the Eastern paradigm what would be important is what can be *given* to the oceans. For only by giving to Nature, by adjusting to it, by following the Divine law can sustainability be attained.

There is also a poetic and spiritual dimension to the oceans. Man has always been fascinated by two things - outer space and the oceans. He has always wanted to reach for the stars while the sea represented for him something vast, bottomless and full of riches. The ancient Indian scriptures referred to the sea as 'Ratnakar' where all jewels are to be found. It was also, in contradiction, a place where, like mountains and streams, meditation was to be practised. The ancient Puranic story refers to the '*Sagara Manthan*', a process whereby the ocean is churned by the *Devas* and *Asuras* (the spiritual and material forces) to yield all its gems and riches, including *Lakshmi*, the goddess of wealth. And after the wealth is exhausted, comes the poison which threatens to destroy the world and which nobody except *Shiva*, the God totally detached from worldly things, could consume and that also only by retaining the poison in his throat.

The Puranic story, like all ancient parables, hints at the coming together of the intellectual, mental (*daivic*) and materialistic (*asuric*) forces if riches are to be gathered from the oceans; and like *Shiva*, the nectar can only be protected by consuming (destroying) the poison if the world is to be saved from being destroyed or polluted: and this has to be through detachment, decrease of wants and voluntary restraint on consumption.

The oceans are one of the last places available to mankind for tapping resources - the others being Outer Space and Antarctica. Covering three quarters of the earth's surface the oceans have since antiquity been regarded as the sources of all kinds of wealth. The Puranic story of the *Devas* and *Asuras* churning up the ocean to recover wealth is also echoed in other traditions as well. Here is what Shakespere sings about the riches in the oceans in the *Tempest*:

Full fathom five thy father lies
Of his bones are corals made;
Those are pearls that were his eyes:
Nothing of him that doth fade,
But suffers a sea-change
Into something *rich* and strange. (emphasis added)

The riches of the oceans, including its aesthetic and life-sustaining properties, are available for humanity, but only if it learns to use them wisely, to accomodate to the law governing them and to give life-enhancing materials to them instead of toxins. This would apply to the other planetary ecosystems, (atmosphere and geosphere) as well and sustainable development would be a harmonious give and take relationship between human beings and Nature.

References

1 Rajni Kothari, "Environment, Technology and Ethics" *Ethics of Environment and Development* (London: Belhoven Press, 1990) p. 27.

2 Quoted in Fritjof Capra, *The Turning Point* (New York: Flamingo, Harper Collins, 1982) p. 144.

3 To Gandhi a Euclidean point - having no length and no breadth - could never be empirically known or attained. But without its definition the elucidiation of Euclidean geometry was not possible.

4 E.M. Borgese, *The Future of the Oceans* (Montreal: Harvest House, 1986) pp. 13-42.

2

Sustainable Development

Human beings draw their sustenance from the environment. The environment has therefore been of interest from time immemorial. Primitive man regarded nature with awe. Agricultural societies harmonized with nature. The growth of the modern industrial system broke the harmonious link between man and nature and gave birth to the idea that nature needed to be 'mastered'. The recent widespread perception of imbalances caused by industrialization, greenhouse gas emissions and the complex set of inter-relationships leading to possible global warming and climate change has led to a re-examination of humanity's relationship with nature.

The result is that environmental issues are today engaging the attention of statesmen around the globe. In a sense, concern about environmental problems is not new. London in the Middle Ages, for example, had a problem with smog as a result of burning logs, and so there were restrictions on the burning of logs. There were also periodic plagues, and these forced public health officials to encourage care about such matters as the cleanliness of water. In the nineteenth century, park areas were created for the preservation of nature and as places of human recreation.

But the current preoccupation with environmental issues is quantitatively and qualitatively different. While destruction and changes of the environment are not new, the size of the problem is. National attempts to address environmental problems have been made over the centuries; what is new are the international attempts to protect the environment.

In the late 1960s, the environmental impact of the postwar economic boom was being felt in various ways. There was growing concern about the spread of pesticides (such as DDT), oil spills from oil tankers, severe river pollution, and the pollution of inland waterways. Questions were being asked by organizations such as the Club of Rome as to whether the high level of consumption of raw materials could be sustained. The result was the convening by the United Nations of an international conference on the human environment.

The 1972 Conference on the Environment (held in Stockholm) was the first of the United Nation's "megaconferences," in which governments from around the world were brought together to discuss the United Nation's work in economic and social cooperation. The megaconference represented a new form of diplomacy. It was not a conference to discuss common problems and suggest ideas on how they could be solved; it was not creating a treaty as such and so was not as ambitious as the usual diplomatic conferences. But it was also, in a sense, more ambitious in that, freed from the requirements to remain focused on a particular issue, it could roam freely over a range of issues and encourage governments to think about these problems. To use the jargon of that era, it was a consciousness-raising conference designed to encourage governments to think more creatively about international cooperation. The main focus of the 1972 Conference was on cleaning up the environment and preventing pollution.

In addition to the various U.N. conferences, the World Bank and the United Nations agencies - the UNDP (United Nations Development Programme) in particular - have at roughly 10-year intervals convened special Commissions to go into the parameters of development. In 1967, the Pearson Commission, which was led by the former Canadian Prime Minister, published its report called *Partners in Development*. Ten years later, in

1977, Willy Brandt, the former Chancellor of the Federal Republic of Germany, chaired the Independent Commission on International Development Issues. The report of the Commission, *North-South: A Programme for Survival*, was published in 1980. In 1987, Gro Brundtland, the former Prime Minister of Norway, headed the World Commission on Environment and Development (WCED). The report of WCED was published in the form of a book entitled *Our Common Future*.

It is interesting to note that none of the three Commissions ever defined development. In fact, Pearson wrote that the word presented semantical difficulties, and that there was more to development than economic and material progress.

Brandt said quite bluntly that development can never be universally defined. In his view, however, development should not be confused with perpetual growth but focus on people, not on machines and institutions. A very important statement made was that the wealthy nations should take into account such matters as health care, education, the role of women in development, democracy and human rights. Brandt pointed out that world development should not be confused with economic growth for development is more than an economic process: fundamentally it is a matter of *moral* commitment to human solidarity and, the new generations of the world need not only economic solutions, they need ideas to inspire them, hopes to encourage them...They need a belief in man, in human dignity, in basic human rights; a belief in the values of justice, freedom, peace, mutual respect, in love and generosity, in reason rather than force.[1]

Growing International Disparity

Pearson, Brandt and Brundtland all laid great emphasis on the need to tackle widening gulf between the rich and poor nations. At the time of the Pearson report, the poorest, which were then called "the least developed countries", represented 66% of the world population and had 12% of global GNP. By the time of the Brundtland report, they had changed the name to "the lowest income countries", who represented 61% of world population but had access to rather less than 6% of GNP. In 10 years the position of the poorest had deteriorated by almost 50% in relative terms.

The position regarding indebtedness of the poor countries was equally alarming. At the time of the Pearson report, the debt of the lowest income countries had risen from $ 20 billion to $ 50 billion between 1960 and 1967. But by the time of the Brundtland report, it had risen to $ 250 billion. At the time of Pearson, the net cash flow between the then so-called developed and developing nations was $ 50 billion from the richer to the poorer. By the time of the Brundtland report, that had been reversed and the net flow was $ 50 billion from the poorest to the richest countries.

The debt interest, as the Brundtland report points out, of the poorest countries exceeds total Official Development Assistance (ODA) they receive by more than 50%. In other words, they are receiving with one hand and giving back much more with the other. Pearson, Brandt and Brundtland all point to the inconsistencies in donor development objectives, but this is not surprising since development has never been precisely defined. Of the three, Pearson was the most optimistic; he forecast that by the end of this century most of the developing countries could be self-reliant, because at that time their economies were growing at 5% per annum.

However, there were still enormous areas of poverty, and Pearson in his report drew the attention of the international community to the difference - the very first sentence of his book is that "the widening gap between the rich and the poor should be a matter of greatest concern" - and he stated that the principal objectives of development should be to reduce poverty and income disparity, because poverty was the principal cause of hunger and malnutrition. The rich nations should help to reduce the debt of the poor ones by stabilizing commodity prices, by improving conditions of international trade, by contributing more assistance for health care, education and agriculture.

By 1977, Willy Brandt was not nearly so optimistic, because during the '70s international trade and world economy was stagnant. The GNP (Gross National Product) and the per capita food production of Africa had declined very seriously, and in 58 developing countries population was growing faster than indigenous food production. Cereal imports into the developing countries in 1967 were 20 million tonnes. By 1977, they had gone up to 80 million tonnes, despite the wonderful work done with the high-yielding varieties of cereal grains in countries like India.

Brandt's urgent needs were almost identical with those of Pearson, to reduce poverty by reducing the debt burden, stabilizing commodity prices, improving conditions of international trade, increasing food production and greater support to agriculture, food research and development.

The Brundtland Commission reiterated that in the last two decades there had been little or no progress in reducing poverty. The excessive farm subsidies in the United States and Europe had depressed commodity prices, while the dumping of surpluses from these countries in the developing world was depriving farmers of developing countries of the opportunity to improve agricultural production, and driving many of them onto marginal land, with serious consequences for the environment.

Sustainable Development

The need to tackle growing poverty and international disparity, and the consequent deterioration of the environment, led to global concern. There is a tendency to think that it was only with the Brundtland report that this was brought to the world's notice. But Pearson had said as early as 1967, "Environment is a global, not a national, concern. Pollution of air, water and land affects lives and economies across all national boundaries. A stable, safe environment is an international responsibility."[2] Brandt said in 1980, "The biosphere is a common heritage."[3] The developed countries' growth, according to them, was being fuelled by the excessive use of resources, causing serious soil erosion, deforestation and desertification. Brandt also bewailed the large energy use and pointed out that in the last 100 years atmospheric carbon dioxide had increased by over

50 per cent. He strongly recommended that stress on the environment be reduced by stabilising population, by better control of industrial waste and pollution and through reducing dependence on non-renewable energies.

However, the concept of sustainable development gained wide acceptance only after it was articulated by the Brundtland Commission (WCED) in 1987. In their report WCED defined sustainable development as the ability, to ensure that it meets the needs of the present without compromising the ability of future generations to meet their needs.[4]

The Chairman of WCED, Gro Brundtland, had earlier elaborated on the concept in her Sir Peter Scott lecture in Bristol on 8 October, 1986,

> There are many dimensions to sustainability. First it requires the elimination of poverty and deprivation. Second it requires the conservation and enhancement of the resource base which alone can ensure that the elimination of poverty is permanent. Third, it requires a broadening of the concept of development so that it covers not only economic growth but also social and cultural development. Fourth, and most important, it requires the unification of economics and ecology in decision making at all levels.[5]

The concept of sustainable development was universally endorsed at the 1992 United Nations Conference on Environment and Development (UNCED). The concept as elaborated by UNCED represents a new paradigm, a new mode of thinking to serve as a guide to action. Achieving sustainable development involves a process of decision-making in which certain questions are asked and appropriate choices and decisions made. Thus there is never an 'end-state' of sustainable development but a process that constantly tries to harmonise the needs of development with the maintenance of the integrity of the environment.

Sustainable development is, a process of change in which the exploitation of resources, the direction of investments, the orientation of technological development, and institutional change are made consistent with future as well as present needs.[6]

Other elements that enhance the likelihood of sustainable development, include a political system that secures effective citizen participation in decision making; an economic system that is able to generate surpluses and technical knowledge on a self-reliant and sustained basis; a social system that provides for solutions to the tensions arising from disharmonious development; a production system that respects the obligation to preserve the ecological base for development; a technological system that fosters sustainable patterns of trade and finance; and an administrative system that is flexible and has the capacity for self-correction.[7]

As against the flow context of development as postulated by Brundtland, Constanza is of the view that sustainability needs to be defined in stock terms. According to him sustainability is the amount of consumption that can be continued indefinitely without degrading capital stocks - including 'natural capital' stocks. Capital stock in business terms means long-term assets such as buildings and machinery that serve as the means of production. Natural capital is the soil and atmospheric structure, plant and animal biomass, etc., that, taken together, forms the basis of all ecosystems. This natural capital stock uses primary inputs (sunlight) to produce a range of ecosystem services and physical natural resource flows. Examples of natural capital include forests, fish populations and petroleum deposits. The natural resource flows yielded by these natural capital stocks are, respectively, cut timber, caught fish, and pumped crude oil.

According to him we have now entered a new era in which the limiting factor in development is no longer human-made capital but remaining natural capital. Timber is limited by remaining forests, not saw-mill capacity; fish catch is limited by fish populations, not by fishing boats; crude oil is limited by remaining petroleum deposits, not by pumping and drilling capacity. He differs from most economists who view natural and human-made capital as substitutes rather than complements. If they are substitutes neither factor can be limiting. However since he sees human-made and natural capital as fundamentally complementary he emphasizes the importance of limiting factors and changes in the pattern of scarcity.

Constanza suggests that the minimum necessary condition for sustainability is the maintenance of the total natural capital stock at or above the current level. While a lower stock of natural capital may be sustainable, given the uncertainty implicit in current knowledge and the dire consequences of guessing wrong, it is best to at least provisionally assume that we are at or below the range of sustainable stock levels and allow no further decline in natural capital. This 'constancy of total natural capital' rule can thus be seen as a prudent minimum condition for ensuring sustainability, to be abandoned only when solid evidence to the contrary can be offered. In fact, the process of reinvesting in natural capital stocks should begin so as to bring them back to safer standards.[8]

Looking at the issue from a decision makers perspective, the Brundtland definition of sustainability as the ability to "meet the needs of the present without compromising the ability of future generations to meet their needs" has been criticized by Starik and Rands as not being adequate in decision-making situations. According to them, the concept is (a) anthropocentric, (b) indefinite on what the needs, whether of the present or the future, are and whose needs havê priority, (c) silent on changes in technology, resource distribution, and quality, and (d) unclear regarding the benefits, costs, and strategies of intergenerational sacrifice and transfer. In a more comprehensive definition of sustainability, in their view, concepts like irreplaceability, biodiversity, carrying capacity, socioeconomic and ecological system resilience, and futurity need to be included.[9]

Another difficulty for decision makers is that, in the broadest sense, sustainable development applies to many different policy areas that are usually thought of separately and appeal to different constituencies. It involves technical, economic, social, environmental, and cultural factors that interact with each other in complex and often unpredictable ways. Thus, it is a highly multidisciplinary concept that is very hard for any one expert analyst or policy maker to encompass.

Also, though intergenerational equity is central to the implementation of the concept of sustainability, it does not follow that achieving it is a zero-sum game between ourselves and our descendants. The reason is that sustainability combines quantities that are finite (resources and environmental assimilative capacity) with others (knowledge and human capacities) that are enhanced rather than depleted when they grow and develop to be used for human benefit. Knowledge wisely added to resources can thus be the source of new wealth and human capacity, both individual and collective, thereby opening up new options and possibilities for making growth and development compatible with sustainability. This implies a shift in emphasis from the material to the mental and spiritual, from the physical to the conceptual.

However, it needs to be noted that though the Brundtland concept of sustainable development cannot be unambiguously applied in specific decision-making situations, it is a very powerful, though simple, idea. As with many powerful and simple ideas, it has become a buzz-word and is used by many different groups to express a wide diversity of value judgments disguised in seemingly value-neutral language.

Ecology, Technology and Sustainable Development

Sustainable development can be seen as a continuous process guided by a basic philosophy which emphasizes development to improve the quality of life for everyone (assuring equity in the distribution of benefits flowing from development) and development that is environmentally appropriate, making proper use (and sometimes non-use) of natural resources and protecting essential ecological processes, life support systems, and biological diversity.

Development thinking based on the above, reaffirms the need for further growth with equity while incorporating explicitly a concern for the environment as a dimension of development conceived as a positive-sum game with Nature. In this view of the matter, the challenge to development thinking becomes one of simultaneously applying three criteria, namely,

- equity in the formulation of social goals of development, as an ethical imperative;
- ecological prudence as an ethical postulate of solidarity with future generations and, a means to improve the present-day quality of life;
- economic efficiency instrumental in making good use of the man-power and material resources from the macrosocial point of view, i.e., by taking into consideration the hitherto externalized social and ecological costs.[10]

The needs of equity, ecology and economic efficiency, or ecodevelopment when considered in the economic perspective, require harmonization of the demand and supply functions as well as consideration of where productive facilities need to be located.

The most decisive variable of the three is the *demand* function. This is also politically the most difficult to manage. Resource conservation through demand management implies one or more of the following solutions:

- resource saving through greater discipline on the part of consumers, improving energy efficiency, reducing traffic at peak hours, and better organization of the production and distribution system;
- a reduction in consumption standards through "voluntary simplicity" and self-restraint;
- acceptance of substitutions between material and non-material consumption: fewer goods and more services or less time spent in market-oriented economic activities and more time allocated to non-economic activities and/or small-scale environmentally benign material production for self-consumption;
- reducing the demand for intra-urban transportation by redesigning cities;
- reducing long distance transportation of materials and goods by better integration of local and regional economies.

The political problems involved in changing lifestyles in line with the above are obvious. Politicians have therefore tended to stress more the supply side.

In the *supply* function, whose locus lies at the intersection between nature and society, technology plays a leading role. Nature provides energy, space, and resources, i.e. those elements that can be transformed by technology into some "use value" deemed as such by society.

Society sets the values and the societal goals, builds the institutions, and produces the knowledge - both traditional and scientific - used to design the goods corresponding to societal needs and aspirations, to identify the resources, to invent the product and process technologies and to provide the necessary equipment. It also supplies the workforce.

The production process combines in a given site resources and energy with work and previously produced equipment to generate a flow of "goods" that go to the market (or reach the consumer through other institutional mechanisms) and of "bads" that are dumped back in nature. The objective would be to optimise the "goods" and minimise the "bads".

The third strategic variable of the harmonization process is the *location of production*. The environmental impact of productive activities depends on the climatic and topographic features and the density and nature of human activities in the proximity. The ecodevelopment approach calls for ecosystem-specific, culture-specific, and site-specific solutions.

On the basis of the above, conventional thought considers that technology constitutes potentially a locus to harmonize the triple concerns of social equity, ecological prudence, and economic efficiency through, inter alia, the following means:

- promoting energy and resource saving through product and process design, as well as upgrading environmentally sound traditional techniques;
- finding novel ways of using the specific resources of each ecosystem, with special emphasis on renewable resources, while recognizing that the conditions of their renewability must be respected;

- minimizing the "bads" by resorting to low-waste technologies;
- recycling and reusing non-renewable resources;
- using the natural ecosystem as a paradigm for man-made production systems.

The attraction of such an approach to politicians is obvious as it does not require change of life styles while simultaneously leading to economic growth. The result is that many, both in the North and South, consider a strong role for technology a *sine qua non* for tackling the environmental crisis. This has led to the articulation of the need for "environmentally sound technologies".

Much effort has been devoted to both the conceptual discussion and practical work on "environmentally sound technologies." They are conceived as covering a wide spectrum ranging from small-scale "soft technologies" and upgrading of traditional know-how to major efforts to produce large-scale modern low-waste technologies, as well as anti-pollution equipment.

The different schools of thought participating in the debate differ about the scope for applying "soft technologies," sometimes narrowly interpreted as a subset of "intermediate technologies," as well as with respect to the relative importance of low-waste and depolluting technologies. The latter subject involves the question of how much effort should go into preventive actions while continuing business as usual - that is, producing "goods" and "bads" and then increasing the national wealth by additional production of equipment to suppress or mitigate the "bads"!

Another variable entering the technology debate is the durability of products. One has to balance the resource-conserving aspects of longer life cycles of products against the need to ensure a reasonable rate of technical change.[11] Developing countries cannot cope with the present trend towards accelerated obsolescence. On the other hand, they can introduce selectively up-to-date technologies in order to achieve competitiveness on international markets. At any rate, better maintenance of infrastructures and equipment offers an excellent opportunity to create jobs financed through the resource saving thus achieved. Discarding the throw-away society, thus, becomes a common objective for both the North and the South.

However technology cannot only be considered in an economic context and in isolation from society and culture. The links of technology with society and culture are multi-dimensional. Recent developments in socio-cultural sciences and in philosophy indicate that modern technology can be regarded as a social construct. It expresses the aspirations, desires and needs of influential social groups. This vision stresses the importance of the mental and cultural conditions that prepare the way for technological developments.

Given these new insights, it is not surprising that historians now agree about the inadequacy of the traditional explanation regarding the emergence of the Industrial Revolution and modern industrial society. Today, it seems to be generally accepted that the newly acquired technical knowledge and the inventions of particularly the late 18th and the 19th century followed logically from the changes that man and society had been undergoing for a long time. To put it simply, typical modern phenomena such as the new sense of time, the disciplining of western man and the mechanization of his world view were the prelude to all the technical developments rather than the result of them. They were the fertile soil in which technology could flourish.

The consideration of social conditions as a precondition for the development of technology has had two impacts. Firstly by introducing the need for diversity in development of technology, it has impacted on the transfer of technology debate. Secondly it has directed attention to the whole question of socio-cultural value systems.

Values and Models of Sustainable Development

The ambiguity inherent in the word "sustainable development" and the lack of a precise definition has meant that there are differing perspectives as to what constitutes sustainability. These not only depend on disciplinary bias but also on cultural value systems and whether the person concerned belongs to the North or South.

Thus while to the developed nations of the North control of population, scientific analysis, control of emissions into the atmosphere (to be mainly implemented by putting a "cap" in the emissions from the developing countries) and the prevention of the destruction of fragile ecosystems like tropical forests, mangroves and coral reefs is the answer to the ecological crisis, for the developing world it is the problems caused by the affluent life styles of the developed nations, deteriorating terms of trade, the consequent intolerable debt burden and lack of development that need to be addressed.

The North-South perceptual confrontation, if so it can be called, could only lead to heightened tensions if basic attitudes, which is what leads to different perceptions, are not altered so as to lead to nonzero sum solutions. Basic attitudes are patterns of values with which people have emotionally identified themselves, as is shown by the images and metaphors that a culture or society identifies itself with. And basic attitudes imply certain world views which get expressed in the perceived relationship of humans with nature, the concept of a good life, and so on. Based on underlying motives, basic attitudes and values often remain concealed, and shift very slowly whether at the individual or the collective societal level.

There is a good deal of vagueness and confusion about the word 'values'. The well-known American psychologist Abraham Maslow writes: "However, 'values' are defined in many ways, and mean different things to different people. As a matter of fact, it is so confusing semantically that I am convinced we will soon give up this catch-all word in favour of more precise and more operational definitions for each of the many submeanings that have been attached to it."[12]

The word 'values' is also often used as a substitute for the words 'virtues' and 'morality'. But values do not mean only virtues. One way to understand what 'value' means is to distinguish values from facts. When we say that the Odyssey was composed a long time ago, we are making a factual statement. But when we say that the Taj Mahal is the most beautiful building in the world, we are making a value judgement.

Another way to understand what 'value' means is to trace its origin. The term 'value' entered philosophical thinking by way of economics. In economics it is mostly used to mean: (a) the capacity of an object to satisfy a human need or desire (this is known as value-in-use), or (b) money (value-in-exchange). It is the first meaning, and human needs, that we need to explore further in the ethical context.

Human beings have a hierarchy of needs which provide the motivation for their behaviour. According to Abraham Maslow, these needs, in the ascending order, are: biological needs, security, love, esteem, knowledge, aesthetic needs, self-actualization and transcendence.[13] Of these the lower needs connected with man's physical existence, such as the need for food, clothing and shelter are called 'basic needs' or simply 'needs'. The needs higher to these constitute values.

However, values are not mere higher 'needs' or desires. Rather, they imply what is desirable or valuable. In the words of sociologist Kluckhon,

> Values do not consist in desires but rather in the desirable, that is, what we not only want but feel that it is right and proper to want for ourselves and for others... [Values are] abstract standards that transcend the impulses of the moment and ephemeral situations.[14]

It is the sense of 'ought' that distinguishes values from ordinary desires and needs. For instance, truth is something not only desirable but we feel that we ought to be truthful. Values are inner imperatives which urge us to seek higher goals.

Values are not only an individual's higher needs and inner imperatives or oughts: they belong to the whole society or community or even the whole of humanity. That is to say, values are certain social norms or standards: they belong to culture.

When we look at diverse cultural values in a global context, problems arise. The whole complex of preconscious and conscious societal and cultural forces when viewed on a global scale is a very intricate phenomenon and one incapable of being expressed by any simple equation of social dynamics. But global society, including its intricate and multiple structures and value systems, has to move harmoniously in a preset direction if the issues posed by the concept of sustainable development are to be resolved. This requires the understanding of the differing cultural and other perceptions so that the various attitudes towards man, nature and the environment can be harmonized.

This is no easy task. There is on the one hand the dominant economic-scientific-technological value system, largely Western in its orientation, but having its resonance in the non-Western world also. In the West a mixture of groups and movements - environmentalists, ecofeminists, New Age followers and others-are acting as pioneers in an attempt to transform the dominant economic-technological paradigm into an ecologically led one. These movements have their echo in the developing parts of the world where groups and individuals are delving into ancient traditions and practices in order to harmonise developments- social, economic, technological-with the requirements of environmental sustainability.

Taking note of the various divergent value systems, the Brundtland Commission pleaded for "elevating sustainable development to a global ethic."[15] The global ethic suggested by Brundtland is largely science, technology and economic-growth oriented. As stated in the Brundtland Report, there is "the possibility of a new era of economic growth" that is based "on policies that sustain and expand the environmental resource base". The Report goes on to say that they are serving an urgent notice based on "the latest and best available scientific evidence".[16] The global ethic recommended by the Brundtland Commission is thus an attempt to harmonise science, environment and economics.

Gro Brundtland was aware of the "different views and perspectives, different values and beliefs" of the Commissioners.[17]

Yet values as such did not figure prominently in the Brundtland Report. There could be a number of reasons for this.

One very obvious one was the need to present a unanimous report. Controversial items had obviously to be avoided. Also anything regarded as being vague or not easy of elucidation. Values, as we have noted, are not only vague but culturally determined and so difficult to get universal agreement on in today's divided, competitive and antagonistic world.

Another reason could be the reliance on the latest and best scientific evidence and the desire to be "objective" and value-neutral. Science too, has its value system though the values are more implicit than explicit. But the traditional Newtonian mechanistic systems, which are the basis of value-free, "objective" science, find it difficult to capture the holistic systemic approach required by planetary scale ecosystems.

A third reason could be its stress on, a new era of economic growth - growth that is forceful and at the same time environmentally sustainable.[18]

Quite obviously values - religious, ethical or Gandhian - could not be included as, while they are all pro-development, they are at the same time anti-growth. Daly, for example, held that while growth was an increase in the flows of matter and energy through the economy and the environment, development was an improvement in non-physical characteristics. Thus while development was possible in a finite biosphere, growth was not.[19]

It was obviously for all, or some of the above reasons, that the Brundtland Report does not go too deeply into value systems. Values became important, however, when the question of global governance was taken up. The Commission on Global Governance co-chaired by Ingvar Carlsson and Shridath Ramphal pleaded for a "global ethic" based on values promoting mutual respect, integrity, liberty, justice and equity and based on a common commitment to a set of core values that can unite people of all cultural, political, religious or philosophical backgrounds.[20]

The need for a core set of values in governance was obviously necessary because decision making has to be concerned with interfacing the natural ecosystem with the human sociocultural system for attaining sustainability. The basic entities of socioeconomic systems are individual human beings. The hierarchical structure of society is formed by their interactions in primary groups, such as the nuclear family, and the incorporation of these groups in organizations progressively more complex and embracing political, legal, economic, and social spheres. The analysis of socioeconomic systems is rendered difficult by the extremely complex behaviour of humans, both individually and as groups: due to widely divergent perceptions arising from cultural, religious and national differences.

Varying perceptions have meant that decision makers have percieved environmental conditions in different ways depending on their psychological and cultural makeup and on the basis of their past experience and external factors, like group pressures and interaction and the social reward system, in deciding what actions to take regarding ecosystem management. It is in this context that a common commitment to core values becomes an essential part of decision making in a global context.

It needs to be noted, however, that the value premises on which decision makers act are not always explicitly stated. More often than not they are implicit in the statements made and have to be inferred.

When we consider methods of attaining sustainable development, broadly two models emerge. They may be called the Western, Euroamerican, or the modern paradigm, and the Asian, Eastern one.[21]

A good example of the Western paradigm is the one posulated by Sachs. Integrating socio-cultural factors with the economical, ecological and spatial dispersal parameters of Brundtland, he postulates five dimensions of eco-development. These are:

> *Social sustainability*, that is, greater equity in asset and income distribution both inter- and intra-nationally;

Economic sustainability, meaning that economic efficiency needs to be evaluated in macrosocial terms;

Ecological sustainability, that is, expanding the carrying capacity of ecosystems, reducing consumption of fossil fuels and waste, increasing self-restraint, and developing technologies which produce low-waste and are resource efficient;

Spatial sustainability which means attaining a balance between rural and urban areas, reducing congestion and concentration in metropolitan areas, eliminating ecosystem destruction, and promoting modern regenerative agriculture and decentralised industrialization;

Cultural sustainability, that is, having ecodevelopment in cultural continuity.[22]

The model elaborated by Sachs basically flows from economics (social equity and economic efficiency) within the constraints of ecological, spatial and cultural constraints. Its value system is based on materialism and it has no "spiritual" dimensions.

Attempts have been made to include what may be called human and spiritual values in the sustainable development matrix. In a Seminar on *Ethical Issues in Development* held by the Marga Institute in Colombo, Sri Lanka in 1986 the concept of development was expanded from the economic-technological paradigm to one including socio-cultural and political parameters and various belief systems. The conclusions of the Seminar were that any adequate definition of development must include five dimensions:

- an *economic* component dealing with the creation of wealth and improved material conditions of life;
- a *social* ingredient measured as well-being in health, education, housing, and employment;
- a *political* dimension embodying values such as human rights, political freedom, enfranchisement, and some form of democracy;

- a *cultural* dimension in recognition of the fact that cultures confer identity and self-worth to people;
- a *human* dimension called the 'full-life paradigm', which refers to the ultimate meanings of life and history as expressed in symbols and beliefs.[23]

In the above definition, development encompasses more than the economic, social, cultural and political parameters of Sachs by including the human dimension of the ultimate meaning of life: a value we may term as 'spiritual'.

Another view is that of Rajni Kothari. Criticising the lack of ethics in the technological-economic paradigm, he writes:

> In the absence of an ethical imperative, environmentalism has been reduced to a technological fix, and as with all technological fixes, solutions are seen to lie once more in the hands of manager technocrats. Economic growth, propelled by intensive technology and fuelled by an excessive exploitation of nature, was once viewed as a major factor in environmental degradation; it has suddenly been given the central role in solving the environmental crisis. The market economy is given an even more significant role in organizing nature and society. The environmentalist label and the sustainability slogan have become deceptive jargons that are used as convenient covers for conducting business as usual.[24]

Kothari goes on to say that as against the existing concept of environmentalism, a different meaning needs to be given to sustainability. In his concept, sustainability has to be rooted in ethics thus leading to an alternative mode of development. The essence of his thinking is that a conflict exists between two meanings of "sustainable development": sustainability as a narrow economic ideal geared to maintaining privileges of ruling elites and compromising the future and Nature for the benefit of a minority, as opposed to the ethical ideal of sustainability of life on Earth. So while at one time the conflict was between "environment" and "development", now it was between the two meanings of "sustainable development."

As an alternative design for development which is environmentally and ethically sound, he identifies four primary criteria for sustainable development: a holistic view of development; equity based on autonomy and self-reliance instead of a structure of dependence founded on aid and transfer of technology with a view to "catching up"; an emphasis on participation at all levels - national, international; and an accent on the importance of local conditions and the value of diversity. He goes on to say,

> Our common future cannot lie in an affluence that is ecologically suicidal, and socially and economically exclusive. It can, and must, lie in a curtailment of wants, as Gandhi constantly reminded his countrymen and others.[25]

As the above concept, sustainability requires ethics to be a crucial parameter it is not something that can be solved by technology or by accelerating financial investments. It is only by a shift to values such that Nature is valued in itself and for its life support functions, and not merely as something to be converted into resources and commodities, that sustainable development would be attained.

Conclusion

The three views, and the two paradigms from which they spring, differ in some respects but have many things in common. They all look at sustainable development as being based on economic, social, cultural and political parameters. The two views in the Eastern paradigm, however, stress the human element in a holistic *spiritual* context while the Western paradigm stress more the *material* aspect through greater income and asset distribution. The Eastern paradigm uses the ethical principle as the overriding principle in ordering the other factors while the Western paradigm uses economics for the same purpose. The value system underlying the Eastern paradigm is a religious one while the Western paradigm is based on the value system flowing from the Rennaisance and the Industrial Revolution of the seventeenth and eighteenth centuries.

We shall deal with the two paradigms, and their attendant value systems in some detail. At the moment it is only necessary to note that sustainable development has many dimensions. An analytical tool capable of harmonising a great diversity of views is general systems theory which looks at ecosystems and their sustainability in terms of the interrelatedness and interdependence of all phenomena. In this framework a system is an integrated whole whose properties cannot be reduced to those of its parts. The system has to be understood through the formulation of a network of interlocking models and concepts with none of the theories being considered more fundamental that the others but all of them being mutually consistent. They also have to go beyond conventional disciplinary distinctions using whatever language is appropriate to describe different aspects of the multilevelled, interrelated fabric of reality.

This holistic approach is the one that we shall use when looking at the two paradigms of sustainable development: the objective, value-free Western one based on science, technology and economics, and the various value-loaded views of Hinduism, Buddhism, Islam and Gandhi of the Eastern paradigm. Then we shall apply the concepts to a planetary ecosystem, namely, the oceans.

We have selected the oceans rather than, say, the atmosphere, because the oceans are not only life-sustaining but also the provider of resources: energy, food, materials, space. They provide services (ecological, resource-based) which flow easily into both the Eastern and Western paradigms. They are also under stress with the latest phase of the industrial revolution penetrating into its depths with technology and, unfortunately, wastes: nuclear, toxic and human. They, thus, form an ideal laboratory for analysing the impact of anthropogenic activities on a critical planetary ecosystem.

References

1. Independent Commission on International Development Issues, *North-South: A Programme for Survival* (London: Pan, 1980) p.12.
2. Quoted in Joseph H. Hulse, "Progress in Development from Pearson to Brandt to Brundtland to Brazil" *Sustainable Management of Coastal Ecosystems*, M.S. Swaminathan and R. Ramesh (eds.) (Madras: M.S. Swaminathan Research Foundation, 1993) p.9.
3. *Ibid.*
4. World Commission on Environment and Development (WCED), *Our Common Future*, (New York: Oxford University Press, 1987) p.8.
5. Brundtland quoted in Christine Blackmore, *Taking Responsibility: Science and Technology* (London: Pluto Press, 1989) p.1.
6. WCED, note 4, p.46.
7. *Ibid.*, p.65.
8. Robert Constanza, "The ecological economics of sustainability: Investing in natural capital" *Environmentally Sustainable Economic Development: Building on Brundtland* (Paris: UNESCO, 1991) p. 87.
9. Mark Starik and Gordon P. Rands, "Weaving an Integrated Web: Multilevel and Multisystem Perspectives of Ecologically Sustainable Organisations" *Academy of Management Review* 20, no. 4 (1995) pp. 908-35.
10. Ignacy Sachs, "The Environmental Challenge", *The Uncertain Quest: Science, Technology and Development*, Jean-Jacques Salomon et. al., (eds.) (Tokyo: United Nations University, 1994) p. 308.
11. Orio Giarini, *Dialogue on Wealth and Welfare* (Oxford: Pergamon Press, 1980).
12. Abraham Maslow, *The Further Reaches of Human Nature* (New York: Penguin Books, 1982) p. 106.

13. Abraham Maslow, *Motivation and Personality* (New York: Harper and Row, 1970).
14. Clyde Kluckhon, *Culture and Behaviour* (New York: Free Press of Glenco, 1962) p. 289.
15. WCED, note 4, p. 308.
16. *Ibid.*, pp.1, 2.
17. WCED, note 4, p. xii-xiii.
18. *Ibid.*, p. xii.
19. See in this context Herman Daly, "The economic growth debate" *Journal of Environmental Economic Management*, 14(1987) pp. 323-26.
20. The Commission on Global Governance, *Our Global Neighbourhood* (New York: Oxford University Press, 1995) p. 48.
21. It needs to be noted that the two paradigms are not geographical: the Western paradigm being confined to the developed countries and the Eastern to the Asian and other developing countries. There are followers of the Western paradigm in the developing world and of the Eastern one in North America and Europe.
22. Ignacy Sachs, "Transition Strategies for the 21st Century" *Nature and Resources*, 28(1), 1992, pp. 4-17.
23. Quoted by Denis Goulet, "Ethics in Development Theory and Practice" *Peace and Development: An Interdisciplinary Perspectives*, Sanders and Matsuoka eds. (University of Hawaii, School of Social Work, 1989) p. 91.
24. Rajni Kothari, "Environment, Technology and Ethics" *Ethics of Environment and Development* (London: Belhoven Press, 1990) p.27.
25. *Ibid.*, p.34.

3

The Western Paradigm

Westerners became aware of the "environmental crisis" in the early 1970s. The public debate that ensued quickly became one between the proponents of continuing economic growth as an answer to the problem and the so-called conservationists. This schism between the proponents of economic growth and those advocating the maintenance of ecological integrity exists, in one form or the other, even today.

Starting with the UN Conference on the Human Environment held in Stockholm in 1972 at the international level, a middle path is being sought between these two extreme and still influential views: the narrowly economic and the unconditionally ecological.

The partisans of the "growth first" narrowly economic approach claim that all the other dimensions of development either would be taken care of automatically by the "trickle down effect" of rapid growth or else could be attended to in better conditions once a much higher per capita Gross National Product (GNP) had been attained. They bolster their argument by the claim that there exists an empirical relation between per capita income and some measure of environmental quality: it having been observed that as income goes up there is increasing environmental degradation up to a point, after which environmental quality improves (the so-called inverted U).

One explanation of this finding is that people in poor countries cannot afford to emphasize amenities over material well-being. Consequently, in the earlier stages of economic development, increased pollution can be regarded as an acceptable side effect of economic growth. Later on when a country has attained a sufficiently high standard of living, people would necessarily give greater attention to environmental amenities.

However Kenneth Arrow, a Nobel prize winner in economics, and others have pointed out that the above relationship has so far been shown to apply to a selected set of pollutants only though, because it is consistent with the notion that people spend proportionately more on environmental quality as their income rises, economists have conjectured that the curve applies to environmental quality generally. They warn about the conclusions that can be drawn from these limited empirical findings. While economic growth may be associated with improvements in some environmental indicators, they imply neither that economic growth is sufficient to induce environmental improvement in general, nor that the environmental effects of growth may be ignored, nor, indeed, that the Earth's resource base is capable of supporting indefinite economic growth.[1]

At the other extreme from those advocating growth first are the partisans of the unconditionally ecological and the proponents of the zero rate of growth. Some apply this concept only to the population. Others extend it to both population and material growth, claiming that real development should concentrate on qualitative rather than quantitative aspects. In their most extreme formulations, the partisans of an end to growth demand the "de-industrialization" of the rich countries and the non-industrialization of the poor ones; the latter could serve in the meantime as a recreational and cultural reserve for the rest of the world.[2]

In between these two extreme views there are other formulations. In this connection, Daly makes a useful but often overlooked distinction between growth and development: that growth is an increase in the flows of matter and energy through the economy and the environment while development is an improvement in non-physical characteristics.[3] Munn equates development with social evolution, suggesting that sustainable development is achievable in a time of increasing global change only through strategies that promote the ability of society to adjust to change.[4] The 1991 Strategy for Sustainable Living defines sustainable development as 'improving the quality of human life while living within the carrying capacity of supporting ecosystems'.[5]

However the debate between the two extreme propositions, the narrowly economic and the ecological, continues. As a way of harmonizing the two views, the World Commission on Environment and Development has called for the integration of economics and the environment, using the concept of sustainable development.

Integrating Economics and Ecology

Arising out of the middle path between the economic and ecological viewpoints suggested by the Brundtland Commission and others have arisen the disciplines of resource economics and environmental economics. Though the two have different viewpoints, and in the end reach differing conclusions with one stressing economics and the other ecology, they both try to reconcile the disciplines of economics and ecology.

Resource economics focuses primarily on methods aimed at broadening conventional neoclassical economic analyses to include the true costs of natural resources, particularly common goods such as air and water, in the determination of the optimal allocation of resources. Non-market valuation methods have been developed which enable economists to determine the cost or benefit attributable to non-priced natural resources. The fundamental precepts of neoclassical economics are incorporated in their analyses. One of these is the circular flow of goods and services in the economy, that is, production factors to firms, goods and services to markets, to consumers, and so on. 'Value added' at each stage ensures continuous economic growth. Economic activity is neat, circular and independent of any other system.[6]

The above solution is being widely accepted by governments. For as the concept of sustainable development is being drawn into mainstream politics, emphasis is being placed on economic growth as a long-term solution to the global problematique. This is because of the political need of finding least cost solutions which do not radically change the status quo. The result is that literature is growing on ways of internalizing the 'externalities' of production and economic growth. These externalities range from global warming to local problems such as soil erosion. The emphasis remains on mobilizing the market mechanism through adjustment of price signals to influence the behaviour of households and enterprises to achieve environmental objectives in tandem with social and economic ones. The liberalisation ethic, that is, market economy in the economic sphere and democracy in the political, is being thus promoted.

Arrow and others have warned against the tendency to equate economic liberalisation and other policies promoting gross national product with environmental policy. They say,

> We conclude that economic liberalization and other policies that promote gross national product are not substitutes for environmental policy. On the contrary, it may well be desirable that they are

> accompanied by stricter policy reforms. Of particular importance is the need for reforms that would improve the signals that are received by resource users. Environmental damages including loss of ecological resilience, often occur abruptly. They are frequently not reversible. But abrupt changes can seldom be anticipated from the systems of signals that are typically received by decision-makers in the world today.[7]

Economic growth is not, in their view, a panacea for environmental quality; indeed, it is not even the main issue. What matters is the content of growth - the composition of inputs (including environmental resources) and outputs (including waste products). This content is determined by, among other things, the economic institutions within which human activities are conducted. These institutions need to be designed so that they provide the right incentives for protecting the resilience of ecological systems.

Environmental economics, also following essentially neo-classical tenets, addresses issues of pollution control, standard-setting, waste management and recycling, externalities of private enterprise action, conservation and use of common property resources, and so on, from the standpoint of providing guidance for efficient allocation of resources and elucidiating a sound environmental policy.

Environmental economics grew out of an increasing realisation that resource economics has left out vital economic/ environmental linkages. The assumption of circular flow in the market economy is not grounded in ecological principles, nor does it recognize ecological inputs or outputs. Essential to an understanding of ecological economics are three concepts: throughput, carrying capacity and entropy.

Our economy, and indeed our very survival, relies on ecological *throughputs*. We need water for production and transportation, minerals and soil for agriculture, and so on. At the other end, we rely on nature to act as a sink for our wastes.

The second concept is *carrying capacity*. Under steady-state conditions, the carrying capacity of an ecosystem can be modelled with reasonable confidence. However, for an ecosystem including people, the real carrying capacity will depend on human consumption patterns and will vary geographically and over decades. Thus it is difficult to estimate the population that the world can sustain. Erring on the side of caution is therefore desirable. According to Daly, minimizing future regret is wiser than maximizing present benefit.[8]

While natural inputs can be easily identified, and carrying capacity is intuitively understandable, *entropy* is neither easily identified nor understood. In entropy terms, the cost of any biological or economic enterprise is always greater than the product and any such activity necessarily results in a deficit. Regardless of how efficient production processes become in terms of minimizing externalities or reducing waste, production will always contribute to the ever-increasing state of entropy, or disorder, in the universe. Economic activity should therefore strive to maintain the desired level of goods in society, while minimizing entropy contribution. It needs to be noted, however, that though entropy is extremely useful as a variable for economic analyses, the framework of thermodynamics in which it originated is quite limited. For in the framework of thermodynamics entropy only applies to closed systems.

A number of voices have been raised against views based on continuing with the dominant economic paradigm after marginally reconciling it with ecological concerns. These critics want to reformulate economics from a holistic, systemic viewpoint. There are others who base their criticism on a nonmaterialist view of life: of the need for curtailing wants instead of maximizing them. These views, mainly of a religious kind, we shall go into later. We proceed to consider the perspectives arising out of various alternative formulations from the purely economic standpoint.

"New" Economics: the Scientific Dimension

To those proposing a shift from the dominant neoclassical economic paradigm there is need for the "new" economics to come closer to reality by taking note of the latest developments in scientific thought. The scientific world view has changed from the rational-mechanistic Newtonian-Cartesian view of classical science to a Einsteinian-Heisenbergian-Prigoginian one which stresses relativity, uncertainty and evolution to new forms of organisation. Today it is being increasingly recognized that ideas based on the world-views of Descartes and Newton are incapable of explaining the present-day reality. The real world is neither linear nor mechanistic; instead it has all sorts of relativities. In physics, the idea that space and time can be separated is no longer acceptable. Relativity introduces many contradictions and ambiguities into concepts and arguments that, considered from the Newtonian logic, appear perfectly consistent. Einsteinian relativity, together with the new quantum mechanics, is slowly but surely making a large number of ideas, held sacrosanct for centuries, increasingly obsolete and irrelevant. The theories of Prigogine and subsequent developments of chaos theory, fractals and self-organising systems have made initial conditions important and thus removed "universality" from science. Following from the concept of non-universality the proponents of the "new" economics stress the need for diversity in economic thought and theories as applied to different societies and cultures.

Science's concept of nature is also undergoing a radical change toward the multiple, the temporal, and the complex. In the mechanistic view the world appeared as a vast automaton. We now understand that we live in a pluralistic world. It is true that there are phenomena that appear as deterministic and reversible, such as the motion of a frictionless pendulum or the motion of the earth around the sun. Reversible processes do not know any privileged direction of time. But there are also irreversible processes that involve an arrow of time. If you bring together two liquids such as water and milk, they tend to mix in the forward direction of time as we experience it. We never observe the reverse process, the spontaneous separation of the mixture into pure water and pure milk. Non-reversibility leads to uncertainty and inability to predict and control.

In the mechanical view, by extrapolating the nineteenth-century theories of the equilibrium of undisturbed Nature at the local level, the biosphere is conceived to be in a steady state. In this view of Nature, it is possible to mathematically model geophysical and ecological systems and to understand how decision-making would affect them. Nature is thus predictable, certain and, therefore, controllable.

Based on the body of ideas that came together in the seventeenth and eighteenth centuries under the heading of "classical science" or "Newtonianism," the world was pictured to be one in which every event was determined by initial conditions that were, at least in principle, determinable with precision. It was a world in which chance played no part, in which all the pieces came together like cogs in a cosmic clock-like mechanism.

The acceptance of this mechanistic view coincided with the rise of factory civilization and the introduction of machines on a large scale. The Age of the Machine enthusiastically embraced scientific theories that pictured the entire universe as a machine. This view of the world led Laplace to his famous claim that, given enough facts, we could not merely predict the future but retrodict the past. And this image of a simple, uniform, mechanical universe not only shaped the development of science, it also spilled over into many other fields, including economics.

In the classical system, the observer was not a part of the system. He observed the world from the outside. By the early twentieth century, Einstein put the observer back into the system: the machine looked different -indeed, for all practical purposes it was different - depending upon where you stood within it. But it was still a deterministic machine, and God did not throw dice. However, developments in quantum mechanics and the principle of uncertainty, which flowed from Einstein's thesis, demolished the certainty of the machine model.

Prigogine and Stengers, in their book *Order Out of Chaos*, have used original arguments to challenge the Newtonian model, but also showed how the still valid, though much limited, claims of Newtonianism might fit compatibly into a larger scientific image of reality. They argue that the old "universal laws" are not universal at all, but apply only to local regions of reality. And these happen to be the regions to which science has devoted the most effort. In broad-stroke terms, Prigogine and Stengers argue that traditional science tends to emphasize stability, order, uniformity, and equilibrium. It concerns itself mostly with closed systems and linear relationships in which small inputs uniformly yield small results.[9]

What makes their paradigm especially interesting is that it shifts attention to those aspects of reality that characterize today's accelerated social change: disorder, instability, diversity, disequilibrium, nonlinear relationships (in which small inputs can trigger massive consequences), and temporality -a heightened sensitivity to the flows of time.

In Prigoginian terms, all systems contain subsystems, which are continually "fluctuating." At times, a single fluctuation or a combination of them may become so powerful, as a result of positive feedback, that it shatters the pre-existing organization. At this revolutionary moment - Prigogine calls it a "singular moment" or a "bifurcation point" - it is inherently impossible to determine in advance which direction change will take: whether the system will disintegrate into "chaos" or leap to a new, more differentiated, higher level of "order" or organization, which he calls a "dissipative structure."[10] (Such physical or chemical structures are termed dissipative because, compared with the simpler structures they replace, they require more energy to sustain them.) In the above perspective, an organic metaphor is linked to the equilibrium, steady state Newtonian system thereby leading the biosphere to be conceived as being in a state of constant change.

Another model of the self-regulating type that has developed in recent times is the Gaian model. Developments in space technology and space travel have profoundly modified humanity's ideas of itself and its place in the universal scheme of things. The Brundtland Commission's report, for example, starts with the following statement:

> In the middle of the 20th century, we saw our planet from space for the first time. Historians may eventually find that this vision had a greater impact on thought than did the Copernican revolution of the 16th century, which upset the human self-image by revealing that the Earth is not the centre of the universe. From space, we see a small and fragile ball dominated not by human activity and edifice but by a pattern of clouds, oceans, greenery, and soils. Humanity's inability to fit its doings into that pattern is changing planetary systems, fundamentally. Many such changes are accompanied by life-threatening hazards. This new reality, from which there is no escape, must be recognized - and managed.[11]

Out of this vision from space grew the science of ecology as a planetary, holistic science. As we looked at the Earth from space a whole set of questions arose. One question which interested Lovelock was the interactions between the living and inorganic elements of Earth and how it made the Earth, unlike Mars and other planets, a fit place for life. Out of this interest grew the Gaia hypothesis in "which the Earth's living matter, air, oceans and land surface form a complex system which can be seen as a single organism and which has the capacity to keep our planet a fit place for life."[12]

The Gaian hypotheses by viewing the Earth as a "living", self-regulating entity has caused a revolution in our world-view which has been diffused to other disciplines as well. But in mainstream economics it is the Newtonian-Cartesian reductionist and mechanistic view that has influenced the discipline. Towards the end of the 19th century, Jevons and Marshall abandoned the term 'political economy' in favour of 'economics'. The former's motivation was that economics sounded much more like mathematics, ethics, aesthetics.[13] The latter's was that political economy seemed to soil the science with the world of politics and the interests of political parties.[14] Economics, on the contrary, seemed to connote "a science pure and applied, rather than a science and an art."[15]

In recent decades, however, a new look is being given to the concept of the "pure" science of economics. For example Bell and Kristol published in 1981 a group of essays under the heading *Crisis in Economic Theory* which called for a shift to a more holistic economics.[16]

According to Hodgson and Screpanti the proclamation of Bell and Kristol of a crisis in economic theory is an understatement for today 'economics is in chaos'. This is due to recent work in game theory which has raised questions about 'hard core' notions of neoclassical economics like rationality, the presence of imperfect or asymmetric information, the intrusion of chaos theory into economics leading to mathematical models becoming over-sensitive to initial conditions and the discovery that general equilibrium theory does not lead to unique and stable solutions.[17]

In their view not only 'economics' but the very definition of 'the economy' is problematic. Considering the question of 'economics', they say that a science is normally defined as the study of a particular aspect of objective reality: physics is about the nature and properties of matter and energy, biology about living things, psychology about the psyche, and so on. But amongst economists, the prevailing practice for many years has been to regard this subject as being defined not principally as a study of a real object - the economy - but primarily by a method or type of analysis.

Apart from being a recipe for intolerance, the aforementioned definition of economics elevates formalism and axiomatics to unwarranted heights. At the outset, the assumptions are taken as given and unquestionable. Economic agents must maximize (consumers to maximize utility and firms to maximize profits) because economists assume they do so, and so on. For the theoretical economist the game becomes one of simply drawing logical conclusions from pre-ordained assumptions, in combination with secondary assumptions which may be more malleable. Attempts to address the real world, or to evaluate basic assumptions on the basis of pragmatic conceptualizations of such a reality, are looked down upon.[18]

Based on developments in scientific thought, Fritjof Capra considers the systems view as an appropriate basis not only for the behavioral and the life sciences but also for the social sciences, and especially for economics. The application of systems concepts to describe economic processes and activities is particularly urgent because, in his view, virtually all our current economic problems are systemic problems that can no longer be understood via reductionist methods of analysis.[19]

According to him, the systems approach to economics would make it possible to bring some order into the present conceptual chaos by giving economists the urgently needed ecological perspective. In the systems view, the economy is a living system composed of human beings and social organizations in continual interaction with one another and with the surrounding ecosystems on which our lives depend. Like individual organisms, ecosystems are self-organizing and self-regulating systems in which animals, plants, micro-organisms, and inanimate substances are linked through a complex web of interdependencies involving the exchange of matter and energy in continual cycles. Linear cause-and-effect relationships exist only very rarely in ecosystems, nor are linear models very useful to describe the functional interdependencies of the embedded social and economic systems and their technologies. The recognition of the nonlinear nature of all systems dynamics is the very essence of ecological awareness, the essence of 'systemic wisdom.'

The nonlinear interconnectedness of living systems immediately suggests to Capra, two important rules for the management of social and economic systems. First, there is an optimal size for every structure, organization, and institution, and maximizing any single variable - profit, efficiency, or GNP, for example - will inevitably destroy the larger system. Second, the more an economy is based on the continual recycling of its natural resources, the more it is in harmony with the surrounding environment. Our planet is now so densely populated that virtually all economic systems are thoroughly interwoven and interdependent: today's most important problems are global problems. The vital social choices we face are no longer local -choices between more roads, schools, and hospitals - nor do they affect merely a small part of the population. They are choices between principles of self-organization - centralization and decentralization, capital-intensity or labour-intensity, hard technology or soft technology - that affect the survival of humanity as a whole.[20]

Other Models

A workshop held in Santa Fe under the co-chairmanship of two Nobel prize winners, Philip Anderson (Physics) and Kenneth Arrow (Economics), examined the potential applications of recent developments in the natural sciences and computer technology to the understanding of the evolution of the global economy. The proceedings of the workshop have been published under the title *The Economy as an Evolving Complex System.*[21]

The workshop, which had as participants ten economists and ten natural scientists, addressed itself to a number of issues. One of the questions addressed was: Why do economists downplay or ignore the role of psychological, sociological, and political forces in economic systems? Answers from the economists included: "such forces really *aren't* important"; "they're important, but too hard to treat"; "they're being studied in certain specific cases"; and "they're automatically included through their economic effects." None of these answers was entirely satisfying to the natural scientists to whom the importance of such forces seemed self-evident and not easily dismissed. Moreover, several felt, that it should not be too hard to build such non-economic forces into models of the economy.

A related issue was the role of *positive* feedback in economic systems. The inclusion of non-economic forces would naturally lead to positive feedback in many cases. However, positive feedback is apparently frowned upon by some economic practitioners because of its conflict with a belief in a basically stable economy.

Another issue was the methodologies to be used in the modelling of the global economy. A number of different viewpoints emerged. Dealing with the prevailing mainstream competitive equilibrium models of economics, Kenneth Arrow points out that the dynamics of the models is characterised by difference equations (or differential equations in continuous-time models). The original tendency was to search for solutions which were constant in time. There was a generally held point of view, which goes back to the origins of economics as a systematic discipline, that solutions which were not constant would tend to the constant solution or *steady state*. But more recent research, partly influenced by the new methods of nonlinear dynamic analysis developed in physics and ecology, has demonstrated that there are solutions to the same equations with cycles and even with chaotic behaviour. Arrow regards the multiplicity of solutions as an embarrassment, since it suggests that economic theory, even if accurate, does not yield a unique pattern of dynamic behaviour and hence its predictions are far from sharp.

Besides there is the question of uncertainty. The last thirty years has seen the systematic incorporation of time and uncertainty into models. Commodities are distinguished not merely by their usual characteristics but also by the unfolding of the events which are uncertain today and will only be resolved some time in the future. Corresponding to the difference equations which define the dynamic equilibrium in the case of certainty are a set of stochastic difference equations. The search for steady states has been replaced by that for stationary distributions.

Arrow points out, however, that the general perspective of mainstream neoclassical economic theory based on certainty has had some empirical successes. From a very broad perspective, there is a considerable degree of self-maintenance or homeostasis. What would appear to be major shocks, especially wars, are absorbed, not immediately of course, but in the sense that after a relatively few years the economy appears to be about where it would be if the shock had not occurred. Similarly, some proportions in the economy, for example, the ratio between capital and output or the share of wages in national income, are broadly constant over time in specific countries.

But it is clear to him that many empirical phenomena are not covered well by either the theoretical or the empirical analyses based on linear stochastic systems. The presence and persistence of cyclical fluctuations in the economy as a whole, of irregular timing and amplitude, are not consistent with a view that an economy tends to return to equilibrium states after any disturbance. The persistence of unemployment undermines the assumption that prices and wages work to reduce imbalances between supply and demand.[22]

Philip Anderson, giving a physicists view on economics, considers that the question of theories of growth lay at the heart of the subject matter of the workshop and one that was least amenable to standard economic methodology.

He referred to the many regimes in which the standard assumptions of equilibrium theory, such as diminishing returns, concave utility functions, etc., manifestly break down and positive feedback behaviour and exponential explosions occur. These include economies of scale and large startup costs, learning-by-doing, infrastructure buildup, education and simple fashion and social conformity. Web-like effects involving the intricate interlocking of technologies are of this type. There were complex economic interrelationships of modern technology, involving not just the invention of new goods but the dependency of these on each other, for example, the hi-fi on the broadcast network, the supply of records or tapes, but also on a complex of technologies and distribution networks for quite technically complicated electronic devices, high-tech speakers, or earphone parts, etc. The analogy in this case is to growth of a whole interrelated organism in biology, which once started in a given direction is often locked in, in the same way that a complex of technologies gets locked in.

Economics, however, differs from biology in that foresight and game-playing exist. For instance, a whole collection of actors can suddenly and simultaneously switch strategies. Also, government action and regulation exist to correct or control lock-in. Nonetheless, Anderson considers the interrelated organism of biology as an attractive model of development, especially of the original breakthroughs of the agricultural and industrial revolutions, seen as an explosion caused by the natural catalysis of many interacting developments. One can also see, in any particular country like England, that the way that explosion took place can lock the economic system into a relatively inefficient mode because of the many essential interrelationships. Whatever one may say about the "web's" effect on macroeconomics, one can accept that it is an excellent metaphor for the effects of technology in the economy.

It also struck Anderson that there are just too many examples of situations where the rich get richer and the poor starve: regional hegemonies as in Europe, tribal hegemonies in Africa, socioeconomic ones in the Latin American model with, often, outside assistance, purely economic ones in the U.S. It should not be a forbidden subject to observe that differences are usually partially enforced by sociopolitical action; and it should be an interesting question whether, in fact, the purely economic interests of the hegemony are not harmed by closing out large groups from the economic engine.[23]

Holland, Professor of Computer Science, develops what he calls the adaptive nonlinear network as a way of modeling the global economy. The global economy has features that, *in the aggregate*, make it a difficult subject for traditional mathematics:

- the overall direction of the economy is determined by the interaction of many dispersed units acting in parallel. The action of any given unit depends upon the state and actions of a limited number of other units;
- there are rarely any global controls on interactions - controls are provided by mechanisms of competition and coordination between units, mediated by *standard operating procedures*, assigned roles, and shifting associations;

- the economy has many levels of organisation and interaction. Units at any given level typically serve as "building blocks" for constructing units at the next higher level. The overall organisation is more than hierarchical, with all sorts of tangling interactions (associations, channels of communication) across levels;
- the building blocks are recombined and revised continually as the system accumulates experience and adapts;
- the arena in which the economy operates is typified by many *niches* that can be exploited by particular adaptations; there is no universal *super*-competitor that can fill all niches: the result is perpetual novelty;
- because the niches are various, and new niches are continually being created, the economy operates far from an optimum so that improvements are always possible and, indeed, occur regularly.

The global economy, thus is an example, par excellence, of an *adaptive nonlinear network* (ANN) like the central nervous system, ecologies and the developmental stages of multi-celled organisms. ANNs provide for a substantial extension of traditional economics. The building blocks of traditional economics are fixed rational agents that operate in a linear, static, statistically predictable environment. In contrast, ANNs allow for intensive nonlinear interactions among large numbers of agents. These interactions are characterised by limited rationality, adaptation (learning), and increasing returns.

The mathematical tools used in linear models prove inadequate to understanding ANNs. Deeper understanding requires a mathematics that puts more emphasis on combinatorics coordinated with computer modeling. In particular, the understanding of ANNs require mathematical and modeling techniques that emphasize the emergence of structure through the combination and interaction of various units.

One major feature of ANNs is well illustrated by the global economy: ANNs do *not* act in terms of stimulus and response, they *anticipate*. In the global economy, the anticipation of an oil shortage or of a significant default of foreign loans can have profound effects upon the course of the economy, whether or not the anticipated events come to pass. Participants in the economy build up models of the rest of the economy and use them to make predictions. These models, sometimes called *internal models* are rarely explicit. They are usually more *prescriptive* (prescribing what should be done in a given situation) than *descriptive* (describing the options in a given situation).

Clearly the selective pressures placed on an ANN come from its environment. Different environments determine different evolutionary paths. Thus, to study the emergence of models, one must characterize the ANN's environment. It is traditional in economics to carry out this characterization by attaching a *utility* to the various states of the environment. The role of utility in economics is quite similar to the role of *payoff* in game theory, the *error function* in control theory, and so on. It puts a worth on the states and, hence, implicitly defines goals for the system. The ANN must search out the valuable states in the environment. For the reasons cited earlier, this is primarily *a search for improvements, not a search for optima.*[24] (emphasis added)

Thus we see that recent developments in scientific thought could impact on economics in various ways: make it more holistic and dynamic; introduce nonlinearity into the models; make economics a subsystem of the overall system by including non-economic forces in the models; make it an evolving and adaptive system; and so on.

The Factor of Technology

Attempts have been made to integrate knowledge and technology with economics. Drucker considers present economics to be no longer relevant. He thinks that the next economics would have to be knowledge based; integrate the micro-economy with the macro-economy; the real economy of commodities and work with the symbol economy of money and credit; and attempt to be both "humanity" and science. It may also have a new theory of value and may proclaim that productivity - that is, knowledge applied to resources through human work - is the source of all economic value.[25]

While Drucker sees growing productivity in "working smarter" and in "capital enhancing labour's productivity", Malpas and Watson see it in technology. They point out that economists have for decades attempted to isolate growth inputs and particularly to quantify the technology input into economies.[26]

One of the first and most influential attempts to quantify the returns from inputs into the macroeconomic system was carried out by Denison. His work highlighted a link between improving capital inputs and educational quality, leading to increased productivity. He discovered that increased productivity could result from improved knowledge, either in technology or in management.[27]

Before Denison, Robert Solow, the 1987 Nobel Prize winner in economics, expounded the view that 50 per cent of economic growth could be attributed to technological improvement. Solow considered technology to be the driving force behind an economy. His thesis argued that technology per se, rather than investment in technology, was the dynamic in economic growth.[28]

Econometric analysis also produced significant and compelling evidence to support the central role of technology in the growth process. Historical studies for the United States by Dale Jorgenson of Harvard University examined the period 1979-85. Jorgenson analyzed productivity growth in this period broken down into a number of elements. His results showed that 28 per cent of growth came from the quality of labour, 30 per cent from the quality of capital, 13 per cent from capital substitution, 24 per cent from R.& D., with an overall residual of approximately 5 per cent. This analysis supports the thesis that the enhancement of labour and capital by technology is the major source of growth.[29]

As against the stress on technology as the factor leading to economic growth, Giarini, while accepting that this was the case in the past, doubts whether this would be the case in the future. His argument is that, in a given historical context, the embodiment of technical progress in the production sphere made a period of high growth possible. But the impact of this new factor has gradually declined, until today it is negligible. In other words, technology has operated like any other factor of production employed in increasing quantities: after an extraordinary successful period, later extended by the injection of science, it has recently reached a phase of declining returns. The *global* marginal productivity of any investment in R & D is today tending towards zero, which explains the slowdown and stoppage of growth.[30]

Kapp takes the case of modern agriculture to make the point that the trend towards technology and mechanization have made agriculture shift from a diversified system of growing food to a monoculture and made heavy and increasing demands on scarce resources especially petroleum and electricity. This has not only made agriculture unsustainable and extremely vulnerable to external shocks, but also led to a dichotomy between economic returns as defined by mainstream economics in terms of "value added" and returns in forms of energy consumption. According to Kapp, while a Chinese wet-rice farmer gets for each unit of energy expended 50 units of energy in return, in the U.S. for each unit of energy expended only a fifth is got in return. This is for a U.S. system which has a very `good' profitability and cost-benefit ratio in terms of financial returns.[31]

Kapp also calls into question the use of exchange values as represented by prices as organising principles of economic systems especially when such values are incompatible with the requirements of ecological systems. Kapp goes on to say:

> As our discussion of modern agriculture has shown, the appropriate unit of analysis is neither

> the individual farm, nor the national farm economy, nor a particular ecological system. The relevant unit of analysis is much larger and the time span that counts is much longer than those in terms of which business enterprise and economic science have traditionally perceived and defined the notions of efficiency, rationality and optimality.

The answer, according to him is a systems view of the economy which makes it possible to deal with the dynamic interactions between economic systems and the whole network of physical and social systems. This approach by its very nature, would be multi-dimensional, multi-disciplinary and integrative.[32]

Efficiency in resource use is another important facet of sustainability. Environmental capacity - the availability of resources and the ability of the environment to absorb and recover - is limited and may already have exceeded its limits. Three factors determine the future demand (D) on the environment by human activities viz.

$$D = M \cdot W \cdot B$$

where:
- W is average wealth per capita
- B is population level
- M is the "metabolism" or the socio-cultural claim on the environment per unit of wealth.

This approach, formulated by Speth, gives a first order indication of the technological challenge in providing society with the technical means (embedded in culture and social structure) to meet its needs within the boundaries of environmental capacity.[33]

The first order figure that emerges from the above equation gives an idea of the amount of increase in "metabolic" efficiency required. This would depend on:

- assumptions with respect to the future development of population and wealth;

- assumptions with respect to the global distribution of eco-capacity across the world; and
- the specific socio-cultural and environmental factors under consideration.

According to Jansen, in the "industrial North" - even in case of conservative and moderate scenarios and assumptions - the efficiencies of production with respect to the claim on the environment, the environmental efficiency factors, should increase in the next twenty five years by factors varying from 5 to 50 (with an average of, say, 20) in relation to the levels of 1990. To meet this challenge, a fundamental shift in the technological availability is necessary. To bring about such orders of increases in efficiency a systemic approach is necessary.[34]

The Human Welfare Approach

The technology approach has been criticised on the ground that it does not take human beings into account and reduces them to mere consumers or factors of production. Human beings, whether as consumers or producers, have needs and values which need to be satisfied. So any theory of economics needs to start with a model of man.

Dopfer points out that part of neoclassical theory's triumph has been that its proponents succeeded in convincing a significant number of other economists that man can be reduced to his typical economic features. It has been argued that economics deals with economic phenomena and therefore requires behavioral assumptions that, self-evidently, rely on economic man - implying that not only this reduction to economic features but also the type of reduction suggested are valid. Neoclassical *homo economicus* comes out as a rational decision-maker who maximises his or her utility, basically as a trading agent in a market.

Taking man as the starting point and extending on Maslow's hierarchy of needs, Dopfer objects to the psychological bias in Maslow's approach and emphasises the necessary co-evolutionary nature of needs. He goes on to say,

> Self-realisation of man takes place in the process of *production*: a basic need to realise one's creative potential is satisfied by participating in a work process. This *process-need* is concealed in the neo-classical context where only tradable end-results come into the picture, while their generation is discounted in its welfare theoretical significance. A further major class of needs refers to the *end-results* themselves, particularly consumer goods and leisure time.
>
> Individuals have an interest in satisfying their needs and so try to actualise their interests by shaping socio-economic processes. Thus they not only act as factors of production but try to self-realise themselves as producers and consumers. This brings work into the picture, whether the work is in paid employment or is done for oneself or as voluntary social work.[35]

Conventional economic theory has reduced leisure to an end-result and counterpoised it as against work. Whether individuals develop their full potential as human beings or are bored and frustrated during their free time, becomes irrelevant. A differentiation is allowed for only when end-results (cars, television sets or sports equipment) can be introduced explicitly as utility variables and constitute a 'coupled consumption' jointly with leisure time. But this procedure implies that the more durable consumer goods we consume the more psychological satisfaction we can derive from leisure time - a disturbing result, but a significant one for the delineation of a *Weltanschaung* which equates material affluence with human well-being.

Parts of today's world have, therefore, been defined as the "affluent society". It is called an affluent society because it is argued that these societies produce a much larger variety and quantity of material things either unknown or available in limited quantities in the past. As a result, a larger percent of the population in these societies possess and enjoy these things than in the past. Put in another way, many things that only the rich and aristocratic could enjoy in the past are commonly owned by the middle class today.[36]

On the other hand if one considers the world as a whole, one also finds that a very large part of the population is extremely poor. Conservative estimates are that close to one fourth of the world population is below the poverty line, that is, not having even enough food to eat. This raises the question as to whether the world is today, in fact, affluent. And how does one distinguish between affluence and poverty?

In mainstream economics the concept of Gross National Product (GNP) has been used to define the difference between affluence and poverty. Such a methodology overlooks non-Western styles of living where simplicity of life-style constitutes the very purpose of individual and social development. With three "Eastern" views, namely, Buddhism, Hinduism and Islam we shall deal later. But it also applies in the African context.[37] Also though a few studies suggest a continuous decline in GNP over a long period of time,[38] yet, the idea that GNP has continuously increased over the past hundreds of years persists even though it runs counter to the accepted facts of the decline and fall of civilizations. Surely, at the height of its ascendancy, the Roman Empire would have produced commodities, then used, in as large quantities as some of the rich societies of today. A meaningful analysis, thus, requires a deeper understanding of the composition of production.

Theoretical and analytical neo-classical economics does not decompose production into various types of products. It abstracts the issue of composition of production by the construct of "commodity" which is, interestingly, synonymously equated with "good". The analysis is based on the following propositions: producers produce commodities, consumers derive utilities from commodities, and the market system ensures the exchange between consumers and producers.

In descriptive economic literature, the production has been classified into various categories: (i) "goods" and services, (ii) durables and non-durables, (iii) consumer, intermediate and investment goods, (iv) public and private goods, etc. Much of this classification scheme is an integral part of the production of "commodities" which assumes that production is only of "goods" and not of "bads". No differentiation is made, for example, between the production of drugs or of food. Both are considered to be different only to the extent to which they have different price tags: the price tag making drugs have more utility for human beings than food! It is only recently with the stress shifting to an environmental perspective that "bads" have been identified. But what are considered "bads" are only those which adversely affect the natural environment and not those which impact adversely on human welfare.

A broadened ecological and human welfare perspective which includes social factors like eradication of poverty would require the concepts of efficiency, productivity and profit being redefined and related to the basic variables of equity, energy, entropy and welfare.

However, in doing so it will be important to keep in mind that, although entropy is extremely useful as a variable for economic analyses, the framework of classical thermodynamics in which it originated is quite limited. Specifically, it is not adequate to describe living, self-organizing systems - whether individual organisms, social systems, or ecosystems. According to Erich Jantsch, the complexity of a system is limited only if the system is rigid, inflexible, and isolated from its environment.[39] Self-organizing systems in continual interaction with their environment are capable of tremendously increasing their complexity by abandoning structural stability in favour of flexibility and open-ended evolution. Hence the efficiency of technologies and social institutions depend not only on their complexity but also on their flexibility and potential for change.

The adoption of a broad human welfare and ecological perspective, and the use of appropriate concepts to analyze economic processes, makes evident that today the economy, social institutions, and natural environment are seriously out of balance. The obsession with growth and expansion has led to the maximising of too many variables for prolonged periods - GNP, profits, the size of cities and social institutions, and others - and the result has been a general loss of flexibility. As in individual organisms, such an imbalance and lack of flexibility can be described in terms of stress, and the various aspects of today's crisis can be seen as multiple symptoms of this social and ecological stress.

To restore a healthy balance we shall have to return those variables which have been overstrained to manageable levels. This will include, among many other measures, the decentralization of populations and industrial activities, the dismantling of large corporations and other social institutions, the redistribution of wealth, and the creation of flexible, resource-conserving technologies. As in every self-organizing system, the restoration of balance and flexibility may often be achieved through self-transcendence - breaking through a state of instability or crisis to new forms of organization.[40]

Values in Economics

The restoration of balance and flexibility in our economies, technologies, and social institutions will be possible only if it goes hand in hand with a profound change of values. Contrary to conventional belief, value systems and ethics are not peripheral to science and economics but constitute their very basis and driving force. Hence the shift to a balanced social and economic system will require a corresponding shift of values -

from self-assertion and competition to cooperation and social justice, from expansion to conservation, from material acquisition to inner growth. Those who have begun to make this shift have discovered that it is not restrictive but, on the contrary, liberating and enriching. According to Walter Weisskopf, the crucial dimensions of scarcity in the context of human life are not economic but existential. They are related to our needs for leisure and contemplation, peace of mind, love, community, and self-realization, which are all satisfied to much greater degrees by the establishment of a new system of values.[41]

In the history of economic ideas a distinction has been made between "values-in-use" and "values-in-exchange". In other words, the total production was classified into two types: those which had values-in-use only and those which had values-in-use also. Part of the so called progress towards "affluence" may lie in the fact that society now produces more value-in-exchange, even though the values-in-use have declined. The GNP type measure weights values-in-exchange by their market price and values-in-use by zero price - since these are not marketed. Therefore, the growth in production seems large though, in fact, only a shift from values-in-use to values-in-exchange has taken place.

Diwan points out that historically, the distinction between values-in-exchange and values-in-use was obliterated for two reasons. Values-in-use were integrated into values-in-exchange by the extension of the market to the poor section of the society so that the poor were forced to sell whatever they had. This integration was rationalized by the following question: who decides what values have use and for whom? Given the assumptions of rational behaviour and utility, the law of demand provided a response to the question. If a person was willing to pay for a value, that person must, by definition, conclude that the value had a use. Accordingly, values-in-exchange do have values-in-use. The institution of market ensures that values-in-exchange automatically contain values-in-use. The distinction between values-in-use and values-in-exchange, thus, seemed unnecessary, even irrelevant.[42]

There are two problems with the above argument. Firstly, the argument does not explain why poverty exists. It is interesting that poverty, even in the rich countries such as the United States, has persisted in spite of - or is it because of? -a very large growth in production of values-in-exchange in these countries. Obviously, if the values-in-exchange contained values-in-use, hunger and malnutrition would have been abolished. In the last analysis, distribution is not independent of the composition of goods. All goods cannot be only measured by their market price. A more meaningful explanation of the existence of poverty, therefore, lies in the distinction between values-in-use and values-in-exchange.

Secondly, the argument based on the rationality and utility of the consumer is a half-truth. This issue becomes clear if one analyses the rationality of a drunk and utility, to such a person, of liquor. In a drunken state, the utility of liquor is positive. Yet, in a sober state, the utility of the same liquor is at best zero if not negative. In the same way, in the general environment of a market system, values-in-exchange have values-in-use. However, in the real world of needs and feelings, there is a clear distinction between the two. Everyone needs food but not everyone needs yachts.

Refining the above scheme of classification, Diwan divides the total production in society into three categories: (i) production that creates values-in-use; these are the "goods". These are the material goods and services that help the advancement of human beings; (ii) production that generates values-in-exchange. This is a set that contains both "goods" and "bads". The nature of this production is defined by the market and exchange relations; (iii) production that promotes values-in-threat. This is a set that contains nothing else but "bads". It has the effect of harming people. Weapons are a clear example. To the above category, we would like to add a fourth category, "values-in-existence". A clear example would be the life-sustaining property of the oceans, atmosphere and other ecosystems.

It needs to be noted that the classification of production in the above four categories is not mutually exclusive. But the classification into the above categories would assist in analysing as to what constitutes sustainable development.

Giarini also points out that the whole question of value needs to be refocused - around two notions. Value is what humankind can and does produce - which means that value can also be negative, and this is indeed the case when destruction is the outcome of human activity, however scientific this might be and however much it might add to the GNP.

The other notion is that this production can and does usually take place both inside the "monetarized" system (which is economics' conventional, if not exclusive, field of enquiry) but as well outside it. Using these two notions, a new discipline, concerned with optimizing value, can be created. Moving from the restrictive interpretation of value given by current economics to that of utilization value, and shifting the accent on life cycle of products and services, it again puts man - with his needs and wants and his potential for satisfying them - exactly where he belongs, in the centre of the picture.

Capital requirements of the future world being immense, and capital formation difficult and uncertain, it is human capital which must be formed. As we are now beginning to perceive, monetary capital without adequate human development will produce little or nothing and may even be counterproductive. Which brings us back to the imperative of learning, of apprehending how to control the direction of our course in a world which is showing an increasingly more disastrous tendency to get out of hand.[43]

Conclusions

We see that though the mainstream Western paradigm is based on classical thought, there are many views being expressed which, as we shall soon see, are more in line with the Eastern paradigm. Herein lies the possibility of finding a synthesis between the two paradigms - the outer-directed Western and the inner-directed Eastern. The views of modern science are especially very much in line with the Eastern ones.

In search for a "new economics", some basic facts must be recognised. The world's ecological systems are being steadily degraded. Their condition, already seriously impaired, is going to become substantially worse before remedial action can be implemented on a large scale. Nature is being overexploited and nobody has yet figured out what the eventual consequences may be. Though a scientific theory or assessment of the Earth's "outer limits" and "life supporting capacity" is badly needed, none exists, not even in outline.

A radical change of outlook, approach and behaviour is imperative. Only by a comprehensive assessment of the ensemble of human needs and demands over a long-period - well beyond our generation - will it be possible to ensure the intelligent combination, use and conservation of whatever resources are available. It is manifestly evident that, without a rigorous global management of resources, the needs of an ever more demanding multi-billion society can never be satisfied.

These tenets of conservation and good management concur with ethical principles whereby the Earth's natural endowment, the "common heritage of humankind", is held as something for which each generation is a trustee for those to come, and only as a income beneficiary. This requires a new concept of wealth and welfare which can embrace diverse cultural views.

As Aurelio Peccei says in his preface to *Dialogue on Wealth and Welfare*,

> the current paradigms of economics and the philosophy underpinning the notions of wealth,

welfare and value derive from a cultural experience that originated in Europe a couple of centuries ago and was later adopted in the so-called developed countries. Whatever its merits, it can no longer offer orientation and support to the heterogeneous community of nations of our time, which, despite the growing global interdependencies and the planetarization of problems, is characterized by a great diversity - and richness - of cultures and by profound cross-purposes.[44]

We turn now to some other cultures and what, if anything, they have to offer to the global ethic of sustainable development.

References

1. Kenneth Arrow, Bert Bolin, Robert Constanza, Partha Dasgupta, Carl Folke, C.S. Holling, Bengt-Owe Jansson, Simon Levin, Karl-Goran Maler, Charles Perrings, David Pimentel, "Economic Growth, Carrying Capacity, and the Environment", *Science*, Vol. 268, 1995, pp. 520-521.
2. See P. Ehrlich and A. Ehrlich, *Population, Resources and Environment: Issues in Human Ecology* (San Fransisco: W.H. Freeman, 1972).
3. Herman Daly, "The economic growth debate", *Journal of Environmental Economic Management* 14(1987), pp.323-26.
4. R.E. Munn, "Towards Sustainable Development," *Proceedings of a Symposium on Managing Environmental Stress* (Australia: University of New South Wales, 1990).
5. IUCN/UNEP/WWF, *Caring for the World* (Switzerland: Gland, 1991).
6. See Partha Dasgupta, "The Environment as a Commodity", *Oxford Review of Economic Policy*, Vol. 6, No. 1, 1990, pp. 51-67 and Pearce and Turner, *Economics of Natural Resources and the Environment* (New York: Harvester Wheatsheaf, 1990).

7. Arrow et.al., note 1.
8. H. Daly, *Steady-State Economics* (San Fransisco: W.H. Freeman, 1977).
9. Ilya Prigogine and Isabelle Stengers, *Order Out of Chaos*, 4th edition (New York: Bantam, 1984).
10. Ilya Prigogine and G. Nicolis, *Self-Organisation in Non-Equilibrium Systems: From Dissipative Structures to Order through Fluctuations* (New York: Wiley Interscience, 1977).
11. WCED, *Our Common Future* (Oxford University Press, 1987) p.1.
12. J.E. Lovelock, *Gaia: A new look at life on Earth* (Oxford University Press, 1979) p.1.
13. W.S. Jevons, *The Theory of Political Economy*, 2nd. ed. (London: Macmillan, 1879).
14. Alfred Marshal and Mary Marshal, *The Economics of Industry* (London: Macmillan, 1879) p.2.
15. Alfred Marshal, *The Principles of Economics*, 8th ed. (London: Macmillan, 1920) p.36.
16. Daniel Bell and Irving Kristol, *Crisis in Economic Theory* (New York: Basic Books, 1981).
17. G.M. Hodgson and E. Screpanti (eds.), *Rethinking Economics: Markets, Technology and Economic Evolution* (Aldershot, Hampshire, U.K.: Edward Elgar, 1991) p.1.
18. Ibid., pp. 6-8
19. Fritjof Capra, *The Turning Point: Science, Society and the Rising Culture* (New York: Flamingo, Harper Collins, 1982) p.431.
20. Capra, ibid., pp.432-434.
21. Philip W. Anderson, Kenneth J. Arrow and David Pines (eds.), *The Economy as an Evolving Complex System* (Reading, Mass.: Addison-Wesley, 1988).
22. Kenneth J. Arrow, "Workshop on the Economy as an Evolving Complex System: Summary", *Economy as an Evolving Complex System*, note 21, pp. 275-279.
23. Philip W. Anderson, "A Physicist Looks at Economics: An Overview of the Workshop" *Economy as an Evolving Complex System*, note 21, pp. 268-272.

24. John H. Holland, "The Global Economy as an Adaptive Process" *Economy as an Evolving Complex System*, note 21, pp. 117-120.

25. Peter Drucker, *Toward the Next Economics and Other Essays* (London: Walter Heinemann, 1981).

26. Robert Malpas and Simon Watson, "Technology and Wealth Creation" *The Economics of Wealth Creation*, James Ball, (ed.) (Aldershot, Hampshire, U.K.: Edward Elgar, 1992) pp. 208-231.

27. E.F. Denison, *Why Growth Rates Differ* (Washington D.C.: Brookings, 1967).

28. R.M. Solow, "Technical Change and the Aggregate Production Function," *Review of Economics and Statistics*, 39, 1957.

29. D. Jorgenson, "Investing in Productivity Growth" *National Academy of Engineering Symposium*, Washington D.C., 1990.

30. Orio Giarini and Henri Louberge, *The Diminishing Returns of Technology* (New York: Pergamon, 1978) p.47.

31. K.W. Kapp, "The Open-System Character of the Economy and its implications", *Economics in the Future*, Kurt Dopfer, ed., (London: Macmillan, 1976) p.90-105.

32. Kapp, ibid., p.96.

33. J.G. Speth, "Can the world be saved?" *Ecological Economics*, vol. 1, 1989, pp. 289-302.

34. Leo Jansen, "Towards a sustainable future enroute with technology" *The Environment: Towards a Sustainable Future* (London: Kluwer, 1994) p. 499.

35. Kurt Dopfer, "Introduction: Sik's Third Way of Economic Evolution," *The Evolution of Economic Systems*, Dopfer and Raible (eds.) (London: Macmillan, 1990) p.3.

36. J.K. Galbraith, *The Affluent Society* (Boston: Houghton - Mifflin Co., 1956).

37. See, for example, Albert Teveodjre, *Poverty: Wealth of Mankind*(New York: Pergamon Press, 1978).

38. See, for example, Daniel Thorner, "Long-Term Trends in Output in India," *Economic Growth: Brazil, India, Japan*, S. Kuznets (ed.) (Durham N.C.: North Carolina Press, 1955) pp. 103-128.

39. Erich Jantsch, *The Self-Organising Universe* (New York, Pergamon, 1980).
40. Capra, note 19, p. 439.
41. Walter A. Weisskopf, *Alienation and Economics* (New York: Dutton, 1971) p.24.
42. Ramesh Diwan, "Economics of Bread Labour", *Essays in Gandhian Economics*, Ramesh Diwan and Mark Lutz (eds) (New Delhi: Gandhi Peace Foundation, 1985) pp. 109-127.
43. Orio Giarini, *Dialogue on Wealth and Welfare* (Oxford: Pergamon Press, 1980), p.ix.
44. Aurelio Peccei, ibid., p. viii.

4

Hinduism: Nature, Society and Economics

For the first time the people of the world have become one interlinked whole, with every one being affected by what happens to others. Science and technology and economic and political phenomena are increasingly imposing on us the obligation to treat the world as a single integrated unit. Currencies are linked, commerce is international, political fortunes are interdependent. And yet the sense that mankind must become one community is still a vague aspiration and not generally accepted as a conscious ideal or an urgent necessity moving us to common citizenship and the call of a common duty. Attempts to bring about human unity through institutional means, through political adjustments, have proved abortive. It is not by these devices, not at any rate by them alone, that the unity of the human race can be accomplished. For this to occur there has to be some common ground, some understanding of other cultures and societies, some accommodation to the thoughts and views of others.

The dominant culture for the last few centuries has been the European. Ever since the Renaissance, the subsequent developments in science, and European colonization of the world in the nineteenth century, the European ethos has been the dominant one. The only past known to the Europeans emerging from the Middle Ages was the Biblical and the Graeco-Roman. So these were the cultures studied and interpreted during the Renaissance. Now that we have the whole world for our cultural base, the process cannot be confined to the study of Isaiah and Paul, Socrates and Cicero. That would be a failure of perspective. For there are others also who have participated in the global human drama - the prophets of Egypt, the sages of China, the seers of India.

Of the living non-European civilizations, the chief are the Islamic, the East Asian (Chinese, Japanese, Korean, and so on) and the Hindu. The Islamic has the same historical background as Judaism and Christianity, and so is somewhat better known in the West than the Hindu and Chinese civilizations. The East Asian system, especially its Confucian aspect has also been studied in recent times, especially since the development of the tiger economies of the Pacific rim. But Hindu civilization has largely been left unstudied in so far as its impacts on economics and nature are concerned. It is in the above context that a study of Hinduism, and later on of Buddhism, and its impact on nature, economics and ecology is being made.

Hinduism

Religion has been the master passion of the Hindu mind, the presupposition and basis of its civilization, the driving force of its culture, and the expression - in spite of its many failures, divisions, and degradations - of its life in God. A study of Hinduism is thus essential before delineating its relationship with nature and the concepts of economics, ecology and sustainable development flowing therefrom.

Hinduism is not really a religion, it is more a culture. It has no central set of beliefs or dogma. It allows every individual the freedom of belief and to practice the faith which one believes in. It is a vast reservoir, which enriches itself by absorbing from various diverse cultural and religious streams. Throughout history, it has evolved through interaction with different cultures and religions. According to Hindu belief, no single religion has the monopoly of truth. Consequently, everyone has to find his or her own way to truth and salvation. In the Hindu scheme of things, the greater the diversity, the greater is the cultural richness of the community and therefore, one should foster, rather than destroy the diversity.

Hinduism also adopts a rationalist attitude in the matter of society, culture and religion. Religion to the Hindu is not so much a revelation to be attained in faith as an effort to unveil the deepest layers of man's being and get into enduring contact with them. And this has to be achieved through the so called spiritual or yogic practices so as to have a direct perception of reality. Stress is thus not on rites and ceremonies but on inner, liberating experience.

This attitude has meant that throughout the ages Hinduism has absorbed, and preserved the thoughts and rituals of other cults and religions only insisting on the other cults and religions understanding the inner significance of the rituals as emanating from the One Divine. Instead of destroying them, therefore, it adapted them to its stress on inner liberating experience. As Sri Krishna says in the *Bhagavad Gita*,

> Let not the wise disturb the mind of the unwise
> in their selfish work. Let him, working in devotion,
> show them the joy of good work. (III.26)[1]

This advice was necessary as otherwise the inability to harmonize the outer with the inner could lead to schizophrenia in spiritually immature minds.

Through the following of this attitude and approach Hinduism ended up by taking so much from the social life of the native inhabitants of India that it is very difficult to disentangle the Aryan elements from others. The interpenetration has been so complex, subtle, and continuous, that there has grown up a distinct Hindu civilization which is neither Aryan nor non-Aryan. But all the time the dream of a unified culture, of a Unity, has persisted and inspired the imagination of its spiritual leaders.

Another result has been the development of innumerable scriptures and books expounding the various aspects of Hinduism. But all of them are unified in a complex and subtle way. The *Rig Veda* (c.6000 BC), the most ancient of Hindu scriptures, has this to say,

> The sages speak of what is One in many ways;
> they call it *Agni*, *Yama*, *Matarishwan* (1.164.46)
>
> Seers and poets with words flowing from their imagination make into many the hidden reality which is but One (10.114.5)[2]

The One is thus said to be spoken of (*vadanti*) by sages or imagined (*kalpayanti*) by poets and seers in different ways. This leads to the concept of diversity in unity.

The *Upanishads*, which are post-Vedic, adopt the same liberal attitude. The oneness of the Supreme is insisted on, but variety of description is permitted. The light of absolute truth is said to be refracted as it passes through the imperfect human nature. In the boundless being of the One are all the powers that Hindus worship as gods (or angels in biblical terminology), not as if they were standing side by side in space, but each a facet mirroring the whole, or a hologram to put it in modern language.

The triumphs of the Hindu method of religious reform have been striking: no less are its failures. It has been able to avoid religious wars and synthesize other cultures in the most peaceful manner. But there are also many deficiencies. Hinduism, for example, goes from the sublime to the most superstitious of beliefs. It is simultaneously admirable and abhorrent, saintly and savage, beautifully wise and dangerously silly, generous beyond measure and yet mean in many ways.

Primitive superstitions when they were taken over by Hinduism were given added respectability. It became difficult, therefore, to make men quit their old ways, overcome indolence and inertia, and venture on new paths. Though the most revolting practices of cannibalism, polyandry, and human sacrifices were soon abolished, others, such as animal sacrifices, repugnant to our moral sentiments still persist.

The Hindu method, being democratic and non-violent, tends to be slow and laborious. Reform by consent is slower than reform by compulsion though it has the human touch. An extensive application of the principle of liberty, equality, and fraternity has made Hinduism the most elastic of all religions, the most capable of adapting itself to new conditions. It is less dependent on historical facts, is freer from authority. Its gods form no exclusive group. Its pantheon has stood wide open for the admission of new deities who are naturalized as aspects of the Supreme godhead. The danger of the Hindu attitude is that what *is* may be accepted because it *is*, and progress and transformation thereby delayed.

Hinduism and Nature

The Vedas, which contain the germ of all the later developments of the Hindu genius, probably took their present shape in the second millennium before Christ, but their roots go back to far more ancient times and take us back to the very beginning of human speech. Perhaps nowhere else can one observe the whole process of human evolution from its primordial utterance to the most elaborate poetic speech and the most profound philosophy. The Vedas are known as *shruti*, that which has been 'heard'; they are not merely the product of human ingenuity but of revelation, that is an 'unveiling' of the truth. They are also called *nitya*, that is 'eternal', signifying that they do not derive from the world of time and change, but are reflections of the eternal. Finally, they are said to be *apauruseya*, 'without human authorship', they are expressions of the eternal word, the *vak*, and the human authors are *rishis*, those who have 'seen' the truth, and 'poets' (*kavi*), those whose utterance is inspired. This shows how in ancient times speech - the word - was held to be something divine, a gift of God, and poets, those who had the gift of speech, were inspired by God.

Ancient man, that is man from the earliest times until the first millennium before Christ (and even after that in the greater part of the world until the present day), lived in the world of the imagination, that is the world of integral wholeness. Of this world of the imagination the supreme expression was the myth. Myth is a symbolic utterance which arises from the depths of the unconscious, or rather from the deep levels of consciousness. The rational mind, with its abstract concepts and logical constructions, is like the tip of an iceberg, while below it are vast levels of consciousness which link our human nature with the universe around us and with the archetypes or transcendent principles which govern the Universe. The myth is the reflection in the human imagination of these archetypal ideas, those cosmic principles and powers, which were known in the ancient world as the gods or angels.

In the Vedic myth there is a constant conflict between light and the darkness. The darkness is represented by Vritra, the primeval monster, who holds back the waters of life and hides the light of the sun. He represents the primeval darkness of the unconscious, conceived as a rocky cavern in which the cows as, symbols of light, are concealed. They represent the rays of the sun, so that the dawn can be described as the releasing of the cows from their pen. But these rays of light are not merely earthly light, they are the light of the mind, and the search of the sages in the Vedas is a search for illumination of mind. Elsewhere the powers of darkness are called the Panis and their chief is named Vala. It may well be that these sources of darkness represent the dark, Dravidian people who were the enemies of the fair-skinned Aryans, or again they may represent the dark thunder clouds which withhold the rain, but this only reveals the multiple symbolism of the Vedas. Everything has at once a physical and a psychological, including a social, meaning and behind all the symbols is the one supreme Reality which is manifesting itself at every level of existence.

The Myth of Creation is another of the great myths of the Vedas. Says the *Rig Veda*,

> There was neither Non-existence nor Existence,
> Nor was there the Earth or Sky beyond,
> What was the covering, whence, and at whose shelter,
> Was there the primeval Water with depth unfathomed?
>
> Death was not then, nor was there Immortality,
> There was no sign of day and night,
> That One in the breathless space breathed on its own,
> Apart from that there was nothing whatever.
>
> Darkness at the beginning was covered with darkness,
> and this All was indiscriminated chaos;
> All was then in the Void contained, only the One
> hath emerged with its mighty radiance.
>
> Thence arose primal Desire in the beginning,
> the first seed of the Mind;
> Wise sages searched into the heart of mystery,
> and found Existence's kinship in Non-existence.[3]

The subject of the above hymn is creation: what existed before creation started and how creation took place. The underlying sense seems to be that absolute transcendence must transform itself into a pure immanence so that creation may emerge out of it, a point more directly expressed in a number of other hymns.[4] The hymn states that the One, the transcendent, is not directly involved in the creative process. In fact, while the One *is*-that is, simply abides as one-no creation can take place, and as a result, there are none of the oppositions that arise within creation, such as existence and nonexistence, death and immortality, earth and sky, day and night. Creation is the process of the One's expansion into the *all*, which at this stage is contained in the void, of the primeval procreative waters, "the darkness covered with darkness" of the undifferentiated chaos. The One's mighty radiance, "the fulfilling energy up yonder," gives rise to the first form, which is desire from within the void of the waters.

The primal desire's arising in this manner evinces two very important factors in the creative process: (1) the transformation of the One's absolute transcendence into pure immanence, whereby the primal desire projects itself as psychic energy, that is, as the "first seed of mind"; and (2) the projection of this psychic energy, which has the immediate effect of distinguishing itself from the corresponding matter (potencies) manifest within the void. Thus, with the arising of desire the ground is ready for creative activity in which psychic energy works on matter to create further forms out of it.

Clearly this hymn is concerned with the grounding of creation in the One. The grounding must be understood in a twofold manner as both immanent and transcendent. The Lord of creation is immanent, but the repose of this immanence is absolute transcendence. This state of creation would thus seem to render its secret beyond even the comprehension of the sages. Indeed, the hymn itself says that the secret of creation is realized only in the depth of the heart, that is, by means of exclusive devotion.

The *Rig Veda* in another hymn, the *Purusha Sukta*, the Primal Man, describes the pervasive nature of the immanent *Purusha* as one "who possesses a thousand heads, arms, and feet".[5] The immanent One, is however, at the same time transcendent:

> Mightier than His might is *purusha*,
> One-fourth of whom is all that has come into being,

While three-fourths of him resides in the region of immortality.
With three-fourths hath *purusha* risen up,
With one-fourth having become again this,
Thence spreading over what eats and does not eat.[6]

The might of *Purusha*, the indweller God, is expressed in creation, which by virtue of God's presence abides as a self-renewing and eternal process. But, lest one misunderstand that God thus immanent in the world process is not distinct from it, we are immediately reminded that God, the indwelling *purusha*, is greater that His might, in the sense that God essentially transcends the world process. Creation itself is divided into two distinct regions: the region of immortality and that of death. Immortality lies in transcending the material world, or of spiritualizing it.

Later in the hymn, there is the sacrifice and dismemberment of the *Purusha* and that leads to creation. In this symbolic sacrifice, the whole, eternal, self-regenerating process, symbolized by the cycle of spring, summer, and autumn, enters as its ritualistic content, the human, the embodied being, as the sacrificial lamb. The hymn goes on to refer to the *Purusha*, the primeval cosmic being, as the source and origin not only of the physical universe but also of religion and the social order. Quite clearly everything in this world was perceived as bodily related to the divine source, the body of God. "The moon was born from his spirit, from his eye was born the sun...from his navel arose the sky and from his head originated the heaven...".[7]

In the above myth, consciousness is not considered as different from nature or matter. Science is slowly recovering the knowledge, which was universal in the ancient world, that there is no such thing as matter apart from mind or consciousness. Consciousness is latent in every particle of matter and the mathematical order which science discovers in the universe is due to the working of this universal consciousness in it.[8] In human nature this latent consciousness begins to come into actual consciousness, and as human consciousness develops it grows more and more conscious of the universal consciousness in which it is grounded. The link between humanity and nature is, thus, through the universal consciousness which manifests itself when the embodied being is sacrificed. Out of this myth has grown the later "giving up of wants" of Hinduism as a sacrifice and so a way of realizing the original state of consciousness.

The Hindu Societal System

In dealing with any social organization we must inquire into the essential ideas on which it is founded, the conception of life which inspires it, and the forms which these ideas of life assume. In the case of Hinduism, there has been from the earliest times the concept of harmonizing pluralities into the unified whole. For as the earlier discussion has shown, those pluralities arose from the dismemberment through sacrifice of the One.

The pluralities were considered to have been created by the relativity of human perception, the refraction of the light of the One as it passed through individual personalities. Even sages and seers, according to the *Rig Veda*, speak of, and conceive, the Unity as a multiplicity: the One of whom the sages speak in various ways.[9] In all its formulations, therefore, the Hindu thinkers try to find unity in the multiplicity, whether in religion, philosophy or society.

It needs to be noted, however, that inspiring ideas are always larger than the historical forms which embody them. This is, as we shall soon see, the case in Hinduism. The Hindu view of the individual and his relation to society in its ideal form can be best brought out by a reference to the synthesis and gradation of:

- the fourfold object of life (*purushartha*), which is, virtuous and ethical living (*dharma*), earning of wealth (*artha*), happiness and pleasure (*kama*), and liberation (*moksha*);

- the fourfold order of society (*varna*), consisting of the man of learning (*brahmin*), of power (*kshatriya*), of skilled productivity (*vaishya*), and of service (*shudra*); and
- the fourfold succession of the stages of life (*ashrama*), namely, student (*brahmachari*), householder (*grihastha*), social servant (*vanaprastha*), and the suprasocial individual (*sanyasin*).

The social structure is conceived on three interlinked axes with four dimensions each, namely, the objectives of life, the ideal order of society, and the stages of life. The last is in the time dimension while the first two are in social space. In this multi-dimensional concept, equality (which is an important aspect of unity) is sought, as we shall presently see, not in the means but in the end, that is, liberation or *moksha*. This liberation is attainable to everyone not on the basis of psycho-technical capacity or position in the social order (which are bound to be different and so unequal) but in how well each individual utilizes his abilities and opportunities. As Sri Krishna says to Arjuna in the *Bhagavad Gita*,

> He who makes pure his work by Yoga, who watches over his soul, who by wisdom destroys his doubts, is the liberated man.[10]

The three axes can also be looked at in a systems analytical framework. The fourfold order of society (*varna*) and the four stages of life (*ashrama*) form a 4x4 matrix which characterises the social structure in the time dimension. And in fact the two have always been referred to together as *varnashrama*.[11] Every element of the social matrix has a quadruple objective function laid down by the ends to be attained (*purushartha*). It will thus be seen that everyone in the social system has to have knowledge (so that he can understand the moral code, *dharma*), means of livelihood (*artha*) and enjoyment (*kama*) so that he can ultimately liberate himself from all social and other bonds (*moksha*). In other words, every individual has to have the possibility of living a full life. Besides the multiple objective function means that no generalised and unique answer as to how to go through life is possible; it varies from individual to individual.

The four ends of life

The chief end of man, according to the Hindu scriptures, is the attainment of liberation through proper development of the individual. Man is not only an assemblage of body, life, and mind born of, and subject to physical nature. The body with which he confuses himself is not his whole or real being. It is but an instrument for the use of the inner spirit which is the real truth of his being. To exceed his apparent outward self is the aim of a human being. To inquire into his true self, to live in it, to determine what it is inwardly and what use it shall make of its outward circumstances, is to attain to spiritual freedom.

The *Katha Upanishad* says,

> The Self-Existent made the senses turn outward. Accordingly, man looks toward what is without, and sees not what is within. Rare is he who, longing for immortality, shuts his eyes to what is without and beholds the Self.[12]

Is such striving for perfection consistent with normal life? Hinduism affirms that it is. While accepting the spontaneous activities of earning wealth and desire Hinduism asserts that their full value cannot be realized without a rule, a guidance, a restraint. *Dharma*, or the art of ethical living, is what gives coherence and direction to the different activities of life. It is the complete rule of life, the harmony of the whole man who finds a right and just law of his living. Each man and group, each activity of soul, mind, life, and body, has its *dharma*. Thus while man is justified in satisfying his desires, to wholly conform to the dictates of his desires is not, and cannot be, the law of his being. He can only get the best out of them if he conforms to the *dharma* which tells us that while our life is in the first instance for our own satisfaction, it is more essentially for the good of the community. The community of man is the whole world and so the *Bhagavad Gita* advises that we should work for *loksangraha* or world-solidarity.[13]

The next end relates to wealth and material well-being. Though wealth is not its own end, it helps to sustain and enrich life. There was never in India a national ideal of poverty or squalor. Spiritual life finds full scope only in communities of a certain degree of freedom from sordidness. Lives that are strained and starved cannot be religious except in a rudimentary way. Economic insecurity and individual freedom do not go together.

There is a widely prevalent idea that the Hindu view concedes no reality to life, that it despises vital aims and satisfactions, that it gives no inspiring motive to human effort. There is little in Hindu thought to support the view that one has to attain spiritual freedom by means of abstaining from normal life. On the other hand, it lays down that we must pass through the normal life conscientiously and with knowledge, work out its values, and accept its enjoyments (*kama*). Spiritual life is an integration of man's being, in its depth and breadth, in its capacity for deep meditation as well as enjoyment of physical life. *Kama* refers to the emotional being of man, his feelings and desires. If man is denied his emotional life, he becomes a prey to repressive introspection as has been pointed out by Freud. Sri Krishna says to Arjuna, "I am *kama* which is not divorced from *dharma*".[14] It is not desire that is to be rooted out but its unrestrained activity.

Dharma, *artha* and *kama* are neither the beginning nor the end of human life, for beyond them is spiritual freedom, of *moksha*, a universality which ennobles the life of the individual and the whole order of society. Man's life is to be passed in the implicit consciousness of this background.

The four ends of life point to the different sides of human nature, the intellectual and the ethical, the economic, the instinctive and the emotional, and the spiritual. There is implanted in man's fundamental being a spiritual capacity. He becomes completely human only when his sensibility to spirit is awakened. So long as man's life is limited to science, technical invention, and socio-economic programmes, he is incomplete. If we are unfair and unkind to one another, unhappy in personal relationships, and lacking in mutual understanding, life cannot be complete. We have to get out of remaining too much on the surface of life and regain contact with its depths.

It is instructive to study human values in the light of the comprehensive Hindu concept of the four *purusharthas*, i.e. values sought after by *purusha* or man. These are as we have noted, *dharma*, *artha*, *kama* and *moksha*. In its scale of values, Hinduism finds an honoured place for all desires and urges of man, from the material and sensory to the moral, ethical, and super-sensory or transcendental. The Sanskrit word and concept, *kama*, desire, constitutes the entire range of human cravings and satisfactions at the sensory level; it is the first of the *purusharthas*. The second *purusartha* is *artha*, wealth, which is the instrument for the satisfaction of *kama*. The third *purushartha* is known as *dharma*, which means ethical sense, and which helps to discipline and regulate the pursuit of the first and the second objectives, namely, desire and the pursuit of wealth, so that all persons in a society get the opportunity to satisfy their urge for them. Human values in socio-economic management proceed from this third *purushartha* of *dharma*; though third in order from the point of view of human experience, it is put first in all enumerations, due to its primacy and importance. This *dharma* is essentially what manifests spontaneously as a by-product of man's inner growth, of man's spiritual growth, from the freedom of individuality to the freedom and social responsibility of personality.

The four classes

The aim of *dharma* is thus to understand the outer life of man and subject it to control through inner development. *Dharma* has two sides: the social and the individual; the social deals with the duties assigned to the position of individuals in society as determined by their character and function; the individual deals with the duties relevant to the stage of life, youth, manhood, or old age. The complex matrix which is created by the interaction of individual and social *dharma* leads to four ideal classes in society. The social *dharma* of the four classes will be dealt with from three different standpoints, the spiritual-social, the ethical-psychological, and the conventional.

The earliest reference to the four classes is in the *Purusha Sukta* of the *Rig Veda*, where they are described as having sprung from the body of the Divine Person (the *Purusha*), from his mouth, arms, thighs, and feet.[15] This poetical image is intended to convey the organic character of society. Man is not only a separated individual but is also in solidarity with his kind: as well as with the Divine. The stress on the universal in its movement towards the goal is the source of man's sociality. Man is also not an abstract entity. He belongs to a certain social group by virtue of his character, behaviour, and function in the community. In the fourfold division of society, the suggestion is that spiritual wisdom, executive power, skilled production, and devoted service are the indispensable elements of any social order: the wise to work out the proper relationships, the powerful to back it by authority, and the skilled to execute it with the help of devoted workers. Dynamism in society (movement) comes from the economic aspects represented by the entrepreneurs (the thighs) and the workers (feet), while the state (arms) regulate and control and the men of knowledge (the head) lay down the basic moral and social parameters.

As the individual is a social being, society is the necessary means by which he attains the development of his personality. A secure and proper place, in line with his psychological make up, has therefore to be found for him in the community so that he can derive the utmost help from it. Society should not be something alien or an imposition. For then man would either be crushed or rebel against society. The social system should be such as to allow him freedom to develop to his full potential.

By his psycho-ethical nature, man falls into four types, the man of learning and knowledge, the man of power and action, the skilled producer, and the laborer. The types are determined by the prominent elements of man's nature.

Those who are pre-eminently intellectual are the *brahmins*, whose function it is to seek knowledge, communicate it to others, and make it prevail in the world. Their activity is not the pursuit of practical aims in the narrow sense. They should seek joy in the practice of an art like yoga, a science, or a philosophy as a disinterested intellectual pursuit.

While it is the business of the *brahmin* to lay down the set of values, draw out a blueprint for social reconstruction, and persuade the world to accept the high ends of life, it is the business of the *kshatriya* to devise the means for gaining the ends. Also how to regulate, preserve and harmonize the social fabric.

The qualities that mark the *kshatriya* type are a determination from which no danger or difficulty can distract, a dynamic daring, a nobility of soul which would do nothing sordid or mean, and an unflinching resistance to injustice and oppression. The worshippers of power, the men of brute force, the selfish tyrants are the perversions of this type. The qualities of the *kshatriya* are as necessary as those of the *brahmin* for the perfection of human nature.

In the above concept, the political is not conceived as the highest category. The State exists in order that its members may have a good life. It is a social convenience. It is not the judge of its own conduct. Though righteousness depends on force, 'it is wrong to say that it is the will of the strong'.[16] The State is not above *dharma*; rather it is bound by *dharma* or the law. It exists essentially for the good of the individual. As Kautiliya says in the *Arthashastra* (Science of Wealth, 4th Century B.C. and arguably the oldest extant book on political economy), the duty of the state is to ensure to every one the undisturbed enjoyment of what they have acquired and have security and well being (*yogakshema*).[17] The elevation of the State to a position where it can even justify killing if the ends of state policy so require is totally opposed to the Hindu view. Rama tells Lakshmana: 'I bear arms for the sake of truth. It is not difficult for me to gain this whole universe but I desire not even the suzerainty of the heavens if it is to be through unrighteousness.'[18]

The third class that of *vaishyas,* brings into relief the tendency of life to possess and enjoy, to give and take. In its outward action, this power appears as the utilitarian and the practical engaged in commerce and industry. But in fact the *vaishya* is also required to be marked by humanity and ordered benevolence. The *vaishya* class being engaged in pursuits where the temptations to the acquisition and hoarding of wealth exist they are expected to develop qualities of humanity and neighbourly service. If they are keen on wealth for its own sake, they are to be 'detested'. It is not their main function to contribute to the spiritual welfare of society or its political power, yet we cannot have these without their co-operation. Practical intelligence and adaptive skill are their chief qualities.

The perversions of this type are familiar to us, as our age is pre-eminently a commercial one. Armament manufacturers, for example foment discords between nations for the sake of profits. Merchants make millions through the sale of drugs that destroy the body, mind, and soul of people. Commerce and industry, which are the life-blood of the human race, are perverted from their proper use by a false standard of values. Property, according to the Hindu view, is a mandate held by its possessors for the common use and benefit of the common weal. The *Bhagavad Gita* tells us that we have a claim only to so much as is deserved by our acts of sacrifice i.e. unselfishness. If any one selfishly desires more, he is a thief.[19]

The fourth variety of human nature finds its outlet in work and service. Labour is the basis of all human activities. While the first three classes are said to be twice born, since they have had spiritual growth, the fourth is said to be once born. It only means that the activities of the members of the fourth class are instinctive and not governed by yogic knowledge. *Manu* has this to say,

> The staff of the *brahmana* shall be made of such length as to reach of the end of his hair; that of a *kshatriya*, to reach his forehead; (and) that of a *vaishya*, to reach the (tip of his) nose.[20]

The above is obviously a reference to the seven yogic centres of consciousness (*chakras*) with the brahmin being one who has attained the seventh or highest centre, the kshatriya the sixth centre, and the vaishya the fifth centre. The staff is the "spiritual spine" in which these *chakras* are supposed to be placed. Frawley has also pointed out the yogic nature of the four classes.[21]

The spiritual differentiation of society is based on the main values we follow in life defined by the Vedic sages as pleasure, wealth, ethics, and liberation. These values create four classes and four mental natures. If we pursue pleasure we develop a servile mentality, as we become dependent upon external sources of enjoyment and stimulation. If we pursue wealth we develop a commercial mentality and judge the world in terms of property and prices. If we pursue fame or power we develop a political or militaristic mentality and its distinctions of ranks and status.

This has to be moderated by an ethical attitude. If we pursue liberation we develop a spiritual mentality and seek the higher knowledge. We then perceive people by their freedom of mind and spirit.

Such a fourfold division of society is not artificial. Our values in life determine how we see the world and how we act within it. We cannot pursue commercial values as the most important thing in life, for example, and yet find the knowledge that liberates our soul. Our commercial preconceptions will colour our knowledge and distort it. They will cause us to use religion for commercial ends. We may pursue wealth as a secondary goal, but if it is our primary goal we cannot expect to understand the truth of things, which requires freedom from the need to gain materially from them.

All cultures have these four groups. Though each culture may not have a specific system for regulating them, they still appear as classes within society. In Western society there are labour, commercial, political, and religious classes; divisions of society with their own laws and territory, particular needs and spokespersons. This is not to say that each group appears in its true form, however. For example, even religion is dominated by political and commercial interests.

Pleasure, wealth and power are outer goals - the things of the external world bound by time. Liberation is the inner goal that alone takes us beyond time. Hence we can divide human cultures into two basic groups: those pursuing outer and those pursuing inner goals. In this context there are only spiritual or materialistic cultures.

However, in life the outer goals commonly mask themselves as the inner. This is the great tragedy from which the greatest confusion and illusion arises. We veil our seeking of wealth and power as a pursuit of truth or as serving religion. Religion is used as a mask for promoting commercial and political goals. This is not something done consciously. Most of the time we are victims of our own desires, which we blindly transfer into the religious realm where they have no place.

It is to prevent such intermingling of the sacred and profane from taking place that the sages have created the concept of the *brahmin* who, according to *Manu*, "is forbidden from taking service under a king",[22] "has to acquire knowledge, teach and give alms",[23] "seek a means of bare subsistence which causes no pain to others".[24] Those who lay down the law, therefore, are to have no link with the state and are to live in poverty. This enables them to be objective in their dealings with the powerful and the wealthy.

It is to be noted that the qualities which are predominant in each of the four classes are not exclusive of one another. As a matter of fact there is no individual who does not possess all these essentials. Classes are marked as wise or heroic, skilled or unskilled, according as one or the other quality predominates in them. None of these can be regarded as complete. The *brahmin* cannot serve truth with freedom if he has not moral courage and heroism, if he has not the practical sense to adapt the highest truth to the conditions of actual life and the needs of the different classes of society, if he has not the sense of service to humanity. Even the man of action, though he is not engaged in the pursuit of wisdom, has to have a sense of the direction of society, the aims it has, and the way in which he has to sanction the details essential for the realization of those aims. He uses his power for the service of the society. He has a general idea of the nature of the social good, has the courage and the enterprise essential for the exploitation of resources, and is anxious to improve the material conditions of life in every conceivable way. The man of labour is a part of the social order and strives to serve society through his special function with knowledge, honour, and skill.

According to Radhakrishnan, the fourfold scheme is, in a real sense democratic. Firstly, it insists on the spiritual equality of all men. It assumes that within every human being there is a self which has the right to grow in its own way, to find itself, and make its life a full and satisfied image and instrument of its being.

Secondly, it makes for individuality in a positive sense. Individuality is attained not through an escape from limitations but through the willing acceptance of obligations.

Thirdly, it points out that all work is socially useful and, from a spiritual standpoint, equally important.

Fourthly, social justice is not a scheme of rights but of opportunities. It is not assumed that all men are alike. Wisdom in action as required by the *Bhagavad Gita* (*yogah karmasu kaushalam*) is specific to individuals and cannot be universal.[25] Equality in the hindu sense thus refers to opportunity and not to capacity. While it recognizes that men are unequal in capability, it insists that every human being shall have the right and the opportunity to contribute to human achievement, as far as his capacity for making the best of life goes.

Fifthly, the essence of democracy is consideration for others. Freedom for the individual means restrictions on absolute power. No one class can make unlimited claims.

Sixthly, the general tendency of men of all classes to strive to climb the social ladder is due to an impression that the position at the top is one of pleasure, profit, and power. But in the Hindu scheme life becomes more difficult as one rises higher. A *brahmin*, for example, as we have noted, should do nothing for the sake of power or wealth. A *kshatriya* has to even give up his life to maintain *dharma* while the *vaishya* is only a trustee and has to answer to the Divine for all that he does. Only the *shudra* is freed from all responsibilities except that of earning his livelihood. The realisation that there is increase of social responsibility and diminution of personal enjoyments as one rises in the social ladder, makes a person more satisfied with his place and work in society. Competition in society is thus transformed into cooperation.[26]

The *Bhagavad Gita* internalises the qualities necessary for each class. According to its psycho-social teaching, in the fourfold scheme each individual has to follow his own nature and arrive at possible perfection by a growth from within. The individual is not to be a mere passive instrument of collective life. The individual's action must be determined by his own essential quality. Through the fulfillment of his nature he contributes to his own good as well as to the good of society. Says Sri Krishna in the *Bhagavad Gita*,

> The works of *Brahmins*, *Kshatriyas*, *Vaishyas* and *Shudras* are different, in harmony with the qualities born of their nature.
>
> They all attain perfection when they find joy in their work.
>
> Greater is thy own work, even if this be humble, than the work of another, even if this be great.[27]

The *Bhagavad Gita* also defines the work of the four *varnas* according to their inborn qualities. The classification of work was; for the *brahmin*: peace, self-harmony, austerity, purity, forgiveness, righteousness, vision, wisdom and faith; for the *kshatriya*: heroic mind, inner fire, constancy, resourcefulness, courage, generosity and noble leadership; for the *vaishya*: trade, agriculture and rearing of cattle; for the *shudra*: service.[28]

With the passage of time, the *varna* system degenerated into the caste (*jati*) system as we know it today. As the system degenerated, birth acquired greater importance than the inborn qualities of human beings.

The chief features of the caste system as existing today are: (i) heredity: one cannot change one's caste; (ii) endogamy: every member of a caste must marry a member of the same caste and may not marry outside it.

The substitution of the principle of birth for virtue, valour, skill and service has been the main factor in the process of social crystallization and caste separatism. Birth is said to indicate real, permanent differences in the mental attitudes of men. It is not realized that the fact of ancestry, parentage, and physical birth may not always indicate the true nature of the individual. When the obligations of the classes do not spring spontaneously from their inner life, they become mere conventions, departing largely from the maintenance of ethical types.

The truth underlying the system is the conception of right action as a rightly ordered expression of the nature of the individual being. Nature assigns to each of us our line and scope in life according to inborn quality and self-expressive function. Nowhere is it suggested that one should follow one's hereditary occupation without regard to one's personal bent and capacities. The caste system is a degeneration of the class (*varna*) idea. Though idealistic in its origin, beneficient in large tracts of its history, still helpful in some ways, it has become disharmonious with our present conditions, owing to arrested development and lack of elasticity.

The four stages of life

The Hindu scheme does not leave the growth of the individual entirely to his unaided initiative but gives him a framework for guidance. Human life is represented as consisting of four consecutive stages, of which the first three fall within the jurisdiction of society. These stages apply to everyone in the social structure.

The four stages are those of the student, the householder, the social worker (called forest dweller in ancient times) and the *sannyasi* or one who leaves the material world in search of self-realisation.

Human offspring are the most helpless of all living creatures. In the absence of parental care, their chances of survival are little. The tending has to be continued for a long period, till the child reaches the status of man. The higher the cultural level the longer is the period required for education. This is the time that man is required to spend as a student.

The aim of education, as per the Hindu scriptures, is not to impose a stereotyped rule of conduct but to help the child to develop his nature, to change him from within rather than crush him from without. The knowledge imparted should not only fit man for his role in life but give him a general idea of the conditions of spiritual life.

The householder contributes to society by marrying, raising a family and earning his livelihood by following the profession most suited to his temperament. Man attains his full being only by living in harmonious social relationships. Sex is a normal human function concerned with the perpetuation of the race. Marriage, love, and motherhood are glorified in the Veda. The wife has an equal position with the husband in all domestic and religious concerns. Every woman has a right to marry and have a home. The things of spirit are in part dependent on the satisfaction of the body. The physical and the economic, though they may not be important in themselves, are important as means to the life of spirit. The position of householder is glorified by Manu who regards the householder as the mainstay of all the other classes.[29]

The object of man is not merely to be born, to grow up, marry, earn a livelihood, found a family, support it and pass away. That would be a purely physical life almost akin to the life of an animal. The object has to be to grow vertically into a mental and spiritual life transcending the animal instincts. This has to be through social service. When the children get settled and no more want his attention, a man should retire with his wife from active life to serve society. This both purifies and enables him to repay his debt to society.

A *sannyasin* renounces all possessions, distinctions of caste, and practices of religion. As he has already purified himself, he is able to give his soul the largest scope and throw all his powers into the free movement of his spirit. He does not merely formulate the conception of high living but lives it, adhering to the famous rule, 'The world is my country; to do good my religion'. Regarding all with an equal eye he is friendly to all living beings and does not injure any living creature, human or animal, either in act, word, or thought. He also renounces all attachments. A freedom and fearlessness of spirit, an immensity of courage, a love that lavishes itself without demand of return are the perfections he seeks.[30]

The scheme of the objectives of life, classes, and stages has for its aim the development of the individual. It helps him to order and organize his life instead of leaving it as a bundle of incompatible desires. It looks upon him not as a mere individual but as a member of a social group which reflects in its organization the scheme of values for the realization of which the group exists. By spiritual education and social discipline the individual is helped to develop the inner conviction essential for social stability. But throughout there is insistence on the fact that the highest values are suprasocial and truly universal.

The societal structure, it may be noted, is modelled on the triune aspect of the One, the *Sacchidananda* (Existence-Consciousness-Beatitude). The three ends man seeks are a full life, knowledge and happiness, and these are the earthly counterparts of *Sacchidananda*. This gives to man three rights: the right to life, the right to knowledge and the right to happiness. The first right has to be provided by the State or society, the second by education and the third by the economic system to which we now turn.

The Hindu Socio-economic System

Of the four objectives of the Hindu societal system, the earning of wealth (*artha*) is juxtaposed between ethics and virtue (*dharma*) and the pursuit of happiness (*kama*). This has been referred to in the literature as the threefold path (*trivarga*) and, according to Manu, it is the integrated and harmonised pursuit of all three that leads to the supreme good.[31] In the Hindu view, therefore, economics cannot be divorced from ethics and the pursuit of happiness: it has to be conceived in a large intersecting set involving ethics, economics and happiness.

Happiness is essentially an emotional or spiritual experience of the individual, though influenced by external circumstances. It is a subjective state and an empirical fact. Ethics, on the other hand, is normative and deals with conduct. Ethical norms prescribe the right conduct for individuals so that one can relate well to one's fellow beings individually and collectively. Ethics is also the organization of conduct in terms of notions like good, right or welfare. In this sense ethics is concerned with, not merely actual conduct, but conduct as it should be, that is, ideals. Economic values involve the understanding of economic phenomena in addition to the way human beings organize their material, as opposed to spiritual, life.

To the Hindu sages, happiness and peace were closely interlinked. One was not attainable without the other. The chant that every Hindu has to make every day is,

> May all be happy and healthy; may all progress spiritually; may nobody be prey to unhappiness. Let there be peace in the universe.[32]

The Sanskrit word *sukkha* (translated happy in the above verse) has many meanings, for example, it may mean pleasure, happiness, well-being, welfare and a lot more. This word is the opposite of *dukkha* (translated unhappiness in the verse) which means sadness, deprivation, unhappiness and a lot more. The English words given as meanings for *sukkha* and *dukkha* are not all synonymous: for example, one can be 'happy' in a state of inebriation, but that may not be tantamount to his real well-being. However the ultimate aim of our economic activities has something to do with *sukkha*, that is to say, as a result of all the labour, people should feel happy or fulfilled, or get a sense of well-being, or an amalgam of all three.

The idea that pleasure or happiness is the highest good that human beings should strive for was widely prevalent in the ancient and medieval worlds. All the Greek thinkers, for example, had subscribed to one or other variants of this view. But the Hindu sages went beyond happiness narrowly defined. They felt that beatitude should be the ultimate goal for human beings. They thought in terms of integration of pleasure (*sukkha*), happiness (*priti*) and bliss (*ananda*). Pleasure was a desirable sentiment, as against other disagreeable experiences such as pain, deprivation, and so on, while happiness and bliss were the next higher stages to be achieved. Of the four objectives posited by the Hindu sages, namely, *dharma*, *artha*, *kama*, and *moksha*, the latter three involve the above mentioned happiness, pleasure and bliss.

It is of course easy to understand why individuals everywhere in the past and present have preferred happiness, and think of it as the ideal to aspire for. It is, simply stated, an obviously preferred mental state. Because even a masochist is 'enjoying' while undergoing pain, since to him *that* is happiness! The real problem is to understand the nature of happiness. What kind of happiness or pleasure should be tried for. It is when these have to be defined that problems arise.

The Indian sages seem to have made a distinction between happiness in relation to the soul and to the body. In other words, happiness secured through material goods and services, and happiness as a result of non-material spiritual endeavours. The Hindu sages distinguished between the good (*shreyas*) and the pleasant (*preyas*). As the *Katha Upanishad* says:

One thing is the good (*shreyas*) and quite another thing is the pleasant (*preyas*), and both seize upon a man with different meanings. Of these whosoever takes the good, it is well with him; he falls from the aim of life who chooses the pleasant.

> The good and the pleasant come to a man and the thoughtful mind turns all around them and distinguishes. The wise chooses out the good from the pleasant, but the dull soul chooses the pleasant rather than the getting of his good and its having.[33]

On a surface view of the matter it would appear that both the good and the pleasant cannot be pursued at the same time. There is hardly any doubt that, since the Vedic times, people have hankered after material things. There are many passages in the Vedic texts seeking material things such as grain, cows, horses chariots, gold and so on. But we must also remember that Vedic hymns are not only poetry but mystic poetry that was perfected over a long process of meditation.

It has been the view from the very beginning that the Vedas are capable of multiple interpretation. Frawley, for example, has given it a yogic interpretation,[34] Vannucci has used an ecological key to interpret the Vedas[35] while Sri Aurobindo has given it a very mystical meaning.[36] It is important to understand, therefore, that while the spiritual quest may have been the goal of the sages who composed the hymns, the same was not the case for others who had to live in the world. This was something well understood by the seers of the Vedas. They felt that man could live a good and happy life, and did not need to escape from the world. What they emphasized was the wholeness of being, resulting from communion bringing about right living as implied in the Vedic prayer: "Grant us those riches that cause the prosperity for all".[37]

Similar was the thinking of the Upanishads which came after the Vedas. The *Upanishads* postulated that happiness based solely on material goods was not possible. The story of Nachiketas in the *Katha Upanishad* makes this clear:

> Yama (God of Death) to Nachiketas: Choose sons and grandsons, choose much cattle and elephants and gold and horses; choose a mighty reach of earth and thyself live for as many years as thou listest

> Yea, all desires that are hard to win in the world of mortals, all available at thy pleasure; lo these delectable women with their chariots and their bugles, whose like are not to be won by men, these I will give thee...
>
> Nachiketas's reply is significant:
>
> These things last till tomorrow, O Death, for they wear out the vigour of all the senses. Even the whole of life is short. Keep the horses, keep dance and song for thyself
>
> No man can be made happy by wealth alone. We already possess wealth, having seen thee.[38]

This raises the question as to how a human being is to enjoy the material pleasures of life. The *Isha Upanishad* has this to say,

> In the heart of all things, of whatever there is in the universe, dwells the Lord. He alone is the reality. Wherefore, renouncing vain appearances, rejoice in him. Covet no man's wealth.[39]

Enjoyment through renunciation of desires and the regarding of all material wealth as belonging to the Lord is the suggested answer. Also to see one's actions as part of an integrated whole encompassing both the material and the spiritual ends, and against the backdrop of infinity, of the One who is everywhere. It means going beyond me and thee, mine and thine.

Commenting on the above verse, Sri Aurobindo has this to say,

> so long as the difference between I and you exists, hatred cannot cease, covetousness cannot cease, war cannot cease, evil and sin cannot cease, and because sin cannot cease, sorrow and misery cannot cease. This is the eternal maya that makes a mock of all materialistic schemes for a materialistic paradise

> upon earth. Paradise cannot be made upon the basis of food and drink, upon the equal division of goods or even upon *the common possession of goods*, for always the *mine* and *thine*, the greed, the hate, will return again if not between this man and that man, yet between this community and that community (emphasis added).

The answer, according to Sri Aurobindo, is to see oneself as part of the whole of creation:

> To see your Self in all creatures and all creatures in your Self - that is the unshakable foundation of all religion love, patriotism, philanthropy, humanity, of everything which rises above selfishness and gross utility.[40]

Selfishness is nothing but mistaking the body for the Self and seeking its gratification and thus seeking a gross narrow and transient pleasure, instead of the stainless bliss of one's true Self. By emphasizing the 'Self' as well as de-emphasizing the material basis of the individual, Indian philosophy harmoniously linked the individual with society. Thus classical Hindu ethics avoided "the two extremes, viz. considering society to be all-important and over-emphasizing the importance of the individual by overlooking the effect that society has on individual development".[41]

One finds in the earliest Indian writings references to correct behavior. Among the ideals of living, giving to others was the ideal to be aimed at. Nowhere do we find accumulation of property castigated as a vice, but it was considered wrong not to share one's riches with others. The *Rig Veda* is clear on the need for being generous:

> The gods surely did not ordain hunger alone for slaughter; various deaths reach the man who is well-fed. The riches of the man who gives fully do not run out, but the miser finds no one with sympathy.

> The man with food who hardens his heart against the poor man who comes to him suffering and searching for nourishment - though in the past he had made use of him - he surely finds no one with sympathy.
>
> The man who is truly generous gives to the beggar who approaches him thin and in search of food. He puts himself at the service of the man who calls to him from the road, and makes him a friend for times to come.
>
> That man is no friend who does not give of his own nourishment to his friend, the companion at his side. Let the friend turn away from him; this is not his dwelling-place. Let him find another man who gives freely, even if he be a stranger.
>
> ...Riches roll like the wheels of a chariot, turning from one to the other.
>
> ...The man who eats alone brings troubles on himself alone.[42]

The *Brihadaranyaka Upanishad* develops on the above. It says that for human beings there are three important duties: to be self controlled, to be charitable and to be compassionate. Self control conquers heaven, charity the earth and compassion the lower worlds: these are also in the language of the Upanishad referred to as the worlds of the *devas* (the spiritual forces), men and *asuras* (the forces of materialism).[43]

The *Upanishads* considered the earning of wealth very much as an integral part of ethics. Virtue (*dharma*) means inner excellence and worthiness for the performance of an individual's duties towards himself and others. So it includes intellectual abilities as well. The *smritis* or *dharmashastras*,[44] which laid down detailed rules on the conduct of individuals, elaborated on this concept. *Manu*, for example, enumerates wisdom and knowledge under virtue (*dharma*), which according to him, consists of ten qualities, namely, contentment, forgiveness, uprightness, nonstealing, cleanliness, self-control, wisdom, knowledge, truth, and equanimity.[45] The reference to nonstealing is interesting; it puts a constraint on economic dealings with others by insisting that they be equitable and "right".

According to the Vedic thinkers the early part of life has to be devoted exclusively to the cultivation of virtue while being a student (*brahmachari*). In this period moral development is emphasised more than the intellectual; unlike the modern system of education which stresses intellectual growth, ignoring the moral. In the *Taittriya Upanishad* we find a preceptor giving the following instruction to his pupil after teaching him all the Veda:

> Speak the truth. Do your duties. Swerve not from your study. After giving the teacher the gift liked by him,[46] you shall marry and have children. Never deviate from truth. Never fail in your duty. Never neglect your welfare. Never neglect your *prosperity*. Never neglect study and teaching. Do not disregard your duties toward God and the ancestors. Serve the mother as a god. Serve the father as a god. Serve the teacher as a god. Serve the guest as a god. You should do such deeds as are unreproachable, and not others. You should do such virtuous deeds as we have done, and not others (emphasis added).[47]

The stress on not neglecting prosperity is to be noted. In this one verse, all the obligations of a human being to God, his ancestors, mother, father, teachers and the rest of humanity - are elucidated. This is what *dharma* in all its complexity is: the discharge of one's obligation to others through the proper and disinterested discharge of one's duty.

Implicit in the above is the need to respect the *trivarga*[48] - *dharma*, *artha* and *kama* - of others. In this connection, *artha* is understood to stand for material well-being as well as the means of securing such well-being, particularly, wealth. Like the other two goals of *trivarga*, *artha* also has primarily the individual in view. It is the individual who is to pursue *artha* as one of the goals of his life. Now, an essential condition of a man's material well-being is security of livelihood. This is probably the reason why *artha* is defined as *vritti* or livelihood by Kautilya in the *Arthashastra*. Kautilya also declares *artha* as the most important of the three since the other two are dependent on it.[49]

Role of the State

The Hindu economic system is not based only on the *dharma* of individuals which comes from an inner purity or yoga. It also lays equal stress on regulation by the State. In the Shantiparvan chapter of the *Mahabharata* we read that at the beginning of creation, in the Golden Age, men acted according to *dharma* though there was no ruler nor any punishment, but that in course of time men were overcome by delusion, greed, love of pleasures and other base passions, and that in consequence there was anarchy everywhere. The gods were filled with apprehension and approached *Brahma*, the Creator, to seek a way out. The latter reassured them and composed a treatise in order that an orderly and peaceful existence may be ensured for men on earth. The treatise, it is said, in addition to the *trivarga* of *dharma*, *artha* and *kama* dealt with state policy and the theory of punishment so that men did not deviate from the right path.[50]

Kautilya elaborates on the need for state regulation. He states in the *Arthashastra*,

"When people were oppressed by the law of the fishes (*matsyanyaya*, according to which the bigger fish swallow the smaller ones), they made Manu, the son of Vivasvat, the king. They fixed one-sixth part of the grains and one-tenth of their goods and money as his share. Kings who receive this share are able to ensure the well-being of their subjects". (I.13.5-7)

As Kangle remarks on the above verse, here is the raison d'etre for regulation by the state. The original state of nature is imagined to be one of total anarchy, where might alone was right. People agreed to pay taxes and to be ruled by one person in order that they may be able to enjoy security and well-being (*yoga-kshema*).[51]

The first and foremost duty of the king (state) is said to be the protection of his subjects and the ensuring of their well-being and welfare. He can only collect legally imposed taxes after he has protected those engaged in economic activity.[52] He has also to ensure the continuance of the societal structure as represented by the *varnashrama* system.[53] Moreover he has to protect the people from anti-social elements like deceitful manufacturers and traders.

The duty of the ruler to protect his subjects implies something more than mere protection of person and property. It also implies *yogakshema*: as is well-known, yoga refers to the successful accomplishment of an object, while *kshema* refers to the peaceful, undisturbed enjoyment of that object. Security, that is, protection by the state is essential for both. But ensuring the two means something more than merely providing security. In fact, *yogakshema* implies the idea of welfare, well-being, including the idea of prosperity, happiness and so on. That is why Kautilya in his *Arthashastra* asserts,

> In the happiness of the subjects lies the happiness of the king, and in what is beneficial to the subjects his own benefit. (I.19.34)[54]

The *Arthashastra* goes on to delineate what the state has to do for the welfare of the subjects. The ruler is to undertake such activities as settlement on virgin land, building of dams, tanks and other irrigational works, providing pastures for cattle, opening trade-routes and ensuring safety on them, working of mines, and so on.

The ruler is to allow the interests of the subjects to prevail over those of the state. It is laid down that the sale of commodities, whether indigenous or imported, should be arranged in such a way that the subjects are benefitted thereby and that any profit that may be harmful to the subjects is avoided. Further it is said that when the subjects are struck down by natural calamities, the ruler should take care of them like a father. The ideal set before the ruler is that of paternalistic rule.

There is another aspect of the protection which is laid down as the ruler's duty. Protection also implies, as already mentioned, the protection of the social order founded on the system of *varnas* and *ashramas*. The ruler is asked to see that every one carries out the duties of the *varna* or *ashrama* to which he belongs as laid down in the *trayidharma* or the Vedic way. The preservation of the Vedic social order is thus a duty laid on the ruler. Consequently, it can be said that the Vedic religion is to be the state religion. That, however, does not mean that a theological state is thought of. No organised theological body was there to intervene in affairs of the state to safeguard religious interests or to enforce religious sanctions.

The protection of the subjects is to be done with help of *danda*,[55] force of punishment, which is the symbol of the ruler's authority. With the help of *danda* the ruler is to maintain peace and order in the realm so that wealth and prosperity may increase.[56]

Manu also requires the ruler to learn the theory of various trades and professions.[57] The ruler has to collect taxes to enable him to conduct the affairs of state. But these are very rigidly regulated. According to *Manu*,

> After (due) consideration the king shall always fix in his realm the duties and taxes in such a manner that both he himself and the man who does the work receive (their due) reward.

> As the leech, the calf, and the bee take their food little by little, even so must the king draw from his realm moderate annual taxes.
>
> A fiftieth part of (the increments on) cattle and gold may be taken by the king, and the eighth, sixth, or twelfth part of the crops.
>
> He may also take the sixth part of trees, meat, honey, clarified butter, perfumes, (medical) herbs, substances used for flavouring food, flowers, roots, and fruit;
>
> Of leaves, pot-herbs, grass, (objects) made of cane, skins, of earthen vessels, and all (articles) made of stone.[58]

Manu specifically warns the ruler to follow the middle path in levying taxes - neither too little nor too much.

Let him not cut up his own root (by levying no taxes), nor the root of other (men) by excessive greed; for by cutting up his own root (or theirs), he makes himself or them wretched.[59]

The intervention of the state in the economic system is a limited one though considered essential. The state has, for example, no distributive or equity functions which are supposed to be performed by individuals considering the interests of others, whether in one's own society or in the other societies, as a part of their drive for liberation. The stress is on the individual who has to labour for his livelihood for the "gods befriend none but him who has laboured".[60] He has to perform all action in a spirit of service and consecrate it to the Lord. This attitude and the fact that his ultimate objective is liberation makes him keep only as much of his earnings and wealth as he needs keeping in mind the Vedic injunction of "not being greedy". This makes him a trustee (on behalf of God) rather than an owner of wealth. There are thus no property rights in the manner in which they exist in modern capitalist societies, that is, as an absolute right without any corresponding responsibilities.

Hindu Economics

Modern mainstream economics, the so-called neoclassical system, is based on a number of implicit value premises and assumptions. The central core of the value premise is materialism defined in terms of raising the standard of living or maximising consumption and thereby optimising the pattern of production. The production philosophy of modern industrialism is based on the corporate need for profits, technological determinism and ecological indifference. On the basis of this value system, the production system is expected to mesh in with the consumption pattern through the mediation of the market.

The system is based on private ownership. There are two kinds of agents, firms and households. Individuals are expected to behave rationally, have perfect information and expectations of the future. The market is expected to signal to the producers about what the households wish to consume, thereby establishing the optimal production pattern. Economics, and the economy, based on Hindu thought differs from the neoclassical system in a number of ways.

The value premise underlying Hinduism is a mixture of materialism and spiritualism. Economics would thus have to take note of nonmaterial values thereby grounding the core elements of economics in the Vedic holistic view of what constitutes human nature. Economics has also to be a subset of the social and political systems. To the Hindu, human beings not only have the need to survive, implying the need for food and shelter, but they also have the need to care for others. A harmonious balance thus needs to be struck between selfishness and self-lessness, or between the needs of the individual and those of others, between spirituality and materialism.

Hindu teachings stress self-control and the regulation of material consumption rather than its maximisation. The Hindu society would thus not be a "consumerist" one. The suggested way is one of self-restraint with desire being subject to ethics and morality (*dharma*). The method to be followed in achieving this is the yogic one. There are four or five meanings to the word 'yoga'. First of all, it is practice as opposed to theory, or philosophy. Secondly, it is a *sadhana*, spiritual practice. Then it is the control or integration that comes about through spiritual exercise; then as a result of that, it is the equanimity through which one sees all living beings as not being different from oneself; and finally, when perfect control and harmony has been found, it is the skill in performing work; it is the yoga in action. According to the *Bhagavad Gita* it is necessary to: "Yoke your intelligence with the Divine and then strive for yoga: yoga is skill in action."[61]

Hindu thought distinguishes between needs and wants. It recognises that the needs of a manual worker would differ from those of a philosopher or an artist as the *dharma* of each is different. But it deplores wants which are unnecessary and have a way of multiplying themselves indefinitely. No doubt the satisfaction of wants brings pleasure, but such pleasure is transient and ultimately ends up in misery. While needs have to be met, greediness is to be adjusted. This is what the *Yajur Veda* has to say:

> Everything in the world belongs to the Lord. So do not be greedy and restrain your desires.[62]

The production system, run by managers and entrepreneurs imbued with Hindu ethics, would not produce articles which are harmful to others. Thus the production of armaments, toxic materials, drugs, films showing violence and sex etc. would not take place. Industries which pollute the air, water or the soil would not be set up. Firms would also not create unnecessary wants through high pressure advertising.

Besides for the sake of profit, there would be no laying off of workers or impacting on the livelihood of traditional communities. For *artha* and *kama*, earning of wealth and attainment of happiness, have not to be at the expense of others.

To deprive others of their livelihood would prevent them from following the *dharma* of the householder, and thus be ethically unacceptable.

The goal of economics would be the maximisation of happiness combined with full spiritual, mental and moral growth. The welfare function would thus radically differ from the neoclassical one. Unlike the uni-order neoclassical Pigovian welfare function, it would be a multi-order one: if a person looks after his own interests he derives a certain order of utility; if he looks after the interests of his family he derives a higher order of utility; if he cares for the society in which he lives, he derives an even higher order of utility; if his vision and goal embraces the entire collection of living beings, human and others, he derives the highest order of utility. This concept of welfare would modify the acquisitive society by shifting acquisition of wealth as being only for private gain to acquisition being for societal or universal gain.

The stress of Hindu thought is on the liberty of the individual. Freedom of the individual is fundamental to human growth; it is also fundamental to a democratic socio-political order. But that freedom becomes a menace, as much to the individual as to society, if it fails to inspire itself with a second value, namely, the sense of social responsibility. The freedom of the individual needs to be enriched with the virtues of self-discipline and a concern for humanity. This constitutes character, character centred in socially oriented action. It is this that makes human beings capable of enriching inter-human relations, with ethical and humanistic impulses and macro-social efficiency. This the Hindu system seeks to achieve through its socio-economic system of four ideal classes, and their four aims, as being subject to *dharma*.

There is the need for unwavering justice and ethical sense. This is what is meant by the word *dharma*. This approach has to be imbibed by the state as much as by the people. *Dharma* is presented by the Hindu system as the principle that integrates man and society. It is basically a by-product of the spiritual growth of the individual, which is expressed as moral law, and which is reinforced by the state laws and regulations. A respect for law and the constant effort to uphold it, on the part of the citizens and of the holders of power in the state, are what make for human integration and the strength and stability of a state. The awakened moral sense of the citizens makes the laws and regulations of the state effective. If the moral sense is absent, the laws become ineffective, as the citizens twist the laws to suit their own advantage. This increases injustice in society and weakens the political and social fabric.

The Hindu tradition teaches that the earning of wealth by right means and honest labour is *dharmic*, but greed, and its impulsion to dishonesty and unscrupulousness, is opposed to *dharma*; it is opposed to *dharma* because it is opposed to general social welfare and inner spiritual growth. Also it is *dharma* that equalizes a strong man and a weak man in society; if the restraint of *dharma* is not there, the strong will have all the wealth and the satisfactions flowing therefrom, and the weak will be deprived of even elementary human satisfactions. According to *Manu*, one has to,

> Give up those *arthas* and *kamas* (wealth and sensory cravings) which are opposed to *dharma*; and (give up) even that *dharma* which results in one's own unhappiness (like donating all wealth without thought for the care of one's children) and in the suffering of the people.[63]

The stress of Hindu thought is on the widest possible dissemination of knowledge throughout society. In the Hindu system, the transmission of knowledge is considered to be a sacred duty to be performed without payment. As Sri Krishna tells Arjuna, it is necessary to,

> Offer as sacrifice wealth, (results of) austerities and spiritual exercises, and learning and knowledge.
>
> But greater than any material sacrifice, is the sacrifice of knowledge.[64]
>
> This would mean that there would be no intellectual property rights like patents, copyright etc. As the Veda says, 'all knowledge comes from God'.[65]

Hindu thought is of the view that society needs to be unified. This has to be through sacrifice, as only that integrates and creates harmony. The Vedas go beyond the society in which a person lives to humanity as a whole. As the *Atharva Veda* puts it,

> Harmony for us with our own men, harmony with foreigners ... harmony through union of mind and union of purpose.[66]

Conclusions

From the above we can arrive at the following premises on which the Hindu socio-economic system needs to function:

* ethics, politics, economics and societal structure constitute an indivisible whole leading to a unified society;
* economics is essentially the science of human happiness. Its goal is the welfare of all. Implicit in the above is the basic presumption of equal dignity of and respect for the life and welfare of every individual. Translated into the sphere of economic policy, it entails top priority for meeting the most basic material needs (water, food, shelter) of everybody;
* the supreme consideration of economics has to be man. Economic systems that ignore humanity and its needs - material, mental, moral, spiritual - are meaningless;
* human welfare economics focusing on man implies importance of a decentralized social economy. The ideal

is a communitarian economy allowing for living interaction, mutual access, and voluntary cooperation of all its members;

* three-fourths of society (the student, the social worker and the *sannyasi)* would be in the non-profit, voluntary sector of free education, social service and service to humanity through the realisation of truth. This would reduce the pressure regarding employment (for money) on the remainder one-fourth and also require changing the concept of national wealth to include non-monetised work as well;
* there would be no absolute right to property but only to its usufruct as a trustee of the Divine;
* there would be full employment in society as everybody would be "employed" whether for earning one's livelihood or for doing service;
* there would be no hoarding of wealth and the economy would have fast circulation of money as the method for attaining development, both material and spiritual.

The Hindu system would also be in perfect harmony with Nature. Based as it would be on the concept that the Divine is immanent in the universe, it would to that extent sacralise Nature and treat it with respect and consideration. The objective would be to take from the Earth as much as it can sustainably give and not to exploit it beyond limits for the attainment of a material affluence.

References

1. Bede Griffiths, *River of Compassion: A Christian Commentary on the Bhagavad Gita* (Warwick, New York: Amity House, 1987) p.55.
2. *Rig Veda*, translated by Ralph T.H. Griffith (London: 1889; reprinted Delhi: Motilal Banarsidas, 1973).

3. Translated and quoted in *Hindu Spirituality*, K. Sivaraman (ed.) (Delhi: Motilal Banarsidas, 1995) p. 3.
4. For example, *Rig Veda*, note 2, 1.164.6 and 1.164.46.
5. Ibid., 10.190.1. The word *purusha* means man; here it means the original Male principle or Consciousness.
6. *Hindu Spirituality*, note 3, p. 13.
7. *Rig Veda*, note 2, 10.90.13,14.
8. See, for example, Fritjof Capra, *The Tao of Physics* (New York: Fontana Books, 1976)
9. *Rig Veda*, note 2, 1.164.46.
10. *Bhagavad Gita*, note 1, 4.41 p. 80.
11. See for example, R.P. Kangle, *Kautilya's Arthashastra*, Vols. I-III, (Delhi: Motilal Banarsidas, 1992), 13.4.62.
12. Swami Sarvananda, *Katha Upanishad*, (Madras: Ramakrishna Math, 1973), 2.4.1.
13. *Bhagavad Gita*, note 1, 3.25, p. 55.
14. *Bhagavad Gita*, note 1, 7.11, p.139. The word *kama* has had connotations of sex because of its connection with the famous *Kamasutra* of Vatsayama. In fact even the *Kamasutra* has been misrepresented: it deals with sex, yes, but also with other relations, aesthetic and moral, between the sexes, as well as how to enjoy life.
15. *Rig Veda*, 10.90.11,12 in *Hindu Scriptures*, translated and edited by R.C. Zaehner (New Delhi: Rupa & Co., 1995) pp. 9-10. See also *Laws of Manu*, hereinafter *Manu*, translated by G. Buhler, 1886, reprinted 1982, Delhi: Motilal Banarsidas, verse 1.31 of which states: "But for the sake of the prosperity of the worlds, He caused the *Brahmana*, the *Kshatriya*, the *Vaishya* and the *Shudra* to proceed from his mouth, his arms, his thighs and his feet."
16. *Mahabharata*, 3.134.3, quoted in S. Radhakrishnan, *Eastern Religions and Western Thought* (Oxford: Oxford University Press, 1939 reprinted 1991) p. 360.
17. Kangle, note 11, Vol.III, p. 116.

18. *Valmiki's Ramayana*, 2.97.6-7, quoted in Radhakrishnan, note 16, p. 360.
19. *Bhagavad Gita*, note 1, III.13, p.50.
20. *Manu*, note 15, 2.46.
21. David Frawley, *Gods, Sages and Kings*, (Delhi: Motilal Banarsidas, 1995) pp. 261-62.
22. *Manu*, note 15, 3.64,153.
23. *Ibid.*, 1.82.
24. *Ibid.*, 4.2,3.
25. *Bhagavad Gita*, note 1, 2.50, p. 32.
26. Radhakrishnan, note 16, pp. 367-70.
27. *Bhagavad Gita*, note 1, 18. 41,45,47, pp. 312-315.
28. *Bhagavad Gita*, note 1, 18. 42,43,44, pp. 313-314.
29. *Manu*, note 15, 4.89,90.
30. See for example the *Bhagavad Gita*, note 1, 2.55-72, pp.36-41, for the qualities that a person of settled wisdom attains.
31. *Manu*, note 15, 2.224.
32. The sanskrit chant is,

    sarve bhavantu sukkhinah
    sarve santu niramayah
    sarve bhadrani pashyantu
    ma kashchid dukkha bhag bhavet
    om shanti, shanti, shanti.

33. *Katha Upanishad*, 2.1.2. The translation is by Sri Aurobindo, *The Upanishads: Texts, Translations and Commentaries*, (Pondicherry: Aurobindo Ashram, 1986) p. 220.
34. Frawley, note 21.
35. M.Vannussi, *Ecological Readings in the Veda*, (Delhi: D.K. Printworld, 1994).
36. Sri Aurobindo, *The Secret of the Veda*, (Pondicherry: Aurobindo Ashram, 1971).
37. *Rig Veda*, note 2, 1.79.9.
38. *Katha Upanishad*, 1. 23,25,26,27. The above follows Sri Aurobindo's translation, note 33, pp. 218 - 219.

39. *Isha Upanishad*, verse 1. The translation is the authors.
40. Sri Aurobindo Birth Centenary Library, Vol. XII, (Pondicherry: Aurobindo Ashram, 1971) pp. 484-48.
41. S. Gopalan, *Hindu Social Philosophy* (Delhi: Wiley Eastern, 1979) p. 55.
42. *Rig Veda*, translated by Wendy O'Flaherty (New York: Penguin, 1984) 10.117.1-6.
43. See Brihadaranayaka Upanishad, 5.2.1-3 in *Hindu Scriptures*, note 15, p. 76.
44. The word *smriti* means to remember or recall. The idea was to recall the moral codes (*dharmashastras*) before taking any action.
45. *Manu*, note 14, 6.92.
46. In ancient India the students lived with the teacher and received education free of all charges. They only paid him when they left and then something inexpensive.
47. *Taittiriya Upanishad*, 1.11.1, 2, in *Upanishads* Prabhavananda and Manchester, (eds.), (New York: Mentor, 1957).
48. *Trivarga* means the threefold way.
49. Kangle, note 11, Vol. III, p.1.
50. *Mahabharata* quoted in Kangle, note 11, Vol. III, p.5.
51. Kangle, note 11, Vol. III, p. 116.
52. *Manu*, note 14, 10.119.
53. *Ibid.*, 7.35.
54. Kangle, note 11, Vol. III, p.118.
55. The *danda* means rod or staff.
56. See Kangle, note 11, Vol. III, pp.118-120.
57. *Manu*, note 15, 7.43.
58. *Ibid.*, 7.128-132.
59. *Ibid.*, 7.139.
60. *Rig Veda*, note 2, 4.33.11.
61. *Bhagavad Gita*, note 1, 2.50, pp. 32-34.
62. *Yajur Veda*, 40.1 (Delhi: Motilal Banarsidas).
63. *Manu*, note 15, 4.176.
64. *Bhagavad Gita*, note 1, 4.28,33, pp. 77, 78.

65. *Sama Veda*, 1462, *Yajur Veda*, 3.17. Both are available from Motilal Banarsidas, Delhi.

66. *Atharva Veda*, translated by W.D. Whitney (Delhi: Motilal Banarsidas, 1996), 7.52.1, 2.

5

Buddhist Teaching, Economics and Ecology

At the time of the Buddha 6th Century B.C., Hinduism had become too much involved in metaphysical discussions and rituals. Buddha rebelled against this and sought to simplify and purify the Hindu doctrine.

The Buddha eschewed metaphysics and sought to develop a system which was understandable by the masses. We will examine the relevance of the Buddha's teachings to the concept of sustainable development, including the economy and the environment. The Buddha lived at a time when the environment was not a matter of concern, the economy was not complex and sustainable development had not become a buzz word. But with his farsightedness the Buddha foresaw that only a moral, nonviolent and humanistic pattern of development could lead to happiness, environmental integrity and peace.

Buddhist Teachings

The Tolerant Buddhist System

Siddhartha Gautama, the historical founder of the system known today as Buddhism, lived in northern India from about

563-483 B.C. In a sense Buddhism grew out of the soil of Hinduism in much the same way as Christianity did out of Judaism. Buddhism is so called because its founder Gautama became the Buddha, the awakened or Enlightened One. It teaches that such awakening or enlightenment is possible for all men to achieve. It is through ignorance and craving that we are impelled through the weary series of rebirths instead of attaining the unutterable peace of *nirvana* (*nibbana* in Pali).[1] Buddhism is sometimes called pessimistic because it sees life in the world as fraught with suffering and frustration. But as we shall see it really is an optimistic philosophy showing as it does a way of release from this situation and delineates how to live a joyful-life.

The Buddha was a dynamic spiritual master teacher whose teachings varied according to the demands of specific situations. Though, by virtue of his attainment, he possessed a certain natural authority, which was apparently quite self-evident (according to accounts he possessed a golden radiance), he never tried to set himself up as a leader figure, nor did he nominate a successor. He obviously wished to inculcate self-reliance in his followers and avoid all the pit-falls that go with power and authority. He indicated that, if there was a need for guidance after his death, his followers might look to his *Dharma*, his teachings.

The Buddha himself foresaw that his teachings would, by stages, lose their vitality and effectiveness. However, by skillfully leaving things flexible and open-ended, he allowed for new waves of creativity and development to periodically revitalise the tradition that he had set going. After his death, we can trace the emergence of three major traditions or new 'turnings of the wheel of the *Dharma*', each with its own component schools and sects:

* basic Buddhism, dubbed Hinayana or 'Little Vehicle' by later schools, whose forms, teachings and practices are probably closest to those of the historical Buddha himself;

* the Mahayana or 'Great Vehicle', which creatively opened up a whole new panoply of approaches; and
* the Vajrayana or 'Thunderbolt Vehicle', the tantric path that yet again revitalised Buddhism by introducing special yogic and other *mantric* technologies.

The above development was a natural one for Buddhism which expressly allows its followers to explore all aspects of the mind. So it was not likely to remain confined to one pattern of thought only, and in the long years of its history Buddhism has happily flowed into a dozen or more channels of thought and practice. Yet all retain three factors in common: the Buddha, as the All-Enlightened One; a large body of doctrine and practice; and a quite remarkable tolerance of differing points of view. There has, for example, never been a Buddhist war, nor has any man been killed or even injured by a Buddhist for holding a different point of view.

In examining the various scriptures that have emerged after the Buddha's passing away, the wisest course therefore would be to read and study the scriptures with an open mind, one that is both appreciative and critical, with a view, not so much to fixing a literal understanding in one's mind, but of imbibing the underlying spirit.

It is with such a spirit that we approach the teachings of the Buddha as available from various texts, especially the *Dhammapada*, to discover their relevance for the post-modern world and especially to the attainment of sustainable development.

Dharma, Karma and Rebirth

Three very important concepts on which Buddha's teachings depend are those of *dharma*, *karma* and rebirth. Since these terms are not very familiar to those brought up in other traditions we will first define them.

The basic meaning of *dharma* is to sustain and uphold. Other English terms are law, norm, duty, teaching. In Asia, Buddhism is called the *Buddha-dharma* or *dhamma* in the Pali form. For a Buddhist *dharma* provides a platform which sustains him; it gives meaning to life, and the purpose and agenda for this life; also the means to cope with his agenda, and the power to achieve it. To him *dharma* is law; in the sense that when his personal will opposes *dharma*, he suffers.

Dharma covers all aspects. It includes the whole day's work - and the period of rest. But the difficulties awaiting the follower of *dharma* are enormous. First, to know what is *dharma* in any particular set of circumstances. Then to accept its limitations. For example where does the unconscious fit in with his conscious understanding of *dharma's* purpose. He must also allow for *dharma* transcendent and immanent, see the Unborn in the born, and using the best of himself attain the highest.

In one sense an individual's *dharma* is the performance of duty. Most people are uneasy with this term because it represents what ought to be done rather than what they want to do. The word ought also connotes a debt which is owed. *Dharma* is thus a list of the debts we owe - to society, humanity, life, the ultimate Whole. As such, *dharma* is its own authority; it needs no Law-giver. It is in itself intelligent, living law.

The answer to what is owed lies in *karma*, and the time for payment is provided by rebirth. The living law of *karma*, that is, as you sow so shall you reap, is based on harmony, the unbreakable harmony of the manifest universe as an expression of the Unborn. Man breaks this harmony while under the delusion of 'self' and pays for the breakage through suffering. The law of *karma* adjusts the damage to the offender, and he pays, some time, somewhere, to the full; none can stay the cold hand of that retribution. Thus we learn, if we are wise, to 'sin no more'.[2]

We see that *dharma*, *karma* and rebirth are closely interlinked. An individuals *dharma* today is an invoice of past debts presented for payment. We cannot blame others for our own past folly. We are ourselves to blame for our body, home or circumstance, our friends and enemies, our job and place in the world. Let us accept and use and better it. We try to run away; into pleasure, religion, toil and ill-health - even into a monastery. But as the *Dhammapada* says; "Not in the sky, nor in the sea, nor in a cave in the mountains can a man escape from his evil deeds."[3] Some *karma* is like Destiny; it is too late to avoid it. Much may be modified by wise action, or even by its mere acceptance. As we accept the *karma* coming to us it becomes our *dharma*. the thing to be done.

The Four Noble Truths

Tradition tells us that when Buddha found *nirvana* under the Bodhi tree, he poured out his joy of liberation in two famous verses of the *Dhammapada*:

> I have gone round in vain the cycles of many lives ever striving to find the builder of the house of life and death. How great is the sorrow of life that must die!
>
> But now I have seen thee, housebuilder: never more shalt thou build this house. The rafters of sins are broken, the ridge-pole of ignorance is destroyed. The fever of craving is past: for my mortal mind is gone to the joy of the immortal *nirvana*. (v.153, 154)

Having got the knowledge of how to get beyond *karma* and rebirth, the Buddha propounded the four noble truths: that life is painful and frustrating (*dukkha*); that the reason for this is in our minds, in the craving which leads us to grasp at that which can never bring satisfaction; that this craving, and hence the frustration born of it, can be overcome; and that there is a path to the end of craving, the end of suffering, to enlightenment and *nirvana*. This is the noble eightfold path of right understanding, right aims; right speech, action, livelihood and effort; right mindfulness and concentration (*samadhi*). The first two steps are aspects of wisdom, the next four deal with ethics, and the last two with the practice of meditation. Without some wisdom, we will never start to tread the path; without some degree of moral purity we shall fail to progress; by meditation (training the mind) we can attain the goal as well as in the intermediate stages use it as a feed-back mechanism to check on our actions.

As the *Dhammapada* puts it very succinctly,

> He who goes for refuge to Buddha, to Truth and to those whom he taught, he goes indeed to a great refuge. Then he sees the four great truths:
>
> Sorrow, the cause of sorrow, the end of sorrow, and the path of eight stages which leads to end of sorrow.
>
> That is the safe refuge, that is the refuge supreme. If a man goes to that refuge, he is free from sorrow. (V.190,191,192)

The first noble truth deals with the question of suffering (*dukkha*). It was the problem of *dukkha*, rather than abstract questions like 'Who made the world?' and 'What happens to us after death?', that started the Buddha on his spiritual quest. *Dukkha* is often translated as 'suffering' but, in fact, it covers a whole spectrum of psycho-emotional states, from a mild sense that things are not quite right to intense physical and mental pain. It may also be taken to mean that there is no lasting peace or rest in life; that we are forever under pressure and subject to disruption. This should not be taken to mean, however, that Buddhists believe that life is all suffering - a common misconception. The opposite of *dukkha*, *sukka* - joy, happiness - is fully admitted. *Dukkha* is problematic, however -and that is why we need to do something about it.

The teaching of the Buddha is not only a negative one of overcoming *dukkha*. It is also positive and asks that human beings live in joy and in harmony. To turn to the *Dhammapada* again, we find,

> ...happy is the teaching of DHAMMA, happy the harmony of (the Buddha's) followers, happy is the life of those who live in harmony. (v.194)
>
> let us live in joy, in love amongst those who hate! Among men who hate, let us live in love.
>
> let us live in joy, in health amongst those who are ill! Among men who are ill, let us live in health.
>
> let us live in joy, in peace amongst those who struggle! Among men who struggle, let us live in peace. (v.197,198,199)

To be joyous is to be in good health, to live in love, in peace and in harmony. It is necessary also to be contented for that is the greatest treasure and wealth. Health is the greatest possession. Contentment is the greatest treasure. Confidence is the greatest friend, but *nirvana* is the greatest joy. (v.204)

It is a fundamental principle of Buddhism that we do not understand what is going on. This is stated in the second of the four noble truths which underpin Buddhist philosophy. While the first noble truth states that there is suffering, the second states that the cause for that suffering is delusion. To remove suffering we must uproot its cause: delusion. At the core of such delusion is separation from the Whole. We each believe we are a solid and lasting self rather than a short-term bundle of thoughts, feelings and impulses.

Says the *Dhammapada*,

> What we are today comes from our thoughts of yesterday, and our present thoughts build our life of tomorrow: our life is the creation of our mind.
>
> If a man speaks or acts with an impure mind, suffering follows him as the wheel of the cart follows the beast that draws the cart.

> If a man speaks or acts with a pure mind, joy follows him as his own shadow. (v.1, 2)

It is because of not understanding the Whole that we feel ourselves to be separate selves in a separate world. We feel separate from each other, separate from the environment that sustains us and separate from the things we use and enjoy. We fail to recognize them for what they are: part of us as we are of them, and the context in which we must painstakingly work out our salvation.

Delusion leads to all manner of problems. The sense of separation reinforces the idea that we, or at least an important part of ourselves, is somehow independent and unchanging. It lures us into believing that by accumulating enough material things - cars, household appliances, clothes, hi-fi systems, fine art or whatever - we will accumulate a sense of well-being. It lures us into believing that the ability to control the world around us will one day cause a state of peace and happiness to arise within us.

The reason for the delusion is desire, craving or thirst (*trishna*) which the Buddha warns against. Says the *Dhammapada*,

> Since a shower of golden coins could not satisfy craving desires and the end of all pleasure is pain, how could a wise man find satisfaction even in the pleasures of the gods? When desires go, joy comes: the follower of Buddha finds the truth. (v.186,187)

Desire is concerned with negatives; we desire what we do not have. What we have we may not like, but we no longer desire it. Buddha's concept is more positive. In defining desire he makes a distinction between need and want. For 'character-building' the difference is profound. The body has needs, such as food and shelter, but all manner of wants arise therefrom which are less legitimate. Sex is a biological necessity for the continuation of the race; when it is exercised in terms of lust for sensual gratification it is no longer a need but has become a want. The same applies to greed for food and wine, or drug addiction or smoking.

The emotions, too, have needs and wants. The need is for expression, and repressed emotion will find an abnormal outlet. Its wants are for violent stimulus for a 'kick' out of violence, sex and all 'sensation', whether in real life or at second-hand from the press and the screen.

The mind itself has needs and wants, but its composition is so subtle and its parts so intertwined that it is hard to define the difference between them.

According to the Buddha, it is of little help to speculate about why there is delusion. The fact is that it is there and something needs to be done about it. So, the spiritual challenge the Buddha set humanity was not simply to adopt a set of beliefs and thereby become good Buddhists. He spoke of 'practice' because the way we are requires urgent attention and action. It requires self-enquiry, discipline and insight sufficient to transform ourselves at our very core, so that we are no longer blinded by the tight addictive grip of delusion.

Buddha wants us to feel a sense of urgency in the solution of our spiritual problem, and use our reason for the solution of our moral problem. A verse of the *Dhammapada* expresses this sense of urgency:

> How can there be laughter, how can there be pleasure, when the whole world is burning? When you are in deep darkness, will you not ask for a lamp? (v.146)

From the standpoint of the Buddha's enlightenment, the universe is a seamless, undivided whole. Only delusion makes it appear fragmented into an infinite number of separate pieces. The task of Buddhist practice is to recover this lost vision of wholeness and put the universe back together again. Practice, then, is healing. Not surprisingly, the Buddha is often referred to as 'the great physician', and his teachings and their practice as 'medication'.

The healing process starts with putting one's own life in order. One must consider the damage being caused to the world. Is one living in such a way as to destroy life; taking things that belong to others; betraying and hurting others through sexual lust; leading a life of deceit and dishonesty; undermining the clarity of mind with drink and drugs. All such behaviour only reinforces the sense of a separated and divided world and leads further away from a vision of unity. If one is going to turn one's life around in a radical way, one has to control the amount of harm inflicted upon others.

The Buddha considers the self of man to be a complex entity existing at every point of the line between its poles of ultimate unity and utter diversity. The polarity is essential to all manifested things, and the tension between the poles is equally necessary. At the 'top' is SELF, at the 'bottom' is self, and the self, the aspiring bundle of thought, emotion, prejudice and karmic sediment, moves slowly upward, life after life, from the darkness of Ignorance to the Light of Enlightenment. It follows that desire varies from the 'wrong' desire for transient and material things to the 'right' desire for Enlightenment. To dub all desire as evil is therefore wrong, for without the urgent will to liberation, there will be no entering on the Buddhist path.

Desire lives and grows by being indulged. When not indulged by the application of ethical restraint and awareness, on the other hand, it stabilises and begins to diminish, though this is not an easy or comfortable process, for the old urges clamour for satisfaction for a long time.

This kind of practice, of course, cuts directly against the main currents of modern consumer society, where desire is energetically encouraged and refined to new pitches and variations by the powerful agencies of marketing and publicity. The implications for the economy of restraining desire will be examined later.

The Eightfold Path

The way to joyful living was given by the Buddha in the eightfold path.

'Walk on the right path and have joy in this world and the world beyond'.[4]

There are two points to be made about the path or the Way. Firstly, the eight stages given are an integrated whole. They all act and interact with each other and have to be seen as a system rather than a linear movement from right understanding to contemplation. Secondly, the Buddha follows the so called Middle Way. The Middle Way is the narrow path of perfection that leads to the top of the mountain. On the right there is the wrong path that leads to desire for things of the earth, and on the left the wrong path that leads to desire for things of heaven. But in the centre there is the narrow path that leads to the top of the mountain. That path suggests a harmony in life: 'not for him who eats too much, nor for him who eats too little; not for him who sleeps too little nor for him who sleeps too much'.

The eight-fold path of the Buddha has to be understood in this context.

As already mentioned, the eightfold path can be considered in three broad categories, namely, wisdom (stages 1 and 2), ethics (stages 3,4,5,6) and contemplation (stages 7 and 8).

The first verses of the *Dhammapada* show us the beginning of the path. In those verses the law of spiritual gravitation is given in sublime simplicity. A pure mind makes it possible to have right understanding, the first stage of the path. A pure mind is like a clear mirror which reflects things but takes nothing, and sees them all under the same light.

The answer to what is 'right' can be found in the words of the *Dhammapada*:

> The perfume of flowers goes not against the wind,
> not even the perfume of sandalwood of rose-bay or

> of jasmine; but the perfume of virtue travels against the wind and reaches unto the ends of the world. (v.54)

In the first stage on the path we also find the four virtues whose perfume 'reaches unto the ends of the world', the four great virtues of Buddhism, and indeed of all spiritual religion or humanism: *maitri*, *karuna*, *mudita*, *upeksha*. *Maitri*, is friendliness, good-will, benevolence, love, loving-kindness to all. *Karuna* is compassion, pity, sorrow for the sufferings of all. *Mudita* is joy in the good of all. *Upeksha* is forgiveness, overlooking the faults of others. These virtues help man to enter the path and are great friends on his journey.

For having a pure mind you need to 'enter the river of life that leads to NIRVANA',[5] to calmly consider what is right and wrong and face different opinions with 'truth, non-violence and peace',[6] and see that all is 'transient', 'sorrow' and 'unreal'. This is the knowledge necessary to go beyond sorrow. As stated by the *Dhammapada*,

> 'All is transient.' When one sees this, he is above sorrow. This is the clear path.
>
> 'All is sorrow.' When one sees this, he is above sorrow. This is the clear path.
>
> 'All is unreal.' When one sees this, he is above sorrow. This is the clear path. (v.277,278,279)

The Buddha says that it is not enough to only perceive what is right or wrong. The aims to be achieved have also to be right. This requires right determination and right thinking so that one has thereafter the right vision. Says the *Dhammapada*,

> Those who have high thoughts are ever striving: they are not happy to remain in the same place. Like swans that leave their lake and rise into the air, they leave their home for a higher home. (v.91)
>
> The man who wisely controls his senses ... In the light of his vision he has found his freedom: his

> thoughts are peace, his words are peace and his work is peace. (v.94,96)

Having the right understanding and aims which lead to a peaceful mind, one is ready to go through life in an ethical frame of mind.

The third stage is right words. According to the Buddha, right words are words at the right time, profitable and kindly. One should "control one's words and mind and not do harm to anybody",[7] not "speak harsh words, for once spoken they may come back to you",[8] not have "anger in words",[9] and, according to the *Dhammapada*,

> Better than a thousand useless words is one single word that gives peace. (v.100)

Words are not substitutes for action, the fourth stage, for they "are like a flower which has colour but no perfume and so are like the words of a man who speaks but does not do anything".[10] Right action is, states the *Dhammapada*,

> Do not what is evil. Do what is good. Keep your mind pure. This is the teaching of the Buddha. (v.183)

The fifth stage is right means of supporting one's life, or right livelihood.

The man who follows the *Dharma* of the Buddha, or indeed the teachings of the great spiritual leaders, cannot earn his livelihood by working for the production and use of things that are useless, harmful or evil. Only an inner light and spiritual heroism can help man in his moral upliftment and path through life's travails. The correct way of earning one's livelihood is to be like the bee which "takes the essence of a flower and flies away without destroying its beauty and perfume".[11]

The sixth of the eight stages of the Path, of those perfections that like spiritual waves impel man to the shore of *nirvana*, is right effort.

Right effort means right tension and right relaxation. In concentration it means the right attention to something whilst there is a relaxing of everything not connected with the object of attention. All right effort is correct in the sense that we never think it is an effort. Says the *Dhammapada*,

> Better than a hundred years lived in idleness and weakness is a single day of life lived with courage and powerful striving. (v.112)

In right effort the effort "has to be made by oneself on the path shown by the Great";[12] anger has to be forsaken and the path of truth, generosity and good traversed. The *Dhammapada* advises,

> Overcome anger by peacefulness; overcome evil with good. Overcome the mean by generosity; and the man who lies by the truth. (v.223)

The seventh stage is right remembrance and the eighth is contemplation. These serve two purposes: in the fullness of time they lead to *nirvana* and till that stage comes about serve as a feed-back mechanism to monitor one's actions. As the *Dhammapada* says, "watchfulness is the path of immortality: unwatchfulness is the path of death" (v.21) and "those who are for ever watchful, who study themselves day and night, all their passions pass away" (v.226). One has to "live in contemplation, be pure and in peace, do what has to be done, be free from passion and (so) reach the Supreme end". (v.386)

Buddhism and Sustainable Development

Sustainable development has, in a systems analytic framework, three important elements: ecological sustainability, economic sustainability or efficiency in macrosocial terms; social sustainability through greater equity in asset and income distribution. We will now see the extent to which Buddhism contributes to these criteria of sustainable development.

Buddhism and Ecological Sustainability

In its search for pleasure and affluence modern humanity has exploited nature without any restraint to such an extent that nature has been rendered almost incapable of sustaining healthy life. Invaluable gifts of nature, such as air and water, have been polluted with disastrous consequences. Humanity is now searching for ways and means of overcoming the pollution problem as its health is being alarmingly threatened. If we are to act with a sense of responsibility to the natural world, to our fellow human beings and to future generations, we must find an appropriate environmental ethic. Hence our search for wisdom and new attitudes in that neglected area of knowledge: religion.

Buddhism being a fully-fledged philosophy of life reflecting all aspects of experience, has a well defined attitude towards nature. Concern for the welfare of the natural world has been an important facet of Buddhism throughout its history. Recognition that human beings are essentially dependent upon and interconnected with their environments gave rise to an instinctive respect for nature. Although Buddhists believe humans have a unique opportunity to realize enlightenment, which other creatures do not, they have never believed humanity to be superior to the rest of the natural world.

The well-known five precepts (*pancha shila*) form the minimum code of ethics that every lay Buddhist is expected to follow. The first precept is non-injury to life. It is explained as the casting aside of all forms of weapons and being careful not to deprive a living thing of life. The Buddhist lay person is also expected to abstain from trading in meat.[13]

The other precepts are to abstain from stealing, adultery, lying and liquor. The monks have much more stringent prohibitions.

In their attempts to understand the meaning of human life, Buddhists throughout the ages have discovered that 'the truth that sets the heart free' is not found in some metaphysical reality outside the place and time in which each one of us lives and breathes. The Buddha and his followers have always been wary of any attempt to endow human existence with a higher or divine purpose - the workings of a remote all-powerful God or eternal soul or even the modern concept of 'progress'. The spiritual meaning of life is to be found right here in the midst of this network of relationships we call 'life'. A modern American Buddhist abbot, Ajahn Sumedho, explains:

> Once you see what it is all about, you really want to be very careful about what you do and say. You can have no intention to live life at the expense of any other creature. One does not feel that one's life is so much more important that anyone else's. One begins to feel the freedom, the lightness in that harmony with nature rather than the heaviness of exploitation of nature for personal gain.[14]

Buddhism also teaches that morality impacts on nature and vice versa as the world passes through alternating cycles of evolution and dissolution.[15] According to a discourse by the Buddha in the *Anguttara Nikaya*, when lust, greed and wrong values grip the heart of humanity and immorality becomes widespread in society, timely rain does not fall. When timely rain does not fall, crops fall victim to pests and plant diseases. Through lack of nourishing food the human mortality rate rises.[16]

For survival, humans depend on nature for their food, clothing, shelter, medicine and other needs. For maximum benefit, humans have to understand nature so that they can usefully utilise natural resources while living harmoniously with nature. By understanding the working of nature - for example, the seasonal rainfall pattern, methods of conserving water by irrigation, the soil types, the physical conditions required for growth of various food crops - humans can get better returns from their farming. But this learning has to be accompanied by moral restraint if the benefits of natural resources are to be enjoyed for a long time. Humanity must learn to satisfy its needs and not feed its greed.

Buddhism advocates the virtues of non-greed, non-hatred and non-delusion in all human pursuits. Greed breeds sorrow and unhealthy consequences. Contentment, as already noted, is a highly-praised virtue in Buddhism. The person leading a simple life with a few easily satisfied wants is held up as an exemplary character.[17] Miserliness and wastefulness are equally deplored as two degenerate extremes. Wealth should only be a means to an end; it is for the satisfaction of human needs. Hoarding is considered a senseless anti-social habit comparable to the attitude of the dog in the manger.

Buddhism commends frugality and the prevention of waste as a virtue in its own right. The disciple Ananda explained to King Udena the thrifty uses of robes by the monks. When new robes were received the old robes were used as coverlets, the old coverlets as mattress covers, the old mattress covers as rugs, the old rugs as dusters, the old tattered dusters are kneaded with clay and used to repair cracked floors and walls. Thus nothing is wasted. Those who waste are derided as 'wood-apple eaters'. A man shakes the branch of a wood-apple tree and all fall. The man collects only what he wants and leaves the rest to rot. Such a wasteful attitude is deplored in Buddhism as not only anti-social but also criminal. The excessive exploitation of nature as carried out today would certainly be condemned by the Buddha in the strongest possible terms.[18]

Buddhism advocates in the *Dhammapada*, as already noted, that a householder should accumulate wealth as a bee collects nectar from a flower. The bee harms neither the fragrance nor the beauty of the flower, but gathers nectar to turn it into sweet honey. Similarly, a human being is expected to make legitimate use of nature so that one can rise above nature and realize one's innate spiritual potential.

Flowing from the above Buddhist analysis emerges what may be called a Buddhist solution. The first thing would be to reverse the process of moral decay which has set in, to restore the *Dharma*.

Yet to be realistic, we also have to accept that selfishness and greed are not going to vanish overnight. It would appear that the first step of a Buddhist solution would be to explain how the present way of life is not in our own self-interest, let alone in the interest of millions of other beings and future generations.

The second step of a Buddhist solution would be to challenge the social structures which sustain and promote values that lead to ecologically destructive results. Two structures of particular importance would be education and economics. In the secular democracies of the West, both of these structures are based on belief in value-free (objective) knowledge, unlimited progress, and individual freedom. The combined effect of these beliefs is the rapid erosion of the moral values (compassion, generosity, self-control etc.) which come from the Western religions. As a force of spiritual renewal, Buddhism would seek to inject into all social structures, including the Western ones, a fresh awareness of undisputed values - but without these depending on belief in God.

To be complete, however, both approaches (appealing to self-interest and renewing social values) must begin with an inner practice of self-transformation. Learning, reflection and meditation would uproot the tendencies of the mind which are destructive to both humanity and the environment. Qualities such as simplicity, balance, compassion and understanding need to be encouraged. In such ways Buddhist practice would work inwardly at transforming the mind and outwardly at transforming the world.

Buddhist Teachings, Society and the Economy

The Buddha did not compartmentalise society and the individual into two distinct categories. He rather wove them together in a complex, interactive web. Though at first glance the Buddhist teachings appear to be oriented towards personal attainment of *nirvana* or enlightenment, in fact that is not so. In the eightfold path, though wisdom and contemplation (stages

1,2,7 and 8) are confined to the individual the other four speak of his interactions with the rest of society.

Also to the Buddha society was not confined to one culture or nation. He took a universal view and according to him the whole of humanity was one family. As the *Hitopadesha* says,

> Of what use are words of wisdom to the man who is unwise? Of what use is a lamp to a man who is blind?
>
> Hear the essence of thousands of sacred books: to help others is virtue: to hurt others is sin.
>
> A man rises or goes down by his own actions: like the builder of a wall, or as the digger of a well.
>
> The narrow-minded man thinks and says: 'This man is one of us; this one is not, he is a stranger. To the man of noble soul the whole of mankind is but one family.[19]

The Buddha lays down in the above saying the essential duty of man towards his fellow beings: not to hurt others but to help them. The Dhammapada goes on to say,

> Pluck out your self-love as you would pull off a faded lotus in autumn. Strive on the path of peace, the path of NIRVANA shown by Buddha. (v.285)

In dealing with others the Buddhist is required to forget the differences of self and self in the greater unity. In the application of this ideal there is as much variety as there is in the human mind, for the *karmic* law, in the long round of successive lives, produces every known relationship. Yet all these human beings are truly brothers, born of one mother, matter, by one father, life. There are older and younger brothers, some to follow and some to lead, but all are members of one family to be served, if need be, at the cost of self and all which the self holds dear.

Buddhist society is thus based on morality. The morality of the Buddhist does not come from following the rules without question but out of love and respect for all of life. One of the most simple statements of this principle was given by the Buddha himself:

Not to commit evil
But to practice all good
And to keep the heart pure;
This is the teaching of the Buddha.[20]

Elsewhere in the scriptures, the Buddha spells out what he means by the right way to lead our lives:

> What is right action? Abstention from killing breathing things, stealing, misconduct in sensual desires: this is called the right action.[21]

The wise man, according to the Buddha, "puts not his own success before the success of righteousness".[22] It is the *Dharma* which has to succeed not the individual. In this sense the Buddhist merges himself into the social system, not by force, whether of society or the state, but by his own free choice and will. This he does because he realises that the success of the Whole is what would sustain him.

Also "noble men find joy in generosity"[23] for it is by this behaviour that an equitable, nonviolent and peaceful society can be attained. For to the Buddhist a peaceful society is the essential desideratum for a joyful, happy and tension-free life. Peacefulness overcomes anger, good overcomes evil and one who controls himself attains the highest. Says the *Dhammapada*,

> Overcome anger by peacefulness; overcome evil by good. Overcome the mean by generosity; and the man who lies by truth.
>
> Speak the truth, yield not to anger, give what you can to him who asks: these three steps lead you to the gods. (v.223,224)

Living peacefully was an important facet of the Buddha's teaching. And living peacefully meant, according to the *Dhammapada*, living in harmony with others.

> Many do not know that we are here in this world to live in harmony. Those who know this do not fight against each other. (v.6)

Speaking holy words only, or preaching to others, was not what led to holiness - but only a life lived free from hate, passion and craving according to the *Dhammapada*.

Whereas if a man speaks but a few holy words and yet he lives the life of those words, free from passion and hate and illusion - with right vision and a mind free, craving for nothing both now and hereafter - the life of this man is a life of holiness. (v.20)

Nonexploitation and nonviolence were other virtues highly praised by the Buddha, for one's happiness should not be at the cost of others. Says the *Dhammapada*,

> He who for the sake of happiness hurts others who also want happiness, shall not hereafter find happiness. (v.131)
>
> All beings tremble before danger, all fear death. When a man considers this, he does not kill or cause to kill. (v.129)

We have already noted the Buddha's emphasis on truth on loving-kindness to all, compassion, joy in the good of all and forgiveness (*maitri*, *karuna*, *mudita* and *upeksha*).

The health, welfare and happiness of all is the goal of Buddhist society. As the Pali text says, "sabbe satta sukhi hontu" (may all beings be well and happy).[24] The *Dhammapada* says that followers of the Buddha find joy in love of all beings.

> The followers of Buddha Gotama are awake and for ever watch; and ever by night and by day they find joy in love for all beings. (v.300)

The Buddha never specifically dealt with economic matters. He looked at the question of earning one's livelihood as a stage on the path leading to Enlightenment. Thus economic activities had to be preceded by wisdom and be based on ethical values. Though the Buddha looked at the earning of ones livelihood as one of the steps to *nirvana* it did not mean that he looked down on the earning of money as a superfluous activity.

One of the misperceptions about the Buddha's teaching is that it is world-renouncing and meant only for monks. But in fact he considered householders to be equal to monks (*bhikkhus*) if they had the correct attitudes. According to the *Dhammapada*,

> But although a man may wear fine clothing, if he lives peacefully; and is good, self-possessed, has faith and is pure; and if he does not hurt any living being, he is a holy Brahmin, a hermit of seclusion, a monk called a Bhikkhu. (v.142)

The Buddha in fact specifically deplores taking refuge away from life in forests or mountains, or shrines as they do not lead to a cessation of suffering. As the *Dhammapada* says,

> Men in their fear fly for refuge to mountains or forests, groves, sacred trees or shrines. But those are not a safe refuge, they are not the refuge that frees a man from sorrow. (v. 188, 189)

But economic activity has to be in the context of relations with others in the societal system. Humankind is one, though infinitely various, and the types of men are profoundly different, not only in bodily structure but in basic pattern of mind. The sexes, East and West, the introvert and extrovert, these are obvious pairs of opposites. It follows, not only that we cannot assume that our neighbour is of the same type as ourselves but that he, being different, must also work out his own salvation with diligence, even though his path is, for the time being, different from that which is, at the moment, ours. In the words of an ancient Buddhist saying, 'The ways to the One are as many as the lives of men'. This leads to a diversity of activities with none being considered superior to the others. The *Dhammapada* says:

> Let no man endanger his duty, the good of his soul, for the good of another, however great. When

> he has seen the good of his soul, let him follow it with earnestness. (v.166)

Certain kinds of activities which harmed society were prohibited. During the simple economy of the Buddha's time, the teaching was,

> There are five trades that a lay follower should not ply. What five? They are: trading in weapons, in breathing things, meat, liquor, and poisons.[25]

In today's much more complex economy many more things would be prohibited: dealing in drugs and arms, indulging in fraud and cheating, exploiting women and children, and so on.

The Buddhist System

The main tenets of Buddhist teachings may be said to be five. Firstly, human beings have to live in peace and harmony with each other, other beings and nature. Secondly, truth and non-violence are essential as it is only then that peace can be achieved. Thirdly, society has to be nonexploitative and human beings have to act in a manner that optimises the health, happiness and welfare of everybody including those in other societies or nations. Fourthly, human beings have to live a life of simplicity. And lastly, there is need for self-control, friendliness, compassion, love and forgiveness.

Having briefly described the Buddhist system, and what it aimed at, it may be worthwhile to critically appraise its approach and what it has achieved. Firstly, Buddhism built up its corpus around a duality expressed in many terms: Truth and Falsehood, Light and Darkness, Violence and Non-violence, Compassion and Harshness etc. Both co-exist, and either defines the other.

Human life as it exists is defined as a struggle, between the two opposing pulls and the aim of Buddhism is to reach the goal by promoting in the individual truth, non-violence, peace, benevolence, compassion. These can be achieved through overpowering or conquering evil, falsehood, violence, injustice and hatred in one's self in dealing with others. Therein lies *nirvana*, human salvation and creation of a peaceful and stable society.

Secondly, it would be clear that the Buddhist system lays down an individual code for human beings and seeks to coalesce them into community life through a philosophy and social code. The main concept which should motivate individual life is the release from suffering through the right vision and the dissemination of it to others.

Thirdly, the needs and demands of material things is to be regulated through proper utilisation, the controlling of waste and a nonexploitative social structure.

Fourthly, the system has cosmological views on time, space, the physical phenomenon and nature. It seeks to establish harmonious human relationships with these phenomenon, as a part of belief. It justifies social structure and practice as a part of the natural order or *dharma*.

Fifthly, with regard to the use of materials and the question of satisfying one's need, there is a defined code against waste, and inefficient use of materials, water and food. Every one is expected to limit one's want and practice a simple life style. The development of humans is, essentially, the degree to which one is able to practice these virtues.

Finally, the paradigm of development is built around man, it aims at the development of man, both to provide leadership and to bring about stability in society. This is to be attained through the practice of a moral code and the observance of a social code. The motor for change in Buddhist society thus is man, in contrast to technology in contemporary society.

Buddhist Economics

Modern mainstream economics, the so-called neoclassical system, is based on a number of value premises and assumptions. The central core of the value premise is materialism defined in terms of raising the standard of living or maximising consumption and thereby optimising the pattern of production. The production philosophy of modern industrialism is based on the corporate need for profits, technological determination and ecological indifference. On the basis of this value system, the production system meshes in with the consumption pattern through the mediation of the market.

The system is based on private ownership. There are two kinds of agents, firms and households. Individuals are expected to behave rationally, have perfect information and expectations of the future. The market conveys a signal about what the households wish to consume to the producers. This is how the optimal production pattern gets established.

Economics, and the economy, based on Buddhist thought differs from the neoclassical system in a number of ways.

Firstly, the value premise underlying Buddhism is a mixture of materialism and nonmaterialism. Buddhist economics would thus have to take note of nonmaterial values thereby grounding the core elements of Buddhist economics in the Buddha's holistic view of what constitutes human nature. To the Buddha, human beings not only have the need to survive, implying the need for food and shelter, but they also have the need to exercise their capacity to care for others. A harmonious balance thus needs to be struck between selfishness and self-lessness, or between the needs of the individual and those of other beings.

Secondly, Buddhist teachings stress self-control and the regulation of material consumption rather than its maximisation. Desire being never satisfied with more and varied consumption, the teaching goes on to say that, "even a shower of gold coins could not satisfy craving desire".[26] Therefore the wise man is,

> He who for himself or others craves not for sons or power or *wealth*, who puts not his own success before the success of righteousness, he is virtuous, and righteous, and wise. (emphasis added) (v.84)

Thirdly, Buddhism distinguishes between needs and wants. It recognises that the needs of a manual worker would differ from those of a philosopher or an artist as the dharma of each is different. But it deplores wants which are, in its opinion, not only unnecessary but also have a way of multiplying themselves indefinitely. No doubt the satisfaction of wants brings pleasure, but pleasure is transient and ultimately ends up in misery.

As the *Dhammapada* says,

> From pleasure arises sorrow and from pleasure arises fear. If a man is free from passion, he is free from fear and sorrow. (v.212)

Fourthly, the production system, run by managers and entrepreneurs imbued with Buddhist ethics, would not produce articles which are harmful to other beings. Thus the production of armaments, toxic materials, drugs, films showing violence and sex etc. would not take place. Industries which pollute the air, water or the soil would not be set up. Firms would also not create unnecessary wants through high pressure advertising.

Besides for the sake of profit, there would be no laying off of workers or the harming of the livelihood of traditional communities. For not only has happiness not to be at the expense of the happiness of others but to deprive others of their livelihood would prevent them from entering on the fifth step of the path to *nirvana*. This would be the equivalent of killing others - something prohibited by the Buddha's teaching.

Lastly, the goal of Buddhist economics would be the maximisation of human happiness combined with full mental and moral growth. The Buddhist welfare function would thus radically differ from the neoclassical one. The utility function of the Buddhist would, like the Hindu utility function be a multi-order one: if a person looks after his own interests he derives a certain order of utility; if he cares for the society in which he lives, he derives an even higher order of utility; if his vision and goal embraces the entire collection of living beings, human and others, he derives the highest order of utility. The Buddhist concept of welfare would thus, modify the present-day acquisitive society by shifting acquisition from private gain to action geared to societal or universal gain.

The fact that Buddhist society is based on peace, nonviolence, harmony and nonexploitation also has some other implications for the economy. A Buddhist economy would, therefore, consider equitable distribution and full employment as an essential component. Such an economy in its international dealings would care as much for other societies as for itself. It would not engage in win-lose games but only in win-win strategies.

Neoclassical theory is based on the premise that all human beings in the economy act rationally and that all have perfect information and anticipations of the future. This makes the actions and perspectives of the human elements of the economy uniform and homogeneous thereby leading to unique equilibria.

Buddhist society, on the other hand, is by its very nature nonhomogeneous and diverse. Every human being has his own *karma*, his own debts to pay. The differing initial conditions for everyone leads to great diversity of actions and behaviour. This leads to intensive nonlinear interactions among the large number of "nonrational" agents in contrast to neoclassical theory where rational agents operate in a linear and statistically predictable environment.

Nonhomogenuity and the inclusion of moral, psychological and sociological factors in the economic system inevitably leads to multiple equilibria thereby making impossible the prediction of unique future states. Different socio-cultural environments therefore determine different evolutionary economic paths. We thus get economic diversity in the world. Also in the Buddhist context, none of the states are considered superior or can dominate over the others as this would be against the doctrines of peace, harmony and nonexploitation.

The Buddha, of course, was fully aware of this and it is for this reason that he laid down values for guiding the actions of different individuals rather than categorical directions of what to do or what not to do. We have already noted how this flexible and adaptive approach led to the flowering of many Buddhist doctrines in different socio-cultural environments. This approach makes a Buddhist economy a learning and adaptive system.

In economics historically two kinds of values have been considered: Values-in-use and values-in-exchange. Modern neoclassical economics, and Gross National Product (GNP), measure only values-in-exchange since they are the only one's marketed. Values-in-threat, that is those which threaten human happiness like armaments, drugs etc. are subsumed under the values-in-exchange and are included in GNP because they are marketed. A Buddhist economy would not only *not* include value-in-threat in "GNP" but would *deduct* it from "GNP" as it is not a "good" but a "bad".

Buddhist economic development is driven by morality and not technology as is the case with the modern system. In the time of the Buddha technology was not as pervasive in society as it is today. But one can be reasonably certain that if he was to rule on technology in today's circumstances he would want it to be such as can only be used for peaceful purposes, does not harm the environment, or lead to poverty, unemployment, and exploitation.

The main features of the Buddhist economy may be briefly enumerated:

- the basic unit of the system is the human being who is conceived as being multidimensional and having multiple orders of utility;
- the goal of the system is the maximisation of human happiness, combined with full mental and moral growth, and the optimisation of health and welfare;

- the societal structures have to be such as to be nonexploitative and nonviolent;
- the overall direction of the economy is determined by the interaction of many dispersed units (human beings) acting in parallel. The action of any one unit depends on the state and actions of a limited number of other units;
- there are very few external controls on interactions - controls are provided by an internal set of values ("self-awareness") and the desire of all to reach the state of *nirvana*;
- the economy has many levels of organisation and interaction: family, community, society, humanity. Units at any one level serve as "building blocks" for the next level but in a nonhegemonic manner;
- the building blocks are continuously being revised and recombined as the system accumulates experience: the system is flexible and adapts;
- the units are not hierarchically arranged and all are free to follow their own way to the goal: the goal is one but the paths are many.

The Buddhist economy is thus an example of an adaptive nonlinear network (ANN hereafter) as defined by Holland.[27] According to Holland, ANNs do not act in terms of stimulus and response, they anticipate. The models are rarely explicit: they are usually more prescriptive than descriptive. ANNs also engender perpetual novelty and though the possibilities are unknown, the use of genetic algorithms leads to evolutionary strategies.

In the Buddhist economy the prescriptions are the main values of Buddhism: nonviolence, nonexploitation, peace, harmony and happiness. The genetic algorithm varies from society to society and culture to culture. So the use of the genetic algorithm leads to varying evolutionary paths. Strategies differ from culture to culture and are evolutionary. As the history of

Buddhism shows, a number of different "visions" can be evolved from the basic teachings of the Buddha: but all these "visions" are complementary to each other and so can live in co-existence and harmony.

Buddhist economies can similarly be expected to be creative in their development in differing socio-cultural environments. But all the different economies would be peaceful and nonexploitative, both internally, in the interactions in society, and externally in their interactions with each other.

Learning and education would be an important element of Buddhist economic systems based as they are on wisdom, ethics and reflection in continuous two-way interactions with each other. Wisdom impacts on ethics while correct actions lead to increase in wisdom: reflection is the feed-back mechanism for ensuring that the dynamics of the economy are propelling it in the right direction. An educated society aware of the imperatives of nonviolence, harmony and happiness would live in peace with its neighbours while its internal dynamics would be in the direction of ensuring a good life for everyone.

However it needs to be pointed out that Buddhist economics can only work in a Buddhist society. For the Buddha was one of those rarely gifted individuals in whom the economist, the philosopher, the moralist, the sociologist, the political scientist were all rolled into one. Therefore the Buddha's teachings are a vast system of thought composed of many sub-systems of which the economy is one. Unless all the sub-systems are in synergetic interaction there is always the possibility of a new subsystem injected into the system being rejected by the social body as an external and nonharmonious foreign body.

In considering Buddhist economics in the context of modern society this point has to be constantly borne in mind. In Buddha's time the external pulls of materialism were not as powerful as they are today. Globalisation of communications and the consequent international "demonstration effect" is having profound impacts on all societies. As an ancient Indian saying goes, `the Eternal has so made the senses that they go outward; only rare individuals look inside and so find peace'.[28] There is thus in todays world a great need for looking inside, for reflection and for attaining ethics and wisdom. This needs a society of like-minded individuals who can build up a powerful counter-movement, of a Buddhist community, a Buddhist *sangha*.

Critique of the Buddhist Model

The Buddhist model would most likely be criticised by the so-called "modernists" on the ground of being impractical in the sense that it is not possible to achieve it in the context of modern society. This is of course true. Buddhist economics needs a Buddhist social structure. But is a Buddhist social structure utopian and unattainable?

In answering the above question, a distinction has to be made between three different social states. One is the desired or the ideal state. This state is as yet unachieved. Buddhist thought persists however in the possibility of achieving this state. For the individual, the ideal state is the achievement of *nirvana*. History records that many have achieved *nirvana* or gone a long way towards achieving it. For the society, the ideal state is freedom: freedom to be ruled by one's own *dharma* and to chart one's individual and unique path. The ruling principle in such a society would be nonviolence and the quest for truth. There is no evidence of any society having achieved this state.

The second state is the transition to the ideal state. Buddhist thought is very clear on this point. The transitional state is achievable through the eightfold path for the individual and the practice of nonviolence and nonexploitation for society.

The third is the state of the present order. This determines what the possibilities are. These differ from society to society and culture to culture. Buddhist thought is emphatic that though each society may follow its own path, change is possible if each society follows its social or collective *dharma* and takes to the nonviolent, nonexploitative path.

Another misconception of the Buddha's teaching is that it leads to asceticism and espouses poverty. This would be a misreading of the Buddha's teaching. Wealth to the Buddha was "contentment"[29] and a man could wear fine clothing (i.e. live in prosperity) if he lives peacefully, is good, self-possessed, pure and does not hurt any living being.[30] It is not riches the Buddha is against but the two extremes of miserly accumulation and conspicuous consumption. He praises generosity and points the way by which wealth can be generated and utilised without any adverse effects: by sharing it with others. Says the *Dhammapada*,

> Misers certainly do not go to the heaven of the gods, and fools do not praise liberality; but noble men find joy in generosity, and this gives them joy in higher worlds. (v.177)

In today's world probably one of the doctrines of Buddhism least acceptable would be the one relating to the control of desire. This comes in direct conflict with one of the most powerful drives of modern economic society: the drive for multiplication of wants. The justification for consumption based on ever-increasing wants is that such consumption is an essential prerequisite for economic growth and stability in an affluent society.

Buddhist teaching would reject this argument on both growth and stability grounds. Growth, according to Buddhist thought is qualitative and not quantitative. In the multi-level Buddhist utility function it is not only self-consumption which is important but meeting the needs of the whole of humanity ultimately, and of the family, society and nation in the meantime. Thus development has to be such that no one is destitute, that there is no poverty. The removal of poverty would make for both the stability and development of society and hence the Buddha stresses generosity as against either accumulation or conspicuous consumption.

Recent work by the World Bank in reassessing the wealth of nations would strengthen the Buddhist argument. In a recent study,[31] the World Bank has divided a country's productive stock into: produced assets (machines, buildings, infrastructure); human capital (education, knowledge and health); natural capital (soils, forests, water, minerals); and social capital (institutional and cultural bases of society).

The World Bank has not yet been able to measure social capital but about the other three forms of capital preliminary results reveal the following picture:

	Developed countries	*Developing countries*
Produced assets	16%	16%
Natural capital*	17%	32%
Human capital	67%	52%

* Most likely underestimated.

Gross national product (GNP) by which economic growth is usually measured thus accounts for only 16% of a nation's capital stock. Human capital accounts for the major part of a nations capital and as countries become developed they will have to have a much faster rate of growth of human capital as compared to produced assets (GNP). If we introduce social capital into the growth matrix, the Buddhist argument becomes even stronger. It also needs to be noted that knowledge is the very first stage of the eightfold path - remarkable evidence of the manner in which great spiritual masters pierce to the heart of reality.

Two further points need to be made at this stage. Though at first stage it may appear that the Buddhist society is noncompetitive this is only true in an external sense. In every human being there is internally intense struggle and competition for realising *nirvana*. Competition is, thus, "internalised" and the "struggle" is against one's own destructive tendencies.

Secondly, the fact that Buddhism encourages diverse economies based on differing socio-cultural environments means that inappropriate development never takes place. Development based on Buddhist thought also leads to creativity, sustainability and the reduction of vulnerability as Buddhist societies tend to be decentralised, flexible and adaptable.

Conclusions

The Buddha never specifically dealt with economics. As we have seen, his main concern was with the problem of suffering. In finding a solution to this problem he developed a holistic paradigm encompassing everything connected with a human being. The Buddha's strong point is that he did not build a systematic model, for he was fully aware that all models become static after having their full run. But he initiated, developed and perfected open-ended concepts amenable and adequate to produce many models, that is, models for a given context, situation and society.

The Buddha's approach and concepts have their own in-built dynamics and close relations with praxis so that once on a Buddhist path, the system is on the path of steady growth towards a peaceful and happy society.

The following of this path leads, as we have noticed, to an economy which is:

- flexible, adaptive and creative;
- nonexploitative so that assets and income get equitably distributed;
- in harmony with the natural environment;
- self-regulated leading to restraint on unnecessary consumption;
- culturally determined.

The Buddhist economy thus meets all the dimensions of eco-development of Ignacy Sachs, namely, sustainability of society, economy, ecology and culture.[32] In addition the Buddhist economy leads to the maximisation of happiness in society and to a peaceful and stable world order.

References

1. Pali: The religious language of Thervada Buddhism. The word means 'text', hence the language of the sacred texts. Its precise origin is disputed, and today few scholars accept the claim that it is the original language of the Buddha himself.
2. The law of *karma* is in the psycho-spiritual sphere akin to Newton's law in the physical sphere: that for every action there is an equal and opposite reaction.
3. *The Dhammapada*, translated by Juan Mascaro, (Penguin Books, 1987) verse 127. All quotations from the *Dhammapada* are from this reference.
4. *Dhammapada*, note 3, verse 168.
5. *Ibid.*, v. 178.
6. *Ibid.*, v. 256,257.
7. *Ibid.*, v. 281.
8. *Ibid.*, v. 133.
9. *Ibid..*, v. 232.
10. *Ibid.*, v. 51.
11. *Ibid.*, v. 49.
12. *Ibid.*, v. 276.
13. *Anguttara Nikaya*, Pali Text Society, London, III.208.
14. Ajahn Sumedho quoted in *Buddhism and Ecology*, Martine Batchelor and Kerry Brown, (eds.) (New Delhi: Motilal Banarsidas, 1994) p.15.
15. This is somewhat akin to Teilhard Chardin's Noosphere interacting with the Biosphere.
16. *Angattura Nikaya*, note 13, I.160.
17. *Ibid.*, IV.2,220,229.
18. *Buddhism and Ecology*, note 14, p.22.

19. Quoted in *Dhammapada*, note 3, p.27.
20. *Ibid.*, v.183.
21. *Samyutta Nikaya*, Pali Society, London, XLV, 8.
22. *Dhammapada*, note 3, v.84.
23. *Ibid.*, v.177.
24. Quoted in *Buddhism and Ecology*, note 14, p.78.
25. *Anguttara Nikaya*, note 13, V.177.
26. *Dhammapada*, note 3, v.186.
27. John H. Holland, "The Global Economy as an Adaptive Process" *The Economy as an Evolving Complex System*, Philip W. Anderson, Kenneth J. Arrow, David Pines eds. (Reading , Massachusetts: Addison Wesley) pp.117-123.
28. *Katha Upanishad*, trans: Swami Sarvananda, (Madras: Ramakrishna Math, 1973), 2.4.1.
29. *Dhammapada*, note 3, v.204.
30. *Ibid.*, v. 142.
31. *Monitoring Environment Progress* (World Bank, 1995).
32. Ignacy Sachs, "Transition Strategies for the 21st Century, *Nature and Resources*, 28(1), 1992

6

Islam and Sustainable Development

The Quran to the average Muslim (that is, those who have submitted to Allah or God) is the book which guides all actions. The Quran for the Muslim is the revelation of God and the book in which His message to man is contained. It is the word of God revealed to the Prophet through the archangel Gabriel. The Prophet (or the Messenger) was therefore the instrument chosen by God for the revelation of His word, of His book of which both the spirit and the letter, the content and the form, are Divine.

It is this belief in the Divine presence and his acting more or less in accordance with this belief that defines the decisive influence of the Quran on a Muslim's (righteous) behaviour. For it is through righteous action that God gives knowledge to a person. As the Quran says:[1]

> And say: "Work (righteousness):
> Soon will ye be brought back
> To the Knower of what is
> Hidden and what is open:
> Then will He show you
> The truth of all that ye did." (9:105).

Indeed, a typical Muslim, with no special claims to piety, seriously believes that he is in direct communion with God, Who listens to his entreaties and rewards (punishes) him for his good (bad) actions. Knowing this, he seeks God's help in every action he contemplates - by saying *Inshaalah* (God willing) every time he plans a new enterprise. And in a substantial number of actions - e.g., feeding the poor, giving alms, helping orphans, not charging interest on loans, not hoarding food items, and in his aversion to gambling and betting - seeking God's pleasure is the mainspring of action. It is under the influence of a firm belief in the Divine presence that certain potent ideas - for example, about the equality of all men before God, about the poor having a right in the rich man's wealth because all wealth belongs to God, about a rich man's obligation to spend with moderation because he is a trustee not owner of his wealth, about man being essentially a free agent with definite social responsibilities to discharge, etc. - are routinely believed in by the Muslims; and, to some extent, also practiced.

In the Islamic concept an individual is an integrated personality who is moved to action by impulses that do not distinguish between the mundane and the spiritual. In this context, the division of man's activity into this-worldly and other-worldly by other systems of thought is considered to be only a stratagem for the resolving of conflicting religious, social, political and economic demands. For to the Islamic vision, the distinction between the secular and the spiritual is both pointless and counter-productive - pointless, because it is artificial and unreal; counter-productive, because it breeds schizophrenic tendencies and tensions. The rewards for deeds can thus be spiritual or material i.e. either in this world or the hereafter. As stated by the Quran:

> ...If any
> Do desire a reward
> In this life, we shall give it

To him; and if any
Do desire a reward
In the Hereafter, we shall
Give it to him.
And swiftly shall We reward
Those that (serve us with) gratitude (3:145)

This unitary character of Islamic philosophy destroys the dichotomy between the secular and the spiritual at both the levels of the individual and of society. As an individual, man is seen as having free will though he has also to be committed to the betterment of society. Thus, driven by a strong ethical impulse, he is supposed to discharge his responsibilities for his own good and that of the society in which he lives. At the socio-economic level, the act of giving to the poor and the needy is linked directly with efforts towards spiritual attainment. At the societal (structural) level, conditions have to be created which enables all its members to freely attain both material and spiritual progress. Thus through a 'unified' framework of thought and action, Islam seeks to create the necessary preconditions for social harmony and economic progress.

Islamic Ethics

Islamic ethics are a result of an interaction between four parameters: God's will and Divine law; the exercise of free will; being in obedience to the Divine command; and the maintenance of social harmony and unity.

In Islamic thought, God is omnipotent and omniscient and His grace and mercy are available to all who conform to His directions. At the same time a person has free will in deciding his course of action. The Quran says:

Let there be no compulsion
In religion: Truth stands out
Clear from Error... (2:256)

Islamic ethics is thus determined by the interaction of man's freedom to act and Divine omnipotence. If man is given absolute freedom of will, then God's omnipotence is compromised. On the other hand, if the belief is exclusively focused on God's omnipotence, then man's responsibility for his actions becomes meaningless. In the Islamic ethical scheme, man is the centre-piece of God's creation; for he is God's viceregent on earth:

> Behold thy Lord said to the angels: "I will create
> A viceregent (*khalifa*) on earth". (2:30)

Since there is no compulsion in Islam, and man has to realize the Truth himself, the entire purpose of man's life as a 'free' agent invested with a free will, able to make a choice between good and evil, right or wrong becomes the realization of his viceregency. By virtue of his freedom, man can either realize his position as God's viceregent on earth or deny himself this exalted niche by making the wrong choice. In other words, man is held accountable for the choices he makes in his individual capacity.

Every human being combines in himself both an 'individual man' and a 'collective man', and there is an essential reciprocity between these two facets of the human personality. The (undivided) individuality aspect highlights freedom; but collectivity at the same time means there being responsibility to society. Far from inducing any schizophrenic tendency, this duality fortifies human nature from within. Armed with a cause, a person is well-placed to reach out to the viceregal ideal by submitting without reserve to God's will.

Another distinctive characteristic of the Islamic view is that it leaves enough 'elbow room' to accommodate under one roof, so to speak, both soaring idealism which takes a person on a spiritual ascent and the mundane concern for personal well-being. The 'space' between the ideal and the reality is filled by the quality of *al'adl* and *al ihsan* (i.e., a state of balance), of which social justice is one aspect. According to this quality, everything is assigned its proper place. Not only that; if anything is not assigned its proper place, then the aim of a free and responsible humanity must be to rectify this undesirable state of affairs by achieving balance, equity and justice.

A key element of man's freedom - and his concomitant responsibility to society - is that both these concepts flow from a Muslim's belief in God's unrivalled supremacy in the universe and beyond. According to the Quran, this belief is the reason why all of humanity is free and equal:

> "...That we erect not
> From among ourselves,
> Lords and patrons
> Other than God" (3:64).

The definition of freedom as an essentially ethical proposition adds a new dimension to it by including freedom from avarice and greed to political and economic freedom. Says the Quran:

> And those saved from
> The covetousness of their own
> Souls,—they are the ones
> That achieve prosperity. (59:9)

Seen from this angle, man's political, social, and economic freedoms are expressions of Islam's ethical perceptions about man and society and the need for being free of avarice and greed.

The Quran places the utmost stress on unity. This flows from the unqualified and unalloyed belief in God's unity. It particularly denotes the vertical dimension of Islam - linking imperfect and finite social institutions with a Perfect and Infinite Being. This link-up is effected by man's unconditional surrender before God, by making his desires, ambitions, and actions subservient to His command:

> Say: "Truly, my prayer
> And my service of sacrifice,

My life and my death,
Are (all) for God,
The Cherisher of the Worlds. (6:162)

Man's submission to God not only helps man to realize his potentiality, but it also releases him from human bondage. By integrating the political, economic, social, and religious aspects, man's life is transformed into a homogeneous whole, consistent from within and integrated with the vast universe without. The integrative social role of unity flows from an awareness of God's omnipotence, knowledge and ownership of everything. Says the Quran:

...for God
Has power over all things. (35:1)
...and God
Hath knowledge of all things. (4:176)
To God belongs the heritage
Of the heavens and the earth. (3:180)

And yet, in such an absolutist world, man's freedom is also ensured. It flows from God being also the judge of human action. From this concept of God being the Judge, in addition to being the Cherisher, the Knower etc. flows the Islamic concept of free will:

'Is not God
The wisest of judges? (95:8)

However, it should be noted that this concept is not meant to dilute human freedom, but only to point out the 'best' way of exercising it. Thus, man is free to own wealth and property, but the best pattern of ownership is to consider it as a 'trusteeship' of what truly belongs to God - and to exercise it according to the Divine law. And once the Divine law is obeyed, man's ownership of property and other things is practically absolute.

Such a perspective becomes a catalytic force in Islamic society and acts on the individual, and through the individual, for the betterment of society. This force, which derives its strength from a deep sense of the Divine presence, transforms man's love for himself into love for God's creation. Thus, an abiding concern for ethical fulfillment raises the level of the individual's consciousness, to a higher plane of consciousness, by adding the force of voluntarism to the altruistic instincts.

Corresponding to unity, the twin Islamic concepts of *al'adl* and *al ihsan* denote a state of an equitable balance of forces - social, economic, national - of which the attainment of social harmony through socio-economic justice is one aspect. The Quran states:

> God commands justice, the doing
> Of good, and liberality...' (16:90).

As a social ideal, the principle of balance or equitableness (*al'adl*) provides a complete description of the interlinking of the basic set of social institutions - legal, political, and economic. On the economic plane, the principle defines a configuration of the production, consumption, and distribution activities, with the needs of the least-privileged members in Muslim society constituting the first charge on the resources of that society.

To understand the full social connotation of the Islamic concept of balance, it should be noted that the antonym of *al'adl* is *zulm*, which denotes harm, wrong, injustice or transgression. In socio-economic terms it would denote an iniquitous system in which the resources of society flow from the poor to the rich. This is not allowed in Islam for the reason contained in the following verse of the Quran:

> In order that it may not
> (Merely) make a circuit
> Between the wealthy among you. (59:7)

Read together with the Quranic verse about justice, good and liberality quoted earlier, it becomes obvious that, starting from a state of disharmony or injustice all steps have to be taken to attain justice and harmony; that the 'rights' of the 'needy and the deprived' are restored to them through a fair distribution of income and wealth; and that this process is a continuous one. Viewed thus, the principle of balance encompasses both the desirable state of affairs and the process by which to get there. Thus, when it is asserted that Islam insists on justice and harmony, such an assertion includes not only the exact point where the social and economic forces are perfectly balanced, but also the territory adjoining this point, where the forces are off-balance. But the condition is that a mechanism must be provided to restore, approximately if not exactly, the state of balance.

As already noted, in the Islamic perspective, man is born with a 'free will' - that is, with the faculty of making an unconstrained choice in various conflictual situations. While man's freedom is both unrestricted and voluntary, so that he is free to make the wrong choice as well, it is in his own interest, says the Quran, to make the 'right' choice for it is thus that he does good to his soul:

> Say: "O ye men! Now
> Truth hath reached you
> From your Lord! Those who receive
> Guidance, do so for the good
> Of their own souls; those
> Who stray, do so to their own loss:
> And I am not (set) over you
> To arrange your affairs." (10:108)

Indeed, God's blessings have been made conditional on man's first making the 'right' choice and taking steps to reach the right state of equilibrium: God has not undertaken to do it. It requires an inner change, a self-sacrifice, a change of heart. The Quran says:

> Verily never
> Will God change the condition
> Of a people until they

Change it themselves
(With their own souls). (13:11)

Thus, the basis of man's freedom is firmly rooted in the need of making the 'right' choice. It should be remembered that it is this faculty of making a choice that makes a human being God's vicegerent on earth, and which defines the central element of a person's character. Insofar as this viceregal stature denotes a potentiality rather than something that actually obtains, we come back to the question of how best to realize it. Also in the Islamic perspective, man is not chained to any historical determinism. While God is all-knowing, he is also the ultimate judge of the manner in which man exercises his inborn right to choose between good and evil and other situations that lie between these two extremes.

The key to an understanding of the ethical basis of individual freedom lies in grasping the fact that Divine omniscience does not necessarily imply any Divine responsibility to see to it that man makes the right choice, even though, if implored, Divine mercy may do just that. Since man is free, he has only two options: either he, obeying the Divine law, takes the right action and is guided to the 'right path' or he makes the wrong choice and is led away from the 'right path' - and may even oppose God. One may look upon the same matter in another way: man is free and potentially God's representative but this potentiality is realized only under the umbrella of following God's prescription of what is best for man. As the Quran says:

Thee do we worship,
And Thine aid we seek.
Show us the straight way,
The way of those on whom
Thou hast bestowed thy Grace,
Those whose (portion)
Is not wrath
And who go not astray. (1:5,6,7).

To assert that man, in any given situation, is guided by rules and procedures based on the Divine law does not necessarily mean that the element of uncertainty facing him in making the right choice will be any less if he was to be guided by man-made laws; or that the demands on human ingenuity would be any the less otherwise. This is because the Divine laws, with few exceptions, lay down only the general guidelines; but within the framework of these guidelines, careful thought is required to interpret - and reinterpret - it within specific societal contexts, and to suit the needs of changing times.

Corresponding to free will is the doctrine of responsibility. Islam lays great emphasis on the concept of responsibility; but this does not imply caring less about individual freedom of choice. Instead, it seeks to establish a proper balance between the demands of the individual and those of the collectivity. According to this view, modern civilization would be defined in terms of a series of steps to constrain individual freedom appropriately so that the inherent conflict between maximizing one's own interests is balanced by the need to maximise the welfare of society - the dividing line between the individual and the society being necessarily *ad hoc* and shifting in accordance with the dictates of time.

The Islamic concept of responsibility includes two fundamental aspects which need to be noted. First, responsibility goes with man's viceregal status - his being God's *khalifa* on earth. But, as noted above, this viceregal status is more something needing to be achieved (potential state) than a fact (realized state). It takes considerable effort on man's part to ascend to this lofty station - indeed, it takes doing good acts, like giving to the poor and the needy, doing justice, praying to God for guidance. Not only that; in doing good acts man has to give away, says the Quran, what he loves most:

> By no means shall ye
> Attain righteousness unless

Ye give (freely) of that
Which ye love; and whatever
Ye give, of a truth
God knoweth it well. (3:92)

Thus, man secures his freedom - especially from avarice and greed - by discharging his responsibility to the disadvantaged and poor in society. Indeed, not discharging one's responsibility in this sense amounts to a denial of faith in God.

Second, the Islamic concept of responsibility is basically voluntaristic in nature and is not an imposition from above. Thus, while this principle implies making a sacrifice, it is not the kind of sacrifice that one would consider a hardship. Instead, the act of giving is linked with the process of becoming a better person in the sense that there will be 'increase in self-purification' (92:18). This is something that an individual would consider to be in his own interest as moral and non-monetary considerations replace monetary and selfish ones in his mind.

Man has a triple responsibility: towards God, to his own self, and to others. These three facets of responsibility underscore the ethical principle that the individual, though possessing a distinctive personality has to consider becoming an integral part of the totality of humankind. There is no virtue in withdrawing into splendid isolation in the pursuit of spiritual excellence, because ascension towards God has to be achieved by doing good to others, says the Quran especially to the disadvantaged, the hungry, the slaves and the poverty stricken:

And what will explain
To thee the path that is steep?-
(It is:) freeing the bondman;
Or the giving of food
In a day of privation
To the orphan
With claims of relationship,
Or to the indigent
(Down) in the dust. (90:12-16)

We may also note what man is not responsible for. First, says the Quran, man is not responsible for what others do:

Every soul draws the meed
Of its acts on none
But itself: no bearer
Of burdens can bear
The burden of another. (6:164)

Second, the Quran does not hold man accountable for what his forefathers did in the past:

That was a People that hath
Passed away. They shall reap
The fruit of what they did,
And ye of what ye do!
Of their merits
There is no question in your case! (2:134)

Thus, freed from the chains of the past, man is required to act positively in the present and in the future.

Third, man's responsibility is in proportion to his financial and physical capacity. In some cases, an individual is absolved of his responsibility because someone else is better equipped than he is to perform a particular duty.

Fourth, one person's responsibility ends where another's freedom begins. Thus, in the discharge of one's responsibility, a person should be careful to exercise it with moderation and good judgement. It is not for any individual to decide what is good for others, and for the society. A person must abide by social norms of good behaviour; and must respect other individuals' rights in discharging their own social responsibility.

Thus, human freedom is not allowed to degenerate into unlimited license for the exercise of private rights; nor is social responsibility designed as a vehicle for human bondage. Also, man is denied the convenient excuse of predestination by making him responsible for his actions. These then are the terms of reference of a consequence-sensitive Islamic ethics, whereby man is committed to the welfare of society - in particular to the amelioration of the lot of its least-privileged members. Another way of looking at the matter is that man is committed to the preservation of his own freedom and that of others. Says the Quran, continue the struggle,

> Until there is no more
> Tumult or oppression
> And there prevail
> Justice and faith in God; (2:193)

The Quran and Ecology

Until a few decades ago it was believed that the space on earth was limitless and that its resources were endless. This wrong impression gave people the idea that they could go on using (and wasting) resources as they liked, and without any risk or danger of exhausting them. Today, in spite of knowledge of the limits of the earth's resources, humanity continues to behave in much the same way when dealing with land and water resources.

It is estimated that the total agricultural land area of the planet was about 4700 million hectares in 1988. This comprised over 3200 million hectares of permanent pasture land and 1500 million hectares of arable land. Of the total available agricultural land about 1230 million hectares or 25% was considered to have been degraded by human-induced soil-degradation.

Nearly three-quarters of the earth's surface is covered by water, 98 per cent of which is sea water and salty and 1 per cent of which is in the form of ice in the Antarctic and Arctic regions. Thus, 99 per cent of the earth's water cannot be used directly for human needs. It is only 1 per cent of the total supply of water on which all the living creatures of the world depend.

The limited land and water resources are diminishing fast because of wasteful and unwise ways of using them. There are vast areas of usable land which are turning into deserts or are being degraded or flooded. For example, the latest research shows that the present area of usable agricultural land diminished by another 300 million hectares by the year 2000.[2] In the meantime world population has almost doubled thus bringing per capita availability to very low levels.

There are repeated warnings in the Quran about this. For example:

Nay, We gave the good things
Of this life to these men
And their fathers until
The period grew long for them;
See they not that We
Gradually reduce the land
(In their control) from
Its outlying borders? Is it
Then they who will win? (21:44)

The Quran does not disagree with scientific theories as far as the laws of nature are concerned, which it tells us are uniform, constant and run according to rules. However, it does not agree with the scientists on certain points which have a great bearing upon man's mental attitude towards nature and, hence, upon his ecological behaviour. It rejects, for example the idea that the laws of nature were devised by nature itself. On the contrary, it says that they have been laid down and are enforced by the Supreme Controller or God. The universe is His scheme; He knows what is needed to properly run this universe and He weighs and measures everything accordingly. The Quran tells us, for example:

Do they not look
At the sky above them?-
How We have made it
And adorned it,
And there are no
Flaws in it?

And the earth -
We have spread it out,
And set thereon mountains
Standing firm, and produced
Therein every kind of
Beautiful growth (in pairs) -

To be observed
And commemorated
By every devotee
Turning (to God). (50:6,7,8)

God is He Who raised
The heavens without any pillars
That ye can see; is firmly
Established on the Throne (of Authority);
He has subjected the sun
And the moon (to his Law)!
Each one runs (its course)
For a term appointed.
He doth regulate all affairs,
Explaining the Signs in detail,
That ye may believe with certainty
In the meeting with your Lord. (13:2)

The Quran considers everything in nature as the common property of all creatures. Humanity's right to use the natural resources is only in the sense of usufruct - which means being given the right to use another person's property on the understanding that we will not damage, destroy or waste what is in our trust. According to Islamic law the basic elements of nature such as land, water, air, fire, forests, sunlight etc. were considered to be the common property of all - not only of all human beings, but of all creatures. The Islamic juristic rules and legal principles on this issue are very specific and clear and are based on the Quran, such as:

For the earth is God's
To give as a heritage
To such of His servants
As He pleaseth; and the end
Is (best) for the righteous.(7:128)

To Him belongs all that is
in the heavens and on earth:(22:64)

This is what an early Muslim legal scholar, Abu al-Faraj, says:

> People do not in fact own things, for the real owner is their Creator; they only enjoy the usufruct of things, subject to the Divine law.[3]

Then the Quran tells us how to use the resources of nature; in moderation and without wastage:

But waste not by excess,
For God loveth not the wasters. (7:31)

Modern scientific findings conclude that everything on earth is interwoven into a beautiful and extremely intricate and complicated balance of nature.[4] This balance is particularly important in the case of the earth which is, perhaps, the only living planet in the universe. The Quran repeatedly enjoins on humanity the need of maintaining that balance and not upsetting order in nature. For upsetting the balance could lead to the extinction of humanity and its replacement by another creation. The Quran says:

See they not how many
Of those before them
We did destroy?-
Generations We had established
On the earth, in strength
Such as We have not given
To you - for whom
We poured out rain

From the skies in abundance,
And gave (fertile) streams
Flowing beneath their (feet):
Yet for their sins
We destroyed them,
And raised in their wake
Fresh Generations
(To succeed them).(6:6)

Seest thou not that God
Created the heavens and the earth
In Truth? If He so will,
He can remove you
And put (in your place)
A new Creation?
Nor is that for God
Any great matter. (14:19,20)

History reveals that it is only humans who exploit the resources of nature carelessly to satisfy their greed. Other species also use the resources of nature for their needs, but they use them in a sustainable way - that is, in such a way that nature can replace what is used. According to the following Quranic verses, animals, herbs etc. understand the laws of God and obey them more than humans:

And the herbs and the trees-
Both (alike) bow in adoration.
And the Firmament has He
Raised high, and He has set up
The Balance (of Justice),(55:5-9).

Seest thou not that
To God bow down in worship
All things that are
In the heavens and on earth,-

The sun, the moon, the stars;
The hills, the trees, the animals;
And a great number among
Mankind? But a great number
Are (also) such as are
Fit for Punishment: and such
As God shall disgrace. (22:18)

Water is essential to life. A total of 20 billion tons of unclean water flows every year from lakes and rivers to the oceans. This water is polluted and poisoned by sewage, agricultural run-off and industrial wastes. One third of rain water on land flows back to the sea. Rivers and streams have no boundaries, therefore one country's polluted water may be another country's drinking water.

Water is also a big divide between the rich and the poor. The range of use varies from up to 20,000 litres per capita a year in the United States of America to less than 500 litres in some developing countries.

In the light of these facts and figures, plus the fact that our earth is the only planet in the universe known so far to contain water, it is not surprising that the Quran lays so much emphasis on the importance of water. Here is one such verse:

It is He who has
Let free flow the two bodies
Of flowing water;
One palatable and sweet,
And the other salt
And bitter; yet, has He
Made a barrier between them,
A partition that is forbidden
To be passed.
It is He Who has
Created man from water;
Then has He established

Relationships of lineage
And marriage... (25:53,54)

Air is another vital element especially in its interaction with the oceans and the land. Here is what the Quran has to say:

It is God Who sends
Forth the Winds, so that
They raise up the Clouds,
And We drive them
To a land that is dead,
And revive the earth therewith
After its death...(35:9).

As already noted, the Islamic view does not make a distinction between the spiritual and the physical. It also makes no distinction between different living creatures. So in dealing with ecology it does not ignore the other species that inhabit the earth. We tend to forget that all living creatures, including human beings, are subject to the same laws of nature.

Animals are generally held in contempt by humans, largely because they are considered to be dumb. We behave towards them as though they had no feelings, and often degrade them or treat them badly. The Quran reminds us that they are communities like the human community; that they are loved by God in the same way as human beings are loved; that they were created the same way as we were; that they are as much a symbol of God's power of creation as human beings are. See how the following verses make these points clear:

There is not an animal
(That lives) on earth,
Nor a being that flies
On its wings, but (forms
Part of) communities like you. (6:38)

Seest thou not that it is
God Whose praises all beings

In the heavens and on earth
Do celebrate, and the birds
(Of the air), with wings
Outspread? Each one knows
Its own (mode of) prayer
And praise. And God
Knows well all that they do. (24:41)

These days, with the advance of science, we know that animals and birds communicate with each other. The Quran told us so some fourteen centuries ago:

And Solomon was David's heir.
He said: "O ye people!
We have been taught the speech
Of Birds and on us
Has been bestowed (a little)
Of all things: this is
Indeed Grace manifest (from God)". (27:16)

In the verse that follows, we are told that God spoke even to the bees:

And thy Lord taught the Bee
To build its cells in hills,
On trees, and in (men's) habitations. (16:68)

The Quran puts the human species in the same class as the other species, by describing man as a two-legged animal who has been created from water like all the others and who, like the others, is subject to God's power:

And God has created
Every animal from water:
Of them there are some
That creep on their bellies;
Some that walk on two legs;
And some that walk on four.
God creates what He wills;
For verily God has power
Over all things. (24:45)

The Islamic view of ecology, it is clear, flows from its ethical postulates.

In the ethical schema of Islam, as we have noted, the individual and society have to strive in the cause of Allah, and to help relocate the sovereignty and power as per: "*La Ilaha Illallahu Muhammadur Rasulallah*" (There is no god but God and Muhammad is His Messenger). This is the concept of *tawhid* or the unity of God; it is the centrepiece of Islamic thought.

The above is not just a group of words; it has three distinct features as well as a message. The three features are (1) *La Ilaha*, no gods: a rebellion against all existing order and superstitions that have bonded people to the orders and beliefs created by human beings; (2) *Illaha*, but Allah, submission to only One, a surrender to the only Authority; and (3) the only method of achieving these two objectives is by following the Messenger. The Message is the essential unity of all creation subject only to God's laws.

Tawhid means that no one can usurp the greatest attribute of God, which is His sovereignty. In Islam all attributes of sovereignty of any conceivable nature reside in God alone, and no one else can share them to the slightest degree.

> To Allah doth belong the dominion
> Of the heavens and the earth,
> And all that is therein,
> And it is He who hath power
> Over all things. (5:123)

It is God who creates and governs, firmly holds all authority, and regulates and governs everything.

> Your Guardian-Lord
> Is Allah, who created
> The heavens and the earth
> In six Days, then He established Himself
> On the Throne (of authority). (7:54)

God made men His viceregent on earth and placed them with (delegated) authority so that men would establish the kingdom of God on earth through righteous deeds and look after creation on behalf of the Almighty. As the Quran says:

> God has promised, to those
> Among you who believe
> And work righteous deeds, that He
> Will, of a surety grant them
> In the land, inheritance
> (Of power), as he granted it
> To those before them. (24:55)

God placed men above others in creation, says the Quran, to test their ability and judgement in the execution of their role as *khalifah*:

> It is He Who hath made
> You (His) agents, inheritors
> Of the earth: He hath raised
> You in ranks, some above
> Others: that He may try you
> In the gifts He hath given you. (6:165)

Human beings have to look at other creatures in the same way as God does, that is, with love, affection and care. This is what the position of viceregent and trustee means.

Viceregency, Trusteeship, and Socio-economic Implications

In Islam the power to rule society is delegated to the whole community: it is not the privilege of any one person or group of persons. All believers living in such a society are to be considered as viceregents of God. Every believer is a *khalifah* of God in his own individual capacity. The Prophet said, "Everyone of you is a ruler and everyone is answerable for his subjects." In an Islamic society, no one is inferior to another.[5]

The Quranic doctrine of unity is a very radical concept which prevents the making of humanity subservient, to anyone: whether in religious attire as priests; in political vesture as kings, revolutionary leaders, and ruling juntas; in the economic sphere as bankers and monopolists; in society as philanthropists and voluntary workers; or in academia as intellectuals and scholars. Human authority should be accepted only as an instrument for collective work, social programme, and civic discipline - not as vehicles for power, authority, or superiority. Superiority in Islam rests solely on one's righteousness.

"The Holy Quran allows privileges only for justice and piety. A pious has privileges; a person with a good spirit has privileges. These privileges, however, do not relate to material things, to property. Such privileges must be done away with. All people are equal, they are all given equal rights".[6]

When in operation the principle of unity (*tawhid*) endows a society with a unity of purpose, function, destiny, and identity. It preconditions the transfer of economic, social, civic and political power to the oppressed and the establishment of *al-'adl* (balance and justice).

The spirit of *tawhid* also means that individuals have no ownership rights over land, water, etc. All is given to them by God to be used righteously for their mental, moral and spiritual benefit:

> Allah hath purchased of the Believers
> Their persons and their goods;
> For theirs (in return)
> Is the Garden (of Paradise): (9:11)

They are also not to be covetous and hoard their possessions. Says the Quran:

> Let not those
> Who covetously withhold
> Of the gifts which God
> Hath given them of His Grace
> Think that it is good for them:
> ...soon shall the things
> Which they covetously withheld

Be tied to their necks
Like a twisted collar,
On the Day of Judgement. (3:180)

Man exercises his social and occupational authority according to the viceregency concept. Under this concept man is charged with responsibility for faithfully sustaining himself and other creatures of the earth. Man accepted this responsibility as a trust (*amanah*) from God, says the Quran, and so he was made the viceregent:

We did indeed offer
The Trust to the Heavens
And the Earth
And the Mountains;
But they refused
To undertake it,
Being afraid thereof:
But man undertook it; (33:72)

It is thus only because of being a trustee that the viceregency has been given to humanity. The faithful execution of the responsibilities of a trustee in the role of a vicegerent is what constitutes true piety in Islam.

The viceregency is bestowed on the whole of humanity through the performance of all individuals. Humans are but trustees of Allah on this earth, and not absolute owners of anything. If one does not perform one's duties voluntarily then pressure should be brought by the community to bring one's behaviour in line with Islamic society's collective behaviour. As already noted, God makes people inheritors of power and property so that He may try them.

....He said:
"It may be that your Lord
Will destroy your enemy
And make you inheritors
In the earth; that so

He may try you
By your deeds." (7:129)

Even family and children, says the Quran, are but a trial for attaining perfection in the doing of righteous deeds so that the highest reward may be obtained from the Divine:

And know ye
That your possessions
And your progeny
Are but a trial;
And that it is God
With Whom lies
Your highest reward. (8:28)

It is our actions in relation to the execution of our duties as viceregent and trustee, that God is going to judge and so the Quran warns us not to betray this trust:

It is your actions that Allah
And His Apostle will observe. (9:94)

O ye that believe!
Betray not the trust
Of God and the Apostle
Nor misappropriate knowingly
Things entrusted to you. (8:27)

The concepts of viceregent and trustee are natural corollaries to God's sovereignty over material wealth. The use of power or of wealth to satisfy an individual's ego is a direct revolt against God. All wealth belongs to humankind and is intended for the support of the members of the particular society in which man lives. In an Islamic society therefore the owners of wealth and those who control the means of production should manage and exercise their economic power, possessions, and resources as per Divine instructions and not as absolute owners or controllers. The Quran looks at the whole of mankind as one people:

Mankind was but one nation,
But differed (later). (10:19)

And all have been sent the Message and are expected to abide by it:

Mankind was one single nation,
And God sent Messengers
With glad tidings and warnings; (2:213)

In all dealings with Muslims or others, the Quran enjoins fair dealings, and the doing of justice, even to those who may hate one, and warns of dire punishment for those who practice fraud:

O ye who believe!
Stand out firmly
For God, as witnesses
To fair dealing, and let not
The hatred of others
To you make you swerve
To wrong and depart from
Justice. Be just: that is
Next to Piety: and fear God.
For God is well-acquainted
With all that ye do. (5:9)

Woe to those
That deal in fraud. (83:1)

The concepts of man's role as a trustee are intended to remove the wide disparity between the rich and the poor. The theme of trust (*amanah*) rests on the belief that capitalists and landlords should transfer the accumulated wealth into a trust for the common use of society. In an Islamic society food, clothing, provision of pure drinking water, shelter, security, peace, and sufficiency are, says the Quran, the inalienable right of all its members:

There is therein (enough provision)
For thee not to go hungry
Nor to go naked,
Nor to suffer from thirst,
Nor from the sun's heat. (20:118,119)

A city enjoying security
And quiet, abundantly supplied
With sustenance from every place: (16:112)

In Islam one is to share one's wealth with those who are of limited means and share in the works that benefit the society as a whole. Surplus wealth should go for the collective welfare of society. The message of the Quran in this regard is categorical and unqualified. It upholds the rights of the needy and destitute, even to those who do not ask, in the wealth of the rich:

And in their wealth
And possessions (was remembered)
The right of the (needy),
Him who asked, and him
Who (for some reason) was
Prevented (from asking). (51:19)

Islam does not recognize a consumption-oriented affluent society. It advocates a low-cost economy and a moderate level of living. It seeks constant human elevation, freedom, and the avoidance of the dehumanization associated with competitive commercialization and industrialization.

Human exploitation of natural wealth, we have seen, is to be subordinated to the will of God. It is obligatory on Muslims to harness the resources of nature to serve the cause of justice, to promote righteousness, and to eliminate evil. However, God's resources must not be allowed to become instruments of exploitation by individuals or groups of individuals - nor for ease, comfort, and affluence. Islam condemns indulgence in luxurious living and the desire to show-off. The Quran opposes the conspicuous consumption of the leisured class:

> And do not eat up
> Your property among yourselves
> For vanities...(2:188)

Wealth in Islam is considered necessary to improve morality, to perfect piety, and to develop good qualities. Wealth is not to be desired for the maximization of standards of living. Wealth is for collective purposes and not for individual utility. According to the Quran it is for social development and not for individual consumption and pleasure.

> To spend of your substance,
> Out of love for Him,
> For your kin,
> For orphans,
> For the needy,
> For the wayfarer,
> For those who ask,
> And for the ransom of slaves;
> To be steadfast in prayer,
> And practice regular charity. (2:177)

While insisting upon a powerful built-in mechanism for income redistribution, Islam insists on alignment with the pleasure of Allah. The Quran also insists on enterprise as a way of earning wealth:

> That man can have nothing
> But what he strives for; (53:39)

Entrepreneurship is highly lauded in Islam. Economic activity, the search for profit, trade, and consequently, production for the market, are looked upon with no less favour by Muslim tradition than by the Koran itself. We even find eulogistic formulations about merchants. It is reported that the Prophet said: 'The merchant who is sincere and trustworthy will (at the Judgement Day) be among the prophets, the just and the martyrs', or: 'The trustworthy merchant will sit in the shade of God's throne at the Day of Judgement', or: 'Merchants are the messengers of this world and God's faithful trustees on Earth.' According to holy tradition, trade is a superior way of earning one's livelihood: 'If thou profit by doing what is permitted, thy deed is a *jihad* (that is, is identified with any vigorous effort undertaken for God's cause) and, if thou usest it for thy family and kindred, this will be a *sadaqa* (that is, a pious work of charity); and, truly, a dirham (drachma, silver coin) lawfully gained from trade is worth more than ten dirhams gained in any other way.'[7]

In an Islamically oriented society thus there would be two classes of people: workers and entrepreneurs. There are moral obligations both on the entrepreneur and the worker - on the entrepreneur to give fair and generous treatment and prompt payment and on the part of the worker hard work, sincere effort and good performance.[8]

Land ownership is also subject to the collective interest of society. Land is the free gift of God, given for use, and not for ownership. Same is true of all other wealth - industries, companies etc. In all cases disposal of this wealth has to be referred back to God:

> To God belongs all
> That is in the heavens
> And on earth: to Him
> Do all questions
> Go back (for decision). (2:109)
>
> Of their goods take alms,
> That so thou mightest
> Purify and sanctify them,
> And pray on their behalf,
> Verily thy prayers are a source
> Of security for them. (9:103)

Wealth is not to be circulated amongst only a few. The Quran lays down that the needs of kin, orphans, the destitute, travellers and the handicapped are to be the first charge:

What God has bestowed
On His Apostle (and taken
Away) from the people
Of the townships-
Belongs to God,-to his Apostle
And to kindred and orphans,
The needy and the wayfarer;
In order that it may not
(Merely) make a circuit
Between the wealthy among you. (59:7)

In an Islamic society every individual's happiness has equal value. It is also essentially a society with equitable income distribution. Wealth has not to be hoarded and miserliness is as much condemned by the Quran as wastage or luxury consumption:

For God loveth not
The arrogant, the vainglorious;
(Nor) those who are niggardly,
Or enjoin niggardliness on others,
Or hide the bounties
Which God hath bestowed
On them. (4:36,37)

According to the Quran those who are deceived by the luxury and life of this world are rejecters of the Faith.

....It was
The life of this world
That deceived them. So
Against themselves will they
Bear witness that they
Rejected Faith. (6:130)

Piling up wealth which is not for use or service to those who need it has been condemned by the Quran in the strongest terms:

Who pileth up wealth
And layeth it by,
Thinking that his wealth
Would make him last
For ever!
By no means! He will
Be sure to be thrown into
That which Breaks to Pieces. (104:2,3,4)

Spending one's honestly earned wealth for social and community is obligatory for a believer in God.

O ye who believe!
Spend out of (the bounties)
We have provided for you. (2:254)

One is asked to spend wealth that is over and above one's need, and need is determined in the context of one being a trustee for others and so is obviously to be minimised rather than maximised.

They ask thee how much
They are to spend;
Say: "What is beyond
Your needs." (2:219)

As already noted, *tawhid* (unity) and *al-'adl* (equity and justice) are two of the basic postulates of the Islamic system. They at one and the same time unify as well as balance. They are also the ultimate aims of one's self-realization which can prevail only in a society where an equal share is given "even unto the last." Justice is, according to the Quran, along with submission to God, the key to the Islamic system:

My Lord hath commanded
Justice; and that ye set
Your whole selves (to Him)

At every time and place
Of prayer. (7:29)

Justice however must be tempered with compassion to avoid unnecessary social hardship. Every individual is entitled to justice from the societal system. Social justice requires the poor to be moved up and the rich to be moved down the scale of the social hierarchy. But this change has to be brought about voluntarily and without there being hatred or envy for to everyone God has given that which they deserve and according to one's efforts. Says the Quran:

And in no wise covet
Those things in which God
Hath bestowed His gifts
More freely on some of you
Than on others: to men
Is allotted what they earn,
And to women what they earn; (4:32)

Covetousness is decried by the Quran because everybody earns wealth by one's enterprise and labour and it is God who 'giveth wealth and satisfaction' (53:48) and:

...man can have nothing
But what he strives for;
That (the fruit of) his striving
Will soon come in sight,
Then will he be rewarded
With a reward complete; (53:39-41)

Certain commercial practices are, however, forbidden. These are, in the first place, of course, practices that are in one way or another fraudulent, together with trade in goods regarded by religion as impure: wine, pigs, animals that have died otherwise than by ritual slaughter, or in goods that are considered to be common to everyone: water, grass, fire. Prohibitions are also directed against various practices that prevent the free working of the economy. Thus, any speculation in foodstuffs, and especially the cornering of them, is forbidden. Above all, however, what is involved is prohibition of any selling in which there is an element of uncertainty. For instance, sale by auction, since the seller does not know what price he will get for the object being sold, or any sale in which the merchandise is not precisely, numerically defined (e.g. the fruits growing on a palm-tree) although the price is expressed in definite terms.

Islam also prohibits what it calls *riba*. The Arabic word *riba* literally means excess or addition. The orthodox view is that this prohibition applies to interest of all kinds while a revisionist view is emerging that this only applies to profiteering and that the Quranic injunction "God hath permitted trade and forbidden usury" (2:275) does not imply abolishing interest but of replacing it by a legitimate financial mechanism that does not perpetuate, or create, distributional inequalities.[9]

The matter is controversial. We shall in this paper go by the orthodox view that interest is not allowed and then evaluate its impact on sustainable development.

Islamic Economics

It is now possible to deduce some of the rules that would characterize an Islamic economy and the general principles that emerge in the context of the Quranic perspective.

The first principle is that the owner of the whole universe, with its wealth and everything else, is God, the Creator. From an economic point of view this principle was regarded quite differently by Islam and modern economics. While Islamic economy is firmly based on this principle, capitalism does not delineate its economic system with this principle in mind. Capitalist societies base their economic doctrine on the concept that man is quite independent in his ownership of wealth. The relationship of the Islamic economy to the Marxist one is scarcely relevant, for communism denies the very existence of God, let alone recognizing that He is the owner and bestower of life.

Various verses of the Quran on which this axiom is based have already been elucidated. This principle is an unvarying element of Islamic economics and society.

The second principle characterising Islamic economy is that God has nominated man to succeed Him in this ownership. Thus, man's right to ownership has come down to him by proxy from God. This requires man to act in compliance with the will of the real owner, in other words, as a trustee. Hence arises the relationship between Islamic economy and ethics, for everything that is ethical is acceptable to the Islamic economic system, and anything unethical is rejected.

The third principle is that wealth is a blessing in the service of man and not his master. God has subjected all that is in the heavens and earth to man, says the Quran:

> And He has subjected
> To you, as from Him
> All that is in the heavens
> and on earth: (45:13)

This sovereignty over wealth that God has bestowed upon man has to be exercised with initiative and courage in taking risks, administering and giving impetus to wealth. But there are strict restraints on this initiative. It is to be neither rash nor heedless and has to seek the grace of God.

The verses in support of the principle of boldness and initiative are numerous. Suffice it to mention that the first attribute of the God-fearing, after belief in the invisible and performing prayers, is good sense in spending according to the Quran:

> To those who fear God;
> Who believe in the Unseen,
> Are steadfast in prayer,
> And spend out of what We
> Have provided for them; (2:2,3)

Spending has to be lawful spending: 'the giving of wealth for love of God to kinsfolk and orphans, the indigent and the wayfarer, to those who ask and those who do not ask' (2:177). Hoarding, as already noted, is prohibited as is prodigality and spending on luxuries. Also says the Quran, give not to the foolish:

> To those weak of understanding
> Make not over your property, (4:5)

The fourth principle is not to earn wealth dishonestly or fraudulently: 'do not substitute worthless things for good ones' (4:2) and 'help one another in righteousness and piety and not in sin and rancour'. (5:3)

Great stress is placed in Islam, as we have noted, on social unity and equality. This is the fifth principle: to equitably distribute wealth so that there is no inequity in society.

From this flows the next principle: not to hoard or to charge interest. This ensures velocity of money flow and increases the efficiency of capital thereby encouraging entrepreneurship.

The noncharging of interest has been considered as a sign of "backwardness" by those professing the mainstream (modern) economic doctrine. But Islamic banks have been opened and are flourishing not on the basis of interest but equity participation in investments. This interestingly is very much like modern venture capital institutions which are the main means in modern society of encouraging innovative developments. In this context, the Islamic system, and the Quranic exhortation to the adventurous and enterprising, would seem to be more in line with post-industrial society where production innovation are considered to be the main driving forces in the economy.[10]

Also the above principles, it is obvious would lead to a system in which no one "owns" wealth and property and which, therefore, would be equitable, entrepreneurial and charitable.

Society emerging from such an economic system would be a brotherhood of equals, non-exploitative and peaceful. The non-charging of interest would also not discount the future as against the present and so lead to the interests of future generations being taken into account.

Conclusions

Any system claiming to be Islamic would have to work within the following parameters:

* the essential unity of all creation subject only to God's laws;
* man having to work as a trustee and being able to achieve the exalted status of God's vice-regent when he acts for the betterment of the global society;
* the least-privileged of the members of society having the first charge on its resources so that economic progress and social harmony are simultaneously attained;
* accepting that the Divine law has to be interpreted within different societal contexts and according to the changing needs of time: thus leading to cultural diversity;
* understanding that man does not have unlimited license in the exercise of private rights: he has to keep in mind the needs of society, especially the least-privileged, and the fact that he has to refer all matters to God whose trustee he is;
* that economic growth and the distribution of wealth are not two distinct processes but are tightly intertwined so as to form a seamless net of causes and effects;
* recognize the right of every human being to a full life of self-fulfillment and happiness;
* recognise the right of all creatures in the bounties of the world; other creatures have to be loved and cherished in the same way as is done by God.

References

1. All quotations from the Quran are from *The Holy Quran*, translated by A. Yusuf Ali (Lahore: Sheikh Muhammed Ashraf, 1938).
2. UNEP, *The World Environment 1972-1992* (London: Chapman and Hall, 1992) pp. 153-54.
3. Quoted in *Islam and Ecology*, Khalid and O'Brien (eds.) (London: Cassel, 1992) p.7.
4. See, for example, J.E. Lovelock, *Gaia* (New York: Oxford University Press, 1979).
5. Syed Abul Maududi, *Islamic Law and Constitution*, trans. and ed. Khurshid Ahmed (Lahore: Islamic Publications, 1983) pp.139-140.
6. Khomeini quoted in *Islam and Nonviolence*, Glenn D. Paige et. al. (eds.) (Honolulu: University of Hawaii, 1993) p.92.
7. Quoted in Maxine Rodinson, *Islam and Capitalism*, tr. by Brian Pearce (London: Allen Lane, Penguin Books Ltd., 1974) pp. 16-17.
8. S.M. Yusuf, *Economic Justice in Islam* (Lahore: Ashraf Press, 1971).
9. See for example, Syed Nawab Haider Naqvi, *Islam, Economics and Society* (New York: Kegan Paul, 1995). For a contrary view see Sheikh Mahmud Ahmad, *Economics of Islam* (Lahore: Muhammad Ashraf, 1974).
10. See for example, Peter Drucker, *Managing the Future* (London: Butterworth - Heinemann, 1992) pp. 21-26.

7

Gandhi: Environment, Economics, Sustainable Development

We now go on to examine the relevance of Gandhi's views to the concept of sustainable development, including economics, technology and the environment. Gandhi was influenced by all the religions we have studied as well as Christianity and the critical thought of Tolstoy, Ruskin and Thoreau. His views thus express a synthesis of western and eastern thought. But it needs to be noted that the synthesis arrived at was peculiarly his own.

Gandhi lived at a time when the environmental crisis had not become a matter of concern but through his commitment to ultimate values, Gandhi foresaw that only a nonviolent and nonexploitative pattern of development could lead to harmony with nature. He made the acute observation that all ancient civilizations were today to be found in deserts because urbanisation drew more from the land that it replaced. Gandhi rejected consumerism and industrialization that was exploitative and led to increasing wants. This to him could never lead to a peaceful and sustainable world.

Gandhi and his Principles

Mohandas Karamchand Gandhi was born on October 2, 1869, and this apostle of peace and nonviolence died a violent death, falling to an assassin's bullet on January 30, 1948, while attending a prayer meeting. Gandhi studied to be a barrister in Britain and thereafter was invited to practice law in South Africa. It was there that he conducted his first experiments in nonviolence in opposition to the practice of Apartheid. He refined his ideas on nonviolence later on in India where he led a peaceful movement for independence from British rule.

Today the concepts of nonviolent resistance, civil disobedience, and silent sit-ins are finding general acceptance. The impact of nonviolence is being felt in many ecological movements. A nonviolent movement to save trees, the so-called Chipko movement, was led by a Gandhian, Sunderlal Bahuguna. The movement was pro- women and pro-nature. Its main aim was to save the forests of the Himalayas as their destruction meant women having to walk long distances to collect water and fuel. A major movement against the World bank assisted Narmada dam project is on in the Gujrat state of India. The basic attitude of this movement is Gandhian and the intention is to prevent disruption to the lifestyles of the indigenous tribal population.

Gandhi was one of those rarely gifted individuals in whom the economist, the political scientist, the sociologist and the philosopher were all rolled into one. The product of his genius was a vast system of thought, composed of many sub-systems. This makes it difficult to look at any of the sub-systems, economics, for instance, in isolation.

The entire Gandhian system is based on two fundamental, interrelated principles: Nonviolence and Truth. One cannot understand any of the structural components of this Gandhian system, economics in particular, without understanding the philosophical foundations of the superstructure.

Also the primary concern of Gandhi in all his thinking was man. His adherence to nonviolence meant that man could not be the cause of the destruction of God's creation. So man had to be considered in a holistic manner including his interlinkages to nature. This is the thinking that underlines the two movements described earlier.

Throughout his life Gandhi immersed himself in all aspects of general welfare and the happiness of human beings. Life was conceived by Gandhi as a field of experimentation. "He practised what he professed, and advocated only what he had tested in his own life...every aspect of human betterment, every problem touching human welfare, whether in the field of politics, or sociology, economics or religion, in every walk of life, commanded his attention and active interest. He owed allegiance to a philosophy and outlook that expresses itself in a multi-sided approach to the many sided problems of life; this makes him, strictly speaking, not a mere individual but a universal personality".[1]

In the realm of technology Gandhi advocated decentralised village industry, after himself experimenting with it, not only because of his dislike for industrial technology, but because of his respect for nature. He considered industrial technology as a form of violence as, among other things, it had brought about large scale unemployment and the decline of indigenous skills and crafts in India - in his view, therefore, it was a nonsustainable system. He understood, perhaps better than many modern ecologists, the intricate web of relationships between all living things and the physical environment that they share. To him each needed the other and both needed God, Who to him was Truth. Also village industry was labour-intensive and led to full employment. We shall deal with this aspect later.

Gandhi's Conceptual Framework

Gandhi, who was influenced by the cultures of India and England, the religions of Hinduism, Jainism, Buddhism, Islam and Christianity, and the writings of John Ruskin, Leo Tolstoy and Henry David Thoreau, put the peculiar stamp of his genius upon the theory of nonviolence. He confronted the problems of imperialism, industrialism, racism, communalism, classism, and the like, in his own way.

The method of inquiry and mode of action that Gandhi used in his search for Truth is what he called *Satyagraha*. *Satya* means Truth and *Graha* means adherence to Truth. *Satyagraha* thus means adherence to Truth, or Truth Force.

Gandhi's life was an experiment with Truth (*Satya*) and the means to achieve the Truth was through *Ahimsa* (nonviolence). The full force of *Ahimsa*, explicitly stated, means "action based on the refusal to do harm".[2] For Gandhi, *Ahimsa* (nonviolence, or love, as he called it) is the means, and *Satya* (Truth) is the end, and the debate on the means-end continuum was meaningless, for they are irrevocably tied to one another. "The means may be likened to a seed, the end to a tree, and there is just the same inviolable connection between the means and the end as there is between the seed and the tree...We reap exactly what we sow".[3]

For Gandhi the means to achieve Truth was through *Ahimsa*, that is, nonviolence or love. Not to hurt any living thing is only a part of *Ahimsa*, that is its least expression. "The principle of *Ahimsa* is hurt by every evil thought, by undue haste, by lying, by wishing ill to anybody".[4] According to Gandhi's interpretation of *Ahimsa*," it is not merely a negative state of harmlessness but it is a positive state of love, of doing good even to the evildoer. However, neither does it mean tolerating injustice. On the contrary, *Ahimsa* requires not only resistance but also conversion of the wrongdoer".[5]

If there is a dogma in Gandhian philosophy, says Bondurant, "it centres here, that the only test to truth is action based on refusal to do harm".[6] This is one principle of *Ahimsa* that Gandhi adhered to until the end. To him the supreme and the only means to the discovery of social truths was through *Ahimsa*.

Because we covet things and seek pleasure, we are in a constant state of competition, obsessively seeking self-gratification at the cost of others, plus putting ourselves in a state of violence. Hence the fulfilment of Ahimsa is difficult, if not impossible, without self-sacrifice and selflessness. Attachment to personal things and loved ones defeats the overall meaning of *Ahimsa*. For Gandhi, *Ahimsa* means universal love; and in its dynamic form it means conscious suffering. It does not mean meek surrender to unjust acts or laws, but confronting the oppressor with a firm conviction and a single-minded honest purpose.

Gandhi kept the *Bhagavad Gita's* (also referred to as the *Gita*) dictum in mind:

> By reason of delusion man takes wrong to be right. Effort is within man's control, not the fruit thereof. All he has to do, therefore, is to decide his course of conduct or duty on each occasion and preserve it unconcerned about the result. Fulfilment of one's duty in the spirit of detachment and selflessness leads to freedom.[7]

Gandhi was profoundly influenced by the *Bhagavad Gita*, which shaped his perspective in general and his economic views in particular. In the eyes of Gandhi the *Bhagavad Gita* was a complete and reasoned moral code which satisfied the heart as well as the intellect. He got from the *Bhagavad Gita* the realization that life is given us for service and not for enjoyment. Man has to, by virtue of being a human being, an innate duty to serve Truth by serving his fellowmen and the life process in general. Such action is to be performed as service for the sake of service. It involves self-sacrifice for the welfare of others. By so rising above self-interest human beings fulfil their destiny and become integrated with the true self within them. As we will see shortly, the implications arising from such a view of human nature for economics are both profound and radical.

Influenced, as he was, by different religions, his concern for the welfare of all made him a firm believer in *sarvodaya* - man's duty to serve all living beings in the universe.[8] But a selfish, self-centred person would be seeking only self-gratification. Hence, "the path of service can hardly be trodden by one who is not prepared to renounce self-interest....The duty of renunciation differentiates mankind from the beast".[9] Renunciation here does not mean abandoning the world, for that would be cowardice. It means detachment from worldly possessions and desires, so that one can immerse himself or herself in selfless devotion for the welfare of all.

Conventional economics emphasises self interest by building upon the notion of utilitarianism. Gandhi, however, rejected Bentham's concept of the greatest good of the greatest number in favour of the greatest-good-of-all or *sarvodaya*. According to him

> I do not believe in the doctrine of the greatest good for the greatest number. It means in its nakedness that in order to achieve the supposed good of fifty-one percent, the interest of forty-nine percent may be, or rather should be sacrificed.[10]
>
> The utilitarian's (sphere of destruction) has no limit. Judged by the standard of nonviolence the late war was wholly wrong. Judged by the utilitarian standard, each party has justified it according to its idea of utility...Precisely on the same ground the anarchist justifies his assassinations. But none of these acts can possibly be justified on the greatest-good-of-all-principle.[11]

The aspect of self-sacrifice, as advocated by Gandhi, may be the least acceptable to the Western mind. "Yet, such sacrifice may well provide the ultimate means of realizing that characteristic so eminent in Western moral philosophy: the dignity of the individual".[12] For Gandhi, flowing from his concept of self-sacrifice, society was not possible without individual freedom and dignity. "No society can possibly be built on a denial of individual freedom".[13]

In making a distinction between man and the system, Gandhi highlighted the primacy of the individual. The system, whether it be social, political, economic, or religious, should be geared toward the betterment of the individual. When a system becomes harmful to the well-being of man, it must be mended or ended, altered or abolished.[14]

Gandhian principles recognize that the individual is primary and the rest of the social institutions are secondary and are there to serve him. Man, the operator of the system, needs all the help available. Thus, we can have a legitimate quarrel with the system that is evil, but we should have no quarrel or hatred for the people in whose name and by whom the system is operated. Gandhi championed the cause of the underprivileged, and the cause of those to whom palpable injustice may have been done, to purify and regenerate society. "While working for the mending or ending of certain outmoded institutional patterns, Gandhi placed his main reliance upon sensitized consciences, upon regenerated human beings for abiding change in society".[15] His prayer for another was "...not, God give him the light that Thou has given me, but give him all the light and truth he needs for the highest development".[16]

To Gandhi it was evident that only in this way could radical social change be brought about in a nonviolent manner.

Gandhian Socio-economics

Gandhi's thought led him to postulate a grand design of an ideal social order: a nonviolent, nonexploitative, humanistic and egalitarian society. This social order embodied the fundamental philosophy of his life. He approached all facets of society - its economics, its politics and sociology - from the philosophical premises - Truth and Nonviolence - that governed his entire life. For him, therefore, economics could not be 'ethically neutral'. In his own words: "Economics is untrue which disregards moral values. This expansion of the law of nonviolence in the domain of economics means nothing less than the introduction of moral values...".[17] With the appearance of morality in Gandhian economics, we also witness the demise of the 'economic man', the core parameter of mainstream economics.

Gandhi was not an economist in the ordinary sense of the term. In his own way, however, he constructed a model which he claimed to be practical and operational in a given environment. He sketched out, in considerable detail, its basic goal(s), its structure, its components, its modus operandi, its data and its variables. Viewed as an economic system, it has its own management scheme and its own techno-structure. It is not a static but a dynamic model, embodying a Gandhian theory of growth. He wrote: "The end to be sought is human happiness combined with full mental and moral growth. I use the adjective moral as synonymous with spiritual".[18]

He did not overlook the purely material goals in his economic system. Any viable economic system, he insisted, must have the production capability to meet social demand for the basic necessities of life - food, clothing, shelter, and other essential prerequisites for survival. But he rejected the pursuit of economic abundance for its own sake. He considered such abundance, dictated by the multiplicity of seemingly insatiable human wants, as demoralising. He was unconvinced that economic abundance, measured by the physical volume of goods and services, is either a necessary or a sufficient condition for individual or social welfare. On the contrary, an incessant drive for economic abundance, through accumulation, competition, and technological innovation, he felt, would promote economic aggression, exploitation, and violence in society.[19]

The production goal of a Gandhian economic system has been stated by Huq as "the maximization of socially necessary goods and services, and the minimization of luxuries and superfluous goods, constrained not only by the availability of scarce resources but also by an overriding moral purpose".[20] The production and consumption of luxuries to stimulate effective demand was repugnant to Gandhian economic philosophy. He was opposed to such `conspicuous consumption' on both moral and economic grounds.

Another parameter of Gandhi's model was localised production or *swadeshi*. Modern economics stresses individualistic mobility and competition on the basis of self-interest. Gandhi's doctrine of non-self-interest, on the other hand, emphasises the social virtues of loyalty and cooperation. No other Gandhian concept illustrates this better than that of *swadeshi*, the spirit in us which restricts us to the use and service of our immediate surroundings to the exclusion of the more remote.

Swadeshi can be seen as the application of the *Bhagavad Gita* to one's immediate environment. In the sphere of economics, it would give a priority or preference for locally grown and manufactured goods. The doctrine of *swadeshi* could also be applied to the labour market: employers are to exhaust first whatever pool of local and unemployed workers there is before hiring more suitable labour from other towns or regions. Similarly, the workers would be more reluctant to leave a local employer in spite of more attractive job offers elsewhere. In short, economic agents living together in a community, region, or country, should first and foremost explore all possibilities to do business with each other before going outside in order to get a better deal. *Swadeshi* demands the sacrifice of utility for the sake of loyalty. The alleged gains of violating *swadeshi* (lower commodity price, higher quality, etc.) would tend to be more than counteracted by almost zero transport costs and the (non-market) costs of community decay. At the same time, Gandhi warned that *swadeshi* should not be made a fetish. Efficiency was also to be maintained. According to him,

> (One) should use only things that are produced by (one's) immediate neighbours and serve those industries by making them efficient and complete where they might be wanting.[21]

The Foundations of Gandhian Economics

We have already stated that Gandhi's is a humanistic and holistic concept encompassing politics, sociology, psychology, ethics, economics and ecology and based on his philosophical outlook. The four parameters of his social philosophy are:

* Truth exists in and beyond man in an absolute, eternal, and living essence.
* The purpose of all life and evolution is to realize Truth. For humankind this translates into the need for self-realization, to know one's self.
* While truth is the end, Nonviolence is the means. Truth and Nonviolence are ultimately two sides of the same coin. One implies the other. Self-realization knows no distinction between ends and means. From this follows the all important principle that we cannot realize truth without giving up the means/ends dichotomy.
* Human truth is always relative. Although we have the innate need to perfect ourselves, no man is perfect. Truth as we can apprehend it is always personal, subjective, and, to that extent, relative to our individual context of culture, history and psychology. In this Gandhi followed the *Rig Veda* which states,

  The wise speak of what is One in many ways.[22]

From these four philosophical parameters emphasizing Nonviolence as the key to the realization of Truth, and stressing the relativity of human perception due to subjectivity and cultural differences, we arrive at the following foundational premises pertaining to Gandhi's economic thought:

* Economics, ethics, politics, and religion constitute an indivisible whole. As such, Gandhi had no kind words about conventional economics which led to a acquisitive and therefore a violent society. According to him,

  "True economics never militates against the highest ethical standard, just as all true ethics to be worth its name must at the same time be also good economics. An economics that inculcates mammon worship, and enables the strong to amass wealth at the expense of the weak, is a false and dismal science. It spells death."[23]

* Economics to Gandhi is essentially the science of human welfare. Its goal ought to be *sarvodaya*, the welfare of all. Implicit in the doctrine of *sarvodaya* is the basic presumption of equal dignity of and respect for the life and welfare of every individual. Translated into the sphere of economic policy, it entails top priority for meeting the most basic material needs (water, food, shelter) of everybody before we allocate resources for goods required for luxury consumption and therefore of a lesser importance.
* The supreme consideration of economics has to be man. Economic theory that ignores humanity and its needs - material, mental, moral, spiritual - is meaningless.
* Human welfare economics focusing on man implies the crucial importance of a decentralized social economy. The ideal is a community economy allowing for a living interaction, mutual access, and voluntary cooperation of all its members.
* Economics has to respect the law of *swadeshi*. As we saw earlier, *swadeshi* was to Gandhi one of the most basic organizational principles consistent with Nonviolence.

Obviously, this basic premise is at odds with both calculated behaviour in an integrated competitive market economy as well as with a highly centralized command economy. Instead, it feeds right into his concept of community economics, or decentralized community planning and of cooperation between all communities at all levels -national, international - thereby leading to a nonexploitative and peaceful world.

* At the very core of Gandhian economics is the concept of rationality. Rather than mere cognitive mental calculations of means, Gandhi broadens the concept to involve harmonious action of body, mind, and soul. Rational action is guided by the inner faculty of conscience which he also calls the inner voice.

From the above foundational premises, can be derived what may be called the seven principles of Gandhian economic thought. It should be kept in mind, however, that unlike the principles of conventional economics, they do not stand on their own, independent of time and place. Instead, they always have to be seen in relation to each other, to their foundational premises, and to the culture and society where they are being applied.

The seven Gandhian principles are:

(i) nonviolent ownership - *trusteeship*: Trusteeship recognizes the right to private property in the means of production as long as it is responsible to the needs of the community. It is *sarvodaya* extended to the firm. Absentee ownership of capital and land, investment and production violating *swadeshi*, excessive salaries, and expense accounts are not consistent with trusteeship. Trusteeship is also consistent with workers' self-management provided they act as trustees;

(ii) nonviolent production - *appropriate technology*: The term appropriate is used to designate the production function that maximizes human needs satisfaction. According to

Gandhi no technology should be used which economizes on manual labour, while there are unemployed workers in the community. This clearly flows from his concepts of *sarvodaya*, *swadeshi*, conscience and trusteeship. Besides appropriate technology should do no harm to the body, mind, or soul. Machinery, according to Gandhi, should not be turned into a craze. Mass production, yes, but in people's own homes;

(iii) nonviolent consumption - *non-possession*: Non-possession follows strictly from the principle of nonviolence. The less you possess, the less you want, the better you are. And better for what? Not for enjoyment of life, but for enjoyment of personal service to fellow beings; service in which you dedicate yourself, body, soul and mind. Everybody is entitled to the consumption of the basic necessities but the golden rule for the elite and those in power is to refuse to have what millions cannot have and not multiply their wants;

(iv) nonviolent work - *bread labour*: Throughout Gandhi's writings runs the thread of the importance of work in humanity's personal growth. The doctrine of bread labour was inspired by Ruskin, Tolstoy, and the *Gita*. According to Gandhi:

> "I cannot imagine anything nobler or more rational than that, say one hour in the day, we should do all the labour that the poor must do and thus identify ourselves with them and, through them, with all mankind."[24]

Gandhi stressed, however, that bread labour could never be forced on anybody, otherwise it would breed poverty, disease, and discontent;

(v) nonviolent allocation - *cooperation*: Gandhi was no believer in competition which more often than not led to violence. He saw in competition the culmination of a materialistic and sensuous paradigm that degraded the population. Competition being predicated on fear and insecurity bred greed and violence. Cooperation, on the other hand, appeals to the human element, our need to serve others.

Yet, Gandhi felt it important to stress that true (nonviolent) cooperation could only take place after provision of the most essential material needs. This is true both of the individual (bread labour) as well as of the local, village (*swadeshi*) levels. The problem of scarcity would also be largely dealt with by the institutional features of bread labour and localized economy with both acting to internally reduce wants thereby leading to a harmonious society;

(vi) nonviolent distribution - *equality*: Equality meant to Gandhi primarily two things: First, everybody has a basic right to live, i.e., to meet the basic vital needs and live a dignified life integrated in the community with one's fellows. As means to such a goal he strongly denounced charity, the flinging of free meals at people unable to find work, but advocated guaranteed employment for everybody who wants to work. Secondly, equality is absence of exploitation. He endorsed non-exploitative capital labour relations as well as non-exploitation of manual by intellectual labour and, above all, non-exploitation of the countryside by the city;

(vii) nonviolence in *reforming economic systems*: Gandhi was no friend of capitalism. On the contrary, he dedicated much of his life to its destruction. But the destruction of an ideology could not be done with violence. The capitalist had to be redeemed and converted to trusteeship.

It should be clear from the above that the core of Gandhi's economic thought flows from his view of human nature, its needs and goals - material and spiritual. At first glance it seems that his economic thought is utopian. But a deeper analysis shows that this is not so. Also that some aspects of his thought can be understood even without going into its metaphysical and spiritual ground. This is especially the case with his concepts of *swadeshi*, non-possession, trusteeship, nonviolence, and *sarvodaya*. Several of Gandhi's other contributions can also be understood and found meaningful without a direct reference to his spiritual and ethical outlook. This is particularly true of his economic theory of growth and development, as well as his theory of structural unemployment.

The Gandhian concepts have been put into a conceptual-analytic framework more familiar to the economist by Amritananda Das.[25] According to Das, conventional development strategy may be summarized in the following way: development is to occur by means of capital-intensive technologies replacing the traditional labour-intensive activities and with it the gradual elimination of the limited (and often non-monetary) exchange systems of traditional village economies. In lieu of an economy operating primarily in a rural setting, a modern, urban oriented national or world-wide market economy is expected to emerge gradually. The pull of labour to the city and the concomitant problems of dislocation, displacement and misery, are seen as regrettable, but as an unavoidable temporary cost well worth the long-run gains in efficiency and growth in per capita income and consumption of the masses.

It is here that the Gandhian perspective differs radically and sheds much additional light. Rather than focusing on the growth of the urban sector, Gandhi foresaw the central and ever-worsening problem of the stagnation and decay of the traditional sector resulting directly from such modernization and the single-minded stress on urban, capital-intensive development. By this development, much of the indigenous skills and crafts get destroyed by the new market competition of mass-produced consumer goods, whether foreign or domestic.

Average earnings in the villages decline more than wages grow in the urban cities. Hundreds of thousands can no longer make a living with the traditional sector, and the growing 'structural unemployment' pushes them into the urban slums or 'shanty towns' in a desperate hope of survival. Against this background, the veritable 'kernel' of Gandhian macroeconomics has to be seen as giving priority to investment in the labour-intensive occupations of the traditional sector. Production by the masses replaces mass production.

Similarly, Das points out, excessive population growth is being overestimated as a primary cause of the economic problems of the Third World. Rather, it is a consequence of excessively capital-intensive development bringing with it the mounting structural unemployment and decay of the economy at the village level. Population control programmes cannot be expected to succeed in a population lacking a regular occupational base and caught in a day-to-day, hand-to-mouth mentality. There is simply no room for any type of prudent, self-imposed voluntary restraint in matters of procreation. Moreover, mounting structural unemployment has an unfavourable negative effect on female labour force participation and education, two sociological factors that are found to be closely associated with a decline in the birth rate.

Since Gandhian development economics see the problem of excessive population growth as chiefly one of a misguided development strategy, the primary focus turns to the issue of a more adequate policy of investment allocation for effectively combating structural unemployment. To create a faster growth in new jobs than the growth in the labour force, available investable surplus needs to be directed into labour-intensive sectors as well as capital-intensive sectors. The latter is necessary in order to assure a sufficiently increased surplus for the years to come. More specifically, the rate of capital accumulation has to be equal at least to the rate of growth of the labour force. But beyond this minimum expansion of the capital goods industries, the bulk of the remaining investable surplus should go towards a revitalization of the village, small-scale, labour-intensive, consumer-oriented sector.

According to Das, the Gandhian system raises an important issue: the possible trade-off between output and employment. Gandhi's social and moral philosophy made him lean towards employment rather than output in defining the objective function to be maximised. One of his deepest concerns was the massive poverty, especially rural poverty in India. At the same time, he had better perception of the nature of massive rural unemployment in India than he is given credit for. That type of unemployment is structural, seasonal, and technological, rather than cyclical. Deficiency of aggregate demand has very little to do with that type of unemployment. In large-scale diffusion of supplementary employment through appropriate low-capital-intensive technology and corresponding restructuring of the economy along the lines of decentralization and small-scale industrialization, he saw the only real, feasible, and meaningful approach to the seemingly insoluble problem of Indian poverty.

Apart from economic feasibility, Gandhi's rationale rested on a moral and metaphysical notion of human labour. To him, labour was not just a commodity for sale in the market in exchange for wages to compensate for the disutility of labour. He was reluctant to measure the opportunity cost of work in terms of sacrifice of leisure. In his system, labour had a dignity and a moral substance which was not for sale. This notion he derived largely from the *Bhagavad Gita*. He was especially influenced by the following passage:

> Not by refraining from action does man attain freedom. Nor by mere renunction he attains supreme perfection.
>
> ....Only a thief would enjoy gifts and not offer them in sacrifice (by working).
>
> This was the Wheel of the law set in motion, and that man lives indeed in vain who in a sinful life of pleasures helps not in its revolutions.[26]

This moral and metaphysical notion of work, as a sacrifice to be performed, greatly influenced Gandhi's economic thinking, the construction of his economic model, and the specification of its techno-structure. The primary behavioural organizational unit in his model is the individual man or household, and the primary organizational unit is the village. It is essentially a decentralized system where the fundamental economic decisions are to be made by the micro-units of the total system - the village communities. Although the individual, village and the community of villages suggest a hierarchy, at the highest level of abstraction, the Gandhian model is, in essence, non-hierarchical. "In this structure," he wrote in a famous passage, "composed of innumerable villages, there will be ever-widening, never ascending circles. Life will not be a pyramid with the apex sustained by the bottom. But it will be an oceanic circle whose centre will be the individual, always ready to perish for the village, the latter ready to perish for the circle of villages, till at last the whole becomes one life composed of individuals, never aggressive in their arrogance, but ever humble, sharing the majesty of the oceanic circle of which they are integral units. Therefore, the outermost circumference will not yield power to crush the inner circle but will give strength to all within and will derive its own strength from it".[27]

Gandhian and Neoclassical Economic thought

Gandhi did not build any systematic model unlike neoclassical economic theory. This was, in a sense, his strong point. All models become static with time and after having their full run. Gandhi systematically went about initiating, developing, and perfecting open-ended concepts which were amenable and adequate to produce many models, that is, models for a given context, situation, and society. Though he did not have any system, but he did have a method, if method is defined as a necessary link between ontology, epistemology, and theory.[28]

The Gandhian method was both scientific and moral. But it was "scientific" only in the sense in which Thomas Kuhn has used the phrase. The critique of a prevailing paradigm on the basis of its internal contradictions and empirical evidence is not enough for its rejection unless a new and alternative paradigm conceptually and empirically assumes the force of calling for the rejection of the earlier paradigm. But without a moral dimension it is difficult to prove the superiority or greater validity of one paradigm over another.

As Sethi states:

> What was scientific has become vulgar empiricism. The moral hollowness of the old paradigm and the moral strength of the new one, along with its scientific dimension, have to be established with relevant concepts and methods. In his life and political activities, Gandhi simultaneously adopted both the approaches and only when he was convinced of the double validity of a new concept or paradigm would he call for the rejection of the old. In his case we must always make a distinction between the critique and the rejection.[29]

The main differences between the neo-classical and the Gandhian system with respect to consumption can be enumerated as below:

Consumption

Neo-classical	*Gandhian*
Resources are limited and wants are insatiable	Resources are abundant enough to satisfy needs of all in a comfortable way

(Contd.)

(Contd.)

Neo-classical	*Gandhian*
Consumer's goal is to maximize utility	Consumer's goal is to satisfy needs
Consumption is budget-determined	Consumption is need-determined
More is better and desirable for its own sake	More is desirable and better only to a point of freedom from drudgery, discomfort, and arduous labour
Multiplicity of material wants becomes the aim of life.	Restraint on material wants is the aim of life.

In the sphere of production, the Gandhian system draws a distinction between basic and luxury goods. In the industrialised countries, whether capitalistic or marketised Marxist, the non-basic or luxury goods form the larger part. In Gandhian societies, the emphasis is to be on the production of basic goods. Some non-basic goods will, no doubt, be produced. However, a very large percentage of total production has to be made up of basic goods. The motivation for this emphasis comes both from sheer need as well as from moral and ethical considerations about love, humanism, and self-restraint.

In capitalistic societies, there is the prevalence and encouragement of an exploitative production and technological structure. The earlier slave system of the United States has been institutionalized in the form of technology. Technology encourages and imposes production modes which require specialization and large-scale organizations. An extreme degree of specialization makes work alienating and creates opportunities for exploiting the labour.

In the Gandhian system the production modes cannot be exploitative by their very nature. For technological change must satisfy the following three major conditions:

- technology must increase the productivity of the worker;
- technology must not replace the worker;
- the worker must have complete control of the technology.

These are stringent conditions and much of modern research and development does not have these worker-oriented goals. The current Appropriate Technology movements all over the world, however, are attempts in this direction.

It has been argued that production in the Gandhian system is less varied. This is a mistaken argument. It is true that the number of commodities in the Gandhian system is far less. However, there are far more varieties of every commodity produced. The diversity of production in the Gandhian system, thus, is much larger than in a capitalistic system. In the neo-classical system production is divorced from distribution, not so in the Gandhian system.

In the neo-classical system, the concept of social equilibrium leads to a set of static equilibrium conditions in the production, consumption and distribution sectors of the economy. The emphasis is on the efficiency in the allocation of scarce resources, on the maximisation of production and material (economic) gains. In Gandhian economics, the notion of equilibrium is lifted to a much higher plane of thought. His social equilibrium is an optimum combination of material and moral progress through continuous movement towards a nonviolent and non exploitative society founded on equality and freedom from economic deprivation and exploitation.[30]

The following details would make clear the distinction between the two systems in the spheres of production and distribution.

Production

	Neo-classical	*Gandhian*
Goal of the economic activity	Multiplicity and quantity of the production of material goods	To provide work for body and to satisfy economic needs of the society so that its members can fulfil themselves within a harmonious society
Measure of success	GNP and ever-rising standards of living	Absence of star-vation among masses
Incentives	Production for the sake of profits	Produce just enough to satisfy one's needs in order to keep one's mind trained and educated for a harmonious growth
How to produce?	Least-cost combination	Full employment of the available manpower
How much to produce?	Restricted only by the production capacity	Constrained by the individual's needs and a socially desirable level
Capital	Essential	Only if it aids human beings
Technology	Essential	Only if it is simple and usable by the masses

(Contd.)

(Contd.)

	Neo-classical	*Gandhian*
Labour	A commodity of production to be exploited	A source of human power which must be utilized for the benefit of its owner.

Distribution

Neo-classical	*Gandhian*
Entrepreneur corporation brings factors and agents together for production by buying/paying wage	Trustees bring together agents and factors of production by example and cooperation
The relationship is of employer-employee	The relationshop is one of trustees and co-operative workers
Capital is owned by the capitalists	Capital is owned by the community
Capitalists substitute capital maximise profits to the capitalist	There is no sub- for labour in order to stitution between capital and worker as long as it leads to displacement of workers. The function of capital is to enhance productivity without replacing the worker
Risks of production are taken by the capitalists	Risks are taken by the community as a whole
Investments are made by the capitalists out of income	Investment is made by the community as a

(Contd.)

(Contd.)

Neo-classical	*Gandhian*
from capital and for future profits	joint decision to improve the quality of life in the community
Distribution is unequal.	Distribution is the essence of the system.

Gandhi's Relevance Today

Gandhi's model, though evolved in the context of India as a part of its religious philosophy and social ethos, the Indian fight against the colonial system and the freedom of the country from foreign domination, has elements of general applicability. Eight elements of his model are particularly relevant in the context of contemporary problems and issues under discussion.

Firstly, the emphasis on dignity of human labour. His symbol for labour amongst other things, was the spinning wheel. Its practice imposed an element of self-discipline and the principle of producing something by one-self for one's need. The use of the spinning wheel, before Gandhi used and popularised it amongst men, was essentially used by women in India. By using it, he probably wanted to break the sex barrier in work. Further, when one produces something for one's own use, by the sweat of one's labour or otherwise, one values it more and is less likely to waste it.

The principle of producing materials for one's own use, or by the community for the use of the community, also envisages a decentralised system of production, and what is more important is that the produce is for one's own or the community's use. Consequently, those elements which are detrimental to humans or to the environment in the use of materials, unlike in the large scale production system for the market economy, are avoided. With the developments in electronics and biotechnology, such an approach of a decentralised production system for use, by the individual or the community, has again become possible. This, however, would require mass education to enable people to understand and utilise the new technologies.

The second major element in his scheme of things is nonviolence. As a principle, it is not passivity or indifference to untruth or tyranny. It is an assertion that injustice, exploitation, tyranny and falsehood can be fought and defeated without violence. The means of protest could be moral or ethical and used for pressurising the perpetrators of injustice or violence, through public demonstration, through non-cooperation and through suffering, instead of taking recourse to violence. If a recourse to violence is avoided, then the possibility of a dialogue to reach an agreement is possible, even though it may take a longer time. It would also help in inculcating respect for others and for their different points of view.

A society based on the principle of non-violence would not need weapons of destruction and all the resources used for developing and producing weapons of war could be utilised for human welfare. In addition, the total perspective of international relations would change and be based on co-operation instead of competition.

The third element in Gandhi's model is austerity and simplicity in life-style. Simplicity, as envisaged by Gandhi, aims at imposing self-discipline on one self by limiting one's needs and wants and the demand one makes on others. It does not mean living marginally or crudely, what it means is having a few things which one needs and which should be of quality, and be of artistic and aesthetic value. This is the life-style which Gandhi endeavoured to promote in sharp contrast to the consumer culture and the life-style of the affluent elite in India, which was an eyesore to a sensitive soul like him especially in a society where the majority of the people lived in abject poverty. A simple life-style would also prevent the colossal wastes which are a part of the consumer culture, and would go a long way in meeting the basic needs of people.

The fourth element of the Gandhian model is, essentially, built around self-control being exercised by human beings leading to the doctrine of non-possession. It also implies, in practice, control of materials. A significant element in it is that it has evolved out of past tradition and takes into account contemporary developments. Its rationality provides a common link between human beings and development and use of materials.

The Gandhian emphasis on self-control and non-possession is in direct contrast to Tawney's model of the acquisitive society.[31] The motive force behind the acquisitive society is the propensity to accumulate wealth composed of goods for current consumption and goods for future consumption. On the positive side, this society has set impressive records in the expansion of productive capacity, advances in technology, exploitation of resources, affluence and abundance of goods and services. On the negative side, the same society has also generated severe strains and stresses on life and powerful tendencies towards the degradation of the total environment - social, economic, ecological, political, and last but not least, moral.

The dominant principle of the acquisitive society is that "it assures men that there are no ends other than their ends, no law other than their desires, no limit other than that which they think advisable. Thus it makes the individual the centre of this universe, and dissolves moral principles into a choice of expediencies...for it relieves them of the necessity of discriminating between enterprise and avarice, energy and unscrupulous greed, property which is legitimate and property which is theft, the just enjoyment of the fruits of labour and idle parasitism of birth or fortune, because it treats all economic activities as standing upon the same level".[32]

Gandhi shared Tawney's incisive insight into the inherent nature of modern, acquisitive societies bent upon accumulation of goods and multiplication of wants as a never-ending process. He had serious doubts about the ability of modern societies to survive on its present course and was fearful of the high probability of the reconstruction of such societies through eruptions of violence. As an alternative to this path of violence, he offered a set of doctrines for social reconstruction consistent with his fundamental principle of nonviolence. In this set, the doctrine of non-possession holds a pivotal spot. In this regard, this doctrine is both a challenge and a response to the 'acquisitive society'. It is a challenge because it proposes a radical transformation of society through the transformation of the individual. It is a response because it suggests a way to fill one of the most serious gaps in modern society, namely the widening gap between moral progress and technological and other material measures of progress.

The fifth element of the model is *swadeshi*: the essence of the *swadeshi* concept lies in the following propositions:

- an individual, as a consumer will reduce his or her wants. In reducing one's wants, consumption will depend upon the commodities that are, or can be, produced locally by the neighbours;
- not only will he or she consume commodities produced, or producible, in the neighbourhood, but also the consumer will make an effort to obtain these commodities from the neighbourhood itself. In other words, the consumer will prefer the commodities produced by an immediate neighbour to the commodities produced by a distant neighbour except when either the immediate neighbour does not produce those goods or refuses to improve the efficiency of production. Only in these cases will the consumer obtain these goods from a distant neighbour;
- the consumer will cooperate with the producer neighbour in the process of improving the efficiency of production.

In this sense consumer and producer do not generate an antagonistic relationship as they are jointly involved in a cooperative effort.

Translated into economic language, and according to Diwan, *swadeshi* involves a downward shift in the cost curve for a commodity produced in the neighbourhood or locality.[33] According to him there are a number of reasons why the cost function shifts downward:

- firstly, because the consumer - a neighbour - helps the producer - another neighbour - there are no costs of marketing, such as advertisements, selling, packaging or providing information;
- secondly, since the production takes place in the community at a local level and the consumer neighbours are helping the producer to become efficient, there is a possibility of skill specialization and thereby reduction in production costs;
- thirdly, the production process employs local materials. This minimizes, if not completely eliminates, the transport costs for both input and the output;
- fourthly, since the materials are obtained from the local sellers, these are likely to be at minimum cost;
- lastly, the labour costs are liable to be low.

The sixth element of the model is trusteeship. Gandhi refused to accept any of the prevailing economic systems, which may be summarized as capitalist, communist, and mixed economy, since all of them produced alienation of one kind or another. He suggested in turn what he called the system of trusteeship. Gandhi claimed that trusteeship was likely to be his most lasting contribution, though the votaries of all the existing systems reject it. Partly it is due to the fact that Gandhi did not elaborate the concept suffiently, and partly because adequate attention has not been paid to it.

Trusteeship has two aspects: its basic principles and structure; and the method to achieve a society based upon the principle of trusteeship. It is the second aspect which has created doubts because Gandhi expected capitalists to relinquish voluntarily their property and act as trustees of the society. But more than once Gandhi made it clear that he was offering a solution or a way out for the capitalists in place of a bloody revolution which they must face if they remain tied down to their wealth and profits. He was also quite emphatic in stating that if the capitalists did not voluntarily surrender, the State is within its right to nationalize their assets. But nationalization to him was only a necessary evil, an intermediate state, which must ultimately be transformed into trusteeship. This is one of the vital differences between Gandhi and Marx.

Gandhi did not leave behind a model of trusteeship; he only stated the basic principles of its organization. These principles were:

- no one has any right over property which is a social phenomenon;
- State ownership of property leads to concentration of economic and political power in the hands of a small bureaucracy which has the monopoly of violence and hence is an antithesis of trusteeship;
- trusteeship is by definition a communitarian system, a kind of general cooperation of efforts and resources;
- trusteeship is a system of social self-management and a kind of socialist democracy from below.[34]

The seventh element of the model is the imperative of full employment. Gandhi believed in the dignity of labour. He argued that nature has intended us to earn our bread with the sweat of our brow. Anyone who idles away a single minute becomes to that extent a burden upon his neighbours and to that extent commits violence.

To Gandhi, full employment was not merely a means to higher production but an end in itself, that is, to eliminate both the dominance of men over men and violence. Full employment economy—the availability of jobs for all those who are willing and able to work at the going social wage - was to him a prerequisite for the moral and spiritual development of all human beings, especially those who are at the bottom of the social scale.

It must be stressed that the Gandhian concept of full employment is slightly different from the concept of full employment in conventional economics. In conventional economics, full employment is attained when 96 per cent of all those willing and able to work at the current wage rate are able to find jobs. It permits voluntary unemployment, commonly referred to as frictional unemployment. Gandhi wanted everyone to earn his or her bread by the sweat of his or her brow. He could not, therefore, approve of voluntary unemployment. In the Gandhian framework, work does not imply disutility that needs to be compensated by money wages, but is a service to fellow persons. This is its positive aspect, that of enabling individuals to realize their best. Work is *yagya* or sacrifice and one can realize God through working for one's fellow-beings.

The eighth element is economic equality. Gandhi maintained that a nonviolent social order has to be constructed on the basis of equality. By equality he meant guarantee of a minimum standard of consumption to all. He argued that everyone must have a balanced diet, a decent house to live in, facilities for the education of one's children, and adequate medical care. True individual freedom - the opportunity for the full moral and spiritual development of human beings - is possible only when the individual is free from hunger and unemployment.

Gandhi accepted the fact that there will be inequalities of skill, industry, intelligence, and opportunity. He recognized that people with talent will earn more. But he wanted them to take only what was required for their legitimate needs and to leave the remainder to be used by the society. He therefore preached the doctrine of non-possession, as he believed that the real happiness and contentment comes not from self-indulgence and multiplication of wants but from self-denial and from deliberate and voluntary reduction of wants.

He wanted the rich and the elite to take an initiative in dis-possession with a view to a universal diffusion of the spirit of contentment. As a practical matter, he was willing to accept, in the transitional phase, income differentials that are considered fair by the society. He proposed to fix a decent minimum living wage and a ceiling for the maximum income that can be allowed to a person in society. The difference between such minimum and maximum income should be reasonable and equitable and variable from time to time, so much so that the tendency will be towards the obliteration of the difference.[35]

Policy Implications of Gandhian Thought

A number of policy prescriptions flow from Gandhian thought. The emphasis of Gandhi is on 'service'- service to one's neighbours, the community, the nation, the world. The current stress on the monetized market economy tends to relegate such activity to the background and to define it as secondary-and this inspite of the fact that even in an economy like that of the United States, nearly 50 percent of services are provided through voluntary, unpaid work! The policy implication is that markets either need to be made more perfect or regulated in favour of voluntary service functions - for example, by recognising the contribution of women, unpaid voluntary workers *et al.* to the production process and including it in GNP.

The *swadeshi* principle implies a number of policies. All of these policies will favour the promotion of local producers. They will involve such activities as demarcating the areas of production between local and large producers and discouraging competition between them. They will also involve differential tax and subsidy policies. The existing policy framework has always provided favourable terms to the large producers as opposed to small producers, for example, by providing cheap capital. In many cases, the large producers have been able to withstand the competition from small producers only because of the tax benefits and subsidies accorded to them in the form of subsidised interest rates, power and other materials. Gandhian economics implies a reversal of such policies.

The proposition of equality implies policies that reduce asset/income inequalities. In many countries the governments have followed income maintenance policies. However, these policies simply counteract the increases in inequalities generated by the biases of imperfect markets. In the Gandhian economic scheme, more forceful policies are needed because the object is to lead eventually to equal distribution of assets. One object of such policies is to raise the costs and prices of luxury goods and reduce the costs and prices of necessities. Gandhian thought leads to a ceiling on personal incomes or wealth.

Gandhi also implies a new paradigm of decision-making. In the past there has been a continuous growth in hierarchy and thereby an increase in the power of people at the top of this hierarchy. Hierarchy and bureaucracy have grown not only in the government but in all other walks of life, including such professions as business and education. Gandhian thought suggests a need to reverse this trend.

Gandhi noted that one of the major sources of maintenance of privilege lay in the high elasticity of consumption of luxury goods. Given the aim of Gandhian thought to reduce privilege, an important policy presumption will involve reductions in the luxury elasticity of production. This has to do with the structure of production. If the production structure remains biased towards basic goods, luxury elasticity of production will keep on falling.[36]

Critique of the Gandhian Model

The Gandhian model is often criticized on the ground that it is anti-industrial and anti-advanced technology and so a feudal, tradition-oriented, static, agrarian model. However this criticism is both unfair and superficial. Gandhi never expressed unqualified opposition to industrialization and modern technology. He was opposed to developing the Indian economy industrially along the same lines as the Western one. Such industrialization, he feared, would spell disaster - moral, economic, social, and political.

Gandhi, however, favoured limited, selective, and socially controlled industrialization: large-scale, heavy, capital-intensive industries, centralized but strictly under public control, and decentralized, small-scale industries to diversify the village economic base. Such a mixed pattern of industrialisation he considered to be responsive to the needs and welfare of a nonviolent society, dedicated to moral and material progress. Writing in the Harijan, he states

> I do visualize electricity, ship-building, iron-works, machine-making and the like existing side-by-side with village handicrafts. But the order of dependence will be reversed. Hitherto industrialization has been so planned as to destroy the villages and village crafts. In the state of the future, it will subserve the villages and their crafts. Nothing will be allowed to be produced by the cities that can be equally well produced by the villages. The proper function of the cities is to serve as clearing houses for village products.[37]

Likewise, he was not opposed to technological innovations *per se*. He recognized that technology has its place and that, wisely used, it can make significant contribution to social welfare. But he was strongly opposed to indiscriminate use of technology which might lead to monopolistić exploitation and displacement of labour.

Again, all through his strictures on technology, his humanism shines through. "The supreme consideration", he wrote, "is man. The machine should not tend to make atrophied the limbs of man".[38]

He was equally concerned about the effect of machines on the human mind. He saw in modern machine technology a powerful, dehumanizing force that alienates man from his product, from his community and, most insidious of all, from himself. Yet, the techno-structure of the Gandhian model of the village economy would not rule out limited use of modern technology. He was receptive to the positive role machines can play in reducing the burden of human drudgery and in increasing labour productivity without degrading the human mind. Of necessity, such machine technology has to be highly selective, controlled, and subservient to higher needs than the simple economic need for efficiency.

Another criticism has been that the self-reliant rural society is without any indication as to how it is to be linked with larger groupings, that of a nation-state and the international system. Further, how to fit in larger transnational systems, such as transportation and communication systems, into the model. Or how to create and support scientific and technological research which has international dimensions and requires international support. The criticism is made that such a system would also lead to localization and narrowing of outlook as it would only tackle local problems.

This criticism too is misconceived and misplaced. Gandhi was not against linking up the village communities with the international community through 'ever widening circles' and in a non-hierarchical way. What he was against was internationalisation which led to domination, dependency and the destruction of traditional societies. He wanted people to live in communities that matched their human size and thought patterns; communities small enough to allow genuine self-government and sharing of responsibilities. Each community would be joined with others, to form a larger unit, but not so large as to tempt any one individual to abuse power by having too much of it. The larger a democratic group grew the less say the individual or local group would be able to have in making their decisions. Therefore limits needed to be placed on the size of a regional group. Only this way could those at the very bottom of the socio-political scale have a say in decision-making that affected them.

Huq has examined the question of international trade from a Gandhian perspective.[39] Huq analyses what the doctrine of *swadeshi* (local self-reliance) means for international trade. He goes on to point out that swadeshi would be anti-international trade only if the concept is interpreted very narrowly and very rigidly - something that Gandhi never did.

Huq mentions that Gandhi anticipated such misinterpretation of his doctrine and he wrote: "Even *Swadeshi*, like any other good thing, can be ridden to death if it is made a fetish. That is a danger which must be guarded against. To reject foreign manufacture merely because they are foreign and to go on wasting national time and money in the promotion in one's country of manufacture for which it is not suited, would be criminal folly and a negation of the *Swadeshi* spirit".[40]

Gandhi was realistic enough to realise that under no circumstances would one country be able to produce all the things needed. And he wrote: "So, though our aim is complete self-sufficiency, we shall have to get from outside the villages what we cannot produce in the villages. We shall have to produce more of what we can in order thereby to obtain in exchange what we are unable to produce".[41]

Huq goes on to suggest that there was a positive doctrine of international trade following from the Gandhian paradigm. The Gandhian perspective leads to the following distinctive features of international trade:

- it accepts the logic of the principle of comparative advantage but rejects it as the sole basis for trade among nations;
- it accepts reciprocal need rather than reciprocal demand as the determinant of terms of trade among nations;
- it postulates an international economic order based on international cooperation and understanding and mutual need, rather than on market forces and competition;
- it is guided by a purpose higher than the purpose of pure economic gain. That is the moral purpose embodied in his notion of 'service' which was to govern the flow of trade among nations;
- it is an economic doctrine into which is infused the philosophical principle of *Ahimsa* or nonviolence and non-exploitation;
- it offers maximum protection against unequal distribution of gains from trade among nations in sharp contrast with the impact of the existing doctrine of international trade.

The Gandhian perspective thus leads to a global economic and political order based on nonviolence, non-exploitation and a high degree of international cooperation.

Gandhi's views on the scale factor are the most misunderstood or misinterpreted. 'Small is Beautiful' is a phrase coined in the name of Gandhi. There is no such absolute hypothesis in Gandhi. Nevertheless, though the scale factor itself cannot be evaluated, other things being given, small is better than large. But other things do not remain the same. Absolute concepts leave one with no choice. But when choice exists, other considerations have to be given full weight. Gandhi was a scientific and post-modern mind. As a searcher and experimenter with truth, he rejected technologies and even scientific research which was repugnant to real human needs just as he rejected those human wants which were detrimental to spiritual and moral development. What he insisted was that technological and scale choices must not be solely determined by economic considerations. Any technology would be acceptable to him if it was found to be consistent with his conceptual system, irrespective of the differences in its productivity components or scale.

In the Gandhian paradigm it is man, and not society or the State, who is the supreme architect of his own destiny. The ways to Truth are many but each person has to proceed towards it in his own way and as dictated by his conscience. For morality is what distinguishes human beings from animals. The path chosen has, thus, to be a moral one.

In relations with others, human beings have always to keep in mind the categorical imperative of nonviolence, that is, while earning their livelihood human beings have to ensure that this was not at the expense of others - whether human beings or nature.

Gandhi also clearly has an ecological orientation. He was led to ecology through his emphasis on nonviolence. Peace in his view was a universal concept. It was not attainable unless harmony - not only in the social sense between individuals but also in the larger sense as between humans, animals and plants — was attained. He was sensitive to the bringing about of a balance between individuals and their environment. His encouragement of the Indian masses to spin cotton for their personal use was not only aimed at instilling self-reliance and self-dignity among them, but also to preserve the environment while using the minimum of capital. His concept was to shift the emphasis of economics from capital to labour.

The question of the feasibility of restructuring society, national or global, in line with the Gandhian paradigm is invariably raised. There is no doubt a great deal of idealism in Gandhian thought. As Gandhi himself often stated, his thoughts pertain to the 'world of tomorrow'. He was convinced that the 'world of today' is moving toward the 'world of tomorrow'. To him national and global orders based on nonviolence, non-exploitation and high degrees of cooperation were no doubt distant goals but were entirely realisable. What was required, to use modern jargon, was 'transvaluation of values' in modern society. This was to Gandhi an entirely realisable goal.

Sachs, as we have noted, postulated the five dimensions of eco-development as sustainability in the social, economic, ecological, spatial and cultural realms.[42] Comparing Gandhi's thought with the model developed by Sachs, it is quite clear that Gandhi was right when he referred to his vision as being for the 'world of tomorrow'. As we can see, Sach's prescriptions for sustainable development in the 21st Century are a mere subset of the Gandhian paradigm. For to Gandhi these would be only a transitional phase - though an important one - to his vision of a world in which peace and nonviolence prevailed. The question that we need to ask ourselves is, therefore, not the question of feasibility of the Gandhian paradigm in the world as it is but whether there is any alternative to it if the world is to attain Peace (*Ahimsa*), which to Gandhi is the ultimate Truth.

References

1. Swami Ranganathananda, *External Values for a Changing Society* (Bombay: Bharatiya Vidya Bhavan, 1971) p. 841.
2. J.V. Bondurant, *Conquest of Violence* (Berkeley: University of California Press, 1965) p. 23.
3. M.K. Gandhi, *Non-Violent Resistance (Satyagraha)* (7th Edition) (New York: Schocken Books, 1972) p.10.
4. *Ibid.*, pp. 41-42.

5. *Ibid.*, p. 161.
6. Bondurant., note 2, p. 25.
7. Mahadev Desai, *The Gospel of Selfless Action or the Gita According to Gandhi* (Ahmedabad: Navjivan Press, 1946) p.145.
8. *Sarvodaya* means the upliftment of all. To Gandhi *sarvodaya* meant *antodaya*, that is, upliftment of the poorest and most downtrodden sections of society. Since the word *anta* means the last, the end, the relation of *antodaya* to Ruskin's *Unto the Last* is obvious.
9. Gandhi, note 3, pp. 48-49.
10. Quoted in Louis Fisher (ed.), *The Essential Gandhi*, (New York: Vintage Books, 1962).
11. M.K. Gandhi, *The Collected Works of Mahatma Gandhi* (Ahmedabad: Navjivan, 1958) Vol. 32, p. 402.
12. Bondurant, note 2, p.29.
13. J.P. Chander, (ed.), *Teachings of Mahatma Gandhi*, (Lahore: The Indian Printing Works, 1945) p. 21.
14. H.T. Mazumdar, *Mahatma Gandhi: Peaceful Revolutionary*, (New York: Charles Scribner and Sons, 1952) p.41.
15. *Ibid.*, p.113.
16. W.S. Nelson, "The tradition of non-violence and its underlying forces", in G. Ramachandran et al., (eds.) *Gandhi: His Relevance for Our Times* (Berkeley: World Without War Council, 1967) p.17.
17. N.K. Bose, *Selections from Gandhi* (Ahmedabad: Navjivan Printing Press, 1948) p.41.
18. *Ibid.*, p.73.
19. See chapter on Gandhi in G.R. Madan, *Economic Thinking in India* (Bombay: S. Chand & Co., 1966).
20. A.M. Huq, "Welfare Criteria in Gandhian Economics" *Essays on Gandhian Economics*, Romesh Diwan and Mark Lutz (eds.) (Delhi: Gandhi Peace Foundation, 1985), p.68.

21. M.K. Gandhi in S. Narayan (ed.), *The Selected Works of Mahatma Gandhi* (Ahmedabad, Navjivan Publishing House, 1968) Vol. VI, p.336.
22. *Rig Veda*, translated by Wendy O'Flaherty (New York: Penguin, 1984) 1.164.46, p.80.
23. Gandhi quoted in Mark Lutz, "Human Nature in Gandhian Economics" in *Essays in Gandhian Economics*, note 20, pp. 27-53 at p. 39. Much of what follows is based on Lutz's analysis.
24. *Ibid.*, p.42.
25. Amritananda Das, *Foundation of Gandhian Economics* (New York: St. Martins Press, 1979).
26. *Bhagavad Gita*, 3-4, 12 and 16, Bede Griffiths, *River of Compassion: Commentary on the Bhagavad Gita* (Warwick, New York: Amity, 1987) pp. 44-52.
27. M.K. Gandhi, *India of My Dreams*, edited by R.K. Prabhu, Bombay, 1947 quoted by Huq, note 20, pp. 69-70.
28. For much of what follows I am indebted to Romesh Diwan and Sushila Gidwani, "Elements in Gandhian Economics", in *Essays in Gandhian Economics* , note 20, pp. 54-65.
29. Sethi, "Foreword", *Essays in Gandhian Economics*, note 20, p.xxiv.
30. Huq, "Welfare Criteria in Gandhian Economics", note 20, p.74.
31. R.H. Tawney, *The Acquisitive Society* (New York: Harcourt Brace & Co., 1921).
32. *Ibid.*, pp.30-31
33. R. Diwan, "Economics of Love" *Essays in Gandhian Economics*, note 20, pp.94-95.
34. For a more detailed exposition see J.D. Sethi, "Poverty, Alienation, and the Gandhian Way Out" *Essays in Gandhian Economics*, note 20, pp. 213-230.
35. R.K. Prabhu and V.R. Rao, *The Mind of Mahatma Gandhi* (Ahmedabad: Navjivan Publishing House, 1967).

36. For a detailed analysis based on conventional economic analysis see Romesh Diwan, "Economics of Love", note 33, pp. 86-108. The mathematical analysis is at pp.103-106.
37. Quoted in Ranchor Prime, *Hinduism and Ecology* (London: Cassel, 1992) p.66.
38. M.K. Gandhi, *All Men are Brothers* (New York: Columbia University Press, 1958) p.126.
39. A.M. Huq, "The Doctrine of International Trade: A Gandhian Perspective "*Essays in Gandhian Economics*, note 20, pp.166-174.
40. M.K. Gandhi, *The Collected Works*, Vol. VI, note 11, p.338.
41. M.K. Gandhi, ibid., p.348.
42. Ignacy Sachs, "Transition Strategies for the 21st Century", *Nature and Resources* , 28(1), 1992, pp.4-17.

8

The Oceans, Seas and Coasts

The oceans are one of the three planetary ecosystems, the others being the atmosphere and the geosphere. In the past two decades there has been a diversification and intensification of the uses of the oceans leading to the oceans playing an increasingly important role in the affairs of the world. The intrusion of the latest phase of the industrial revolution, the so-called third industrial revolution based on information, robotics, and biotechnology, into the oceans has created new opportunities-and dangers-for humankind.

Besides 60% of the world's population - nearly 3 billion people -now lives within 60 kilometres of the coast. This number is increasing rapidly due to a combination of population growth, migration and urbanization. Two thirds of cities with populations over 2.5 million are situated near estuaries. This creates its own environmental pressures on the oceans.

The unrestrained pursuit of activities in coastal areas has led to competition for finite resources, environmental degradation and often social conflict. Furthermore, development practices which ignore the dynamics of coastal systems can be catastrophic, as evidenced by the increasing loss of lives, property and investment due to coastal flooding, erosion, cyclones and hurricanes.

The oceans thus are an ecosystem needing to be studied in the context of sustainable development. This we will do by applying the paradigms developed earlier, namely, the Western, and the Eastern and the Gandhian, to the oceanic ecosystem.

The Oceanic Ecosystem: the Western Perspective

The Western perspective is not a homogeneous and unitary one. While the dominant paradigm is based on classical science - Newtonianism and Darwinism - the global ecological crisis is leading scientists to a new understanding of the relationship of man with nature, and the need to take a holistic approach to problems. According to the holistic view, solutions are not likely to be technical, or economic, or social or spiritual but a combination of all. The emerging paradigm will mean a radical departure from a worldview where man has been dominating nature to his advantage. Modern science is, thus, converging towards the Eastern and Gandhian paradigms.

In what follows, however, we will look at the oceans from the viewpoint of the dominant paradigm: economic growth through the application of science and technology. In this view of the matter, it is generally accepted that if the oceans and coastal areas are to maintain their productivity and natural functions, there must be major improvements in the way coastal and ocean development is managed. Effective coastal management has to be based on a solid scientific foundation taking into account the limitations of natural systems, while balancing and integrating the demands of the various sections of humanity which depend on these systems for their livelihood. This requires the balancing of human needs with the resilience of the oceanic ecosystem.

Dramatic advances in the planetary sciences are changing our concept of the planet earth and man's place it. They are stressing the need for looking at ecosystems in a holistic and integrated manner. Technology is also available to generate and utilize new living, nonliving, and energy resources from the oceans. This could make a significant contribution towards solving the world's food and energy problems, among others.

Marine sciences and technology - remote sensing, sonar, robotics, magnetology, seismology, deep-sea photography, - have altered our concept of the oceans. Previously the ocean floor was regarded as flat and deep. We now know that like the back-bone of a giant reptile, the mid-ocean ridge curves beneath the world ocean. Forty thousand miles long, this mountain chain is far longer, and has peaks far taller, than anything on land. Transverse faults are attached to the giant backbone like rib cages. A new world has been discovered on which our known world of continents floats like a minor appendage.[1]

However, it is not only the physical aspect of the oceans that needs to be considered. The oceans, as an integral part of the planetary life processes, a provider of living organisms and minerals and resources are worthy of study as an ecosystem. Besides, as Arthur Clarke has observed: 'How inappropriate to call this planet Earth, when clearly it is Ocean.'[2] Nearly three-quarters of the Earth's surface is sea, which is why photographs taken from space show the planet as a sapphire blue globe, flecked with soft wisps of cloud and capped by brilliant white fields of polar ice.

The oceans are a living entity, and thereby a good object to study in the context of sustainability: being one of the three planetary ecosystems; an essential component of the complex system that maintains life on earth; the provider of many resources to humanity; and the ultimate sink for all waste products generated by human activities.

The discharge of wastes, and the consequent pollution of the oceans, is today causing the most concern. This raises the question: How "sick" are the oceans? To what extent have human activities altered the natural structure of marine communities, by means direct and indirect, obvious and obscure?

To what extent are the more dramatic consequences of pollution - brought to mind by such names as Minamata and Torrey Canyon - really indicative of the long-term and perhaps irreversible damage we may be doing to our ocean environment? To answer such questions we must first decide where to look and what criteria to use.

The obvious place to look for pollution is where we expect to find it in its greatest concentrations - in coastal waters, estuaries and areas where population and industry are concentrated. Here we can observe directly the physical transport of polluting materials, their entry into and accumulation within local food webs, the effects on marine organisms, communities, and sometimes on humans themselves. The next place to look is where we *least* expect to find evidence of man's polluting activities - far-removed areas such as the polar ice caps, the deep sea, the upper layers of the atmosphere.

When a substance such as DDT is ubiquitous and can be found in the tissues of Antarctic organisms (marine invertebrates, fish, and penguins), in the livers of bottom-dwelling ocean fish, and in the atmosphere over the Sargasso Sea, there is obvious cause for concern.[3]

In the Western paradigm, pollution has to be prevented and the oceans sustainably managed. Sustainable management of a complex system like the oceanic ecosystem requires the use of powerful tools. Systems analysis is the methodology often used for analysing methods necessary for sustainably managing complex and unpredictable physico-ecological ecosystems. We shall examine as to what extent systems analysis, and models based on it, would help in managing the oceans.

Systems analysis was introduced in the early 1950s to facilitate cooperation among different disciplines. Boulding defined systems analysis as a level of theoretical model-building which lies somewhere between the highly generalized constructions of pure mathematics and the specific theories of the specialized disciplines.[4]

At the highest level of abstraction, the theory of model building prevails, and more or less generally applicable definitions and procedures are used for system building. For practical applications, this theoretical framework usually has to be filled in by using a further simplification of the real world into components and interactions relevant to the problem being studied.

General system theory, on which systems analysis is based, arose specifically as a response to the need to counterbalance fragmentation and duplication induced by Western ultraspecialized modes of inquiry. It has benefited from the parallel emergence and rise to eminence of cybernetics and information theory and their widespread applications to originally quite unsuspected fields. Presently, the rise of this theory is aided by societal pressures calling for the development of theories capable of interdisciplinary application. The specific contribution of general system theory derives from its de-emphasis of traditional concepts of matter, substance, idea, or spirit and its explicit orientation toward grasping phenomena in terms of organization.

Organizations are composed of entities in interaction with each other. According to Laszlo, the simplest conceptualization of an entity as defined by its organizational invariance is the system. A system in this definition is a collection of parts conserving some identifiable set of (internal) relations, with the summed relations (that is, the system itself) conserving some identifiable set of (external) relations to other entities (systems). The system also has to have pattern-maintenance and pattern-evolving characteristics if it is to be regarded as a natural system.[5]

In the context of sustainable management of the oceanic ecosystem, it is necessary to consider the internal and external relations of two suprabiological organizations, namely, the oceanic ecosystem and the human sociocultural system. This has to be done in a decision-making perspective and the managerial issues that arise therefrom considered thereafter.

It is legitimate to conceptualize the oceanic ecosystem as a dynamic open system, receiving energy from the sun, recycling it in various ways among many trophic levels, fixing some of it in biomass, and radiating off some proportion into space in the form of heat. Being a vast, complex and planetary system there are many unknowns.[6]

Oceanic processes are extremely complex and do not always lend themselves to providing even an approximate working knowledge of observed input/output relationships as a basis for the creation of system linkages. Since nearly all oceanic parameters shift constantly at variable rates, magnitudes, and frequencies, those changes need to be tracked in real time. This is made difficult, if not impossible, because of the large number of environmental unknowns, including discontinuities and synergisms. This hinders the establishing of systemic relationships between the parameters of the oceanic ecosystem.

Bennett and Chorley point out that, when considering environmental systems, analysts have incomplete and partial knowledge of the system that they seek to understand and control. As we have seen this is the case with the oceanic ecosystem. In such cases, according to the authors, the nature of analysts' knowledge has to be incremental in that greater insight is gained as analysis or control continues. But elements in the analysis of such systems will necessarily be indeterminate (or even counterintuitive) both because of the complexity of the system and because of the intimacy of human/environment interrelations that constrain understanding. In particular, knowledge of such a system is limited by the methods of measurement and observation, the presence of stochastic variation resulting largely from methods of measurement and system analysis adopted, the manner in which systems knowledge is obtained and accumulated, and the practical stages of systems analysis.[7]

Management, however, requires some sort of model so that the impact of interventions can be evaluated. The impediment to the successful modelling of the oceanic physico-ecological system derives from its inherently uncertain nature. Uncertainty arises in terms of the magnitudes and the space/time (i.e. areal location) attributes of inputs, outputs, and states of the system. In the oceans plankton, for example, are found on the surface where there is light, while nutrients are in the deeper, colder waters. This raises the problem of connectivity between inputs and outputs.

Ideally, the oceanic system, limited at the air-sea interface with the atmosphere and the land-sea interface with the coast and the sea floor, should cover the entire ocean for all time. Clearly, this is not possible and, in practice, models have been created during some given period of time, of an estuary, a gulf, a coastal region, a channel, a sea, according to the particular objective to be attained.

An important aspect of the model of the oceanic system has to be the interactions of the system with the atmosphere and the land which provide the inputs and outputs to the system. The identification of all inputs and outputs is essential to the construction of the mathematical model. The geographical delimitation of the system introduces coastal and open boundaries where exchanges with the exterior occur in the form of boundary inputs and outputs. Boundary interactions also occur at the sea surface and at the sea floor.

It is in delineating inputs and outputs into and from the oceans that problems arise. The energy and mass transfers from the land and atmosphere to the oceanic system, and vice versa, are complex and nonlinear. Nonlinearity implies that some or all of the mathematical parameters employed in the description of the system operation are not identical over all magnitudes and regimes of system operation - in other words, that they are free, within certain limits, to change their values in harmony with changes in the system variables. As a consequence, the nonlinear oceanic ecosystem cannot be accurately described mathematically by linear algebraic or linear differential equations. Since in most situations nonlinear systems will not satisfy the principle of superimposition (that is, the addition or subtraction of subsystem outputs to produce a total system response) or exhibit simple proportionality between the amplitudes of input and output, this makes the system indeterminate. Whereas linear systems possess single, unique steady states, nonlinear systems exhibit multiple states, which makes their behaviour not only indeterminate but also, to a degree, unpredictable.

As an ecosystem, it is illuminating to compare the actual coastal ecosystem, composed of discrete organisms, with a hypothetical model in the form of a continuously connected system from the watershed up to the deep ocean that is generally being formulated. While the former is a discontinuous system, the hypothetical one is a continuous one.

There is also the question of indeterminacy in the actual oceanic ecosystem. Processes associated with demography, for example, add to indetermination in the coastal ecosystem. Other instabilities apply, inter alia, to the dynamically changing ocean system, where all physical parameters are not only discontinuous but in a state of constant change, There is also the impact of the rapidly advancing technological and information systems which make the oceanic ecosystem extremely volatile.

The predictable and mathematical model being difficult, if not impossible, to formulate, the attention of model builders has shifted to the maintenance of ecosystem integrity. When we talk of the integrity of ecosystems, the reference is to the interaction between the physical ecosystem and anthropogenic activities. In a larger concept of ecosystem including both man and nature, this would mean internal relations between two parts of the (larger) ecosystem. If the ecosystem is taken to be physical, then it would reflect its external relations with man-made activities.

Analysing the way such ecosystems work, the concepts of the decay of energy and the accretion of information emerge as important factors. Change in ecosystems is twofold: (a) rapid changes (disasters, catastrophes) that destroy structures and that are unpredictable from inside the system, and (b) gradual and slow changes that vanish gradually in a generalised situation of flow of energy and that admit a considerable degree of local diversification. The change is towards segregation, and persistently situations are encountered in which things are found to be misplaced. In the oceanic world, as already noted, plankton live where there is light. Physically the situation in the oceans is that where there is light there are no nutrients; nutrients accumulate in the depths, where there is no light. Integrity of an ecosystem could thus be conceived as bringing about connectivity between events seperated in time and space. This is a subject of considerable importance to ecosystem management if synergy of anthropogenic activities and the physical coastal zone ecosystem is to be brought about.

However to date no such method of bringing about synergy of activities, or of preventing the ecosystem from disintegrating has been discovered. The result is that from the viewpoint of the Western paradigm, the oceanic system is a "black box" whose inner workings are not known: the way to handle the system is through minimising future regret through the precautionary principle. The use of the Western paradigm based on "the best available scientific evidence", thus, does not lead to a manageable system due to discontinuities, in time and place, and the presence of too many unknowns in the oceanic ecosystem. Sustainable development being crucially dependent on management, the Western paradigm would require accretion of knowledge which would take quite some time to reach adequate levels. It is only when knowledge of intractions between the various parameters is available that the Western paradigm can lead to sustainability.

Oceans: An Eastern Perspective

The Western concept of "managing" the oceans or coastal zone would take on a different hue in the Eastern paradigm. In the Asian (Eastern) concept, the Divine (Natural) laws, have to be followed and decisions taken according to well established principles and guidelines. In establishing trade-offs between different activities, in the Eastern view, neither scientific analysis nor logical precision would lead to unique solutions. The attaining of sustainable development needs an ethical perspective. To quote Kothari

> In the absence of an ethical imperative, environmentalism has been reduced to a technological fix, and as with all technological fixes, solutions are seen to lie once more in the hands of manager technocrats.[8]

Management of the oceans, in the Eastern sense, would require commitment to the ideal of sustainability in a spiritual sense thus enabling the harmonisation of apparently disparate activities and objectives. For this the intuitive mind, the mind of the poet or sage is necessary.

We have already looked at values regarding nature in three religions: Buddhism, Hinduism and Islam. But in all cultures there are values respectful of the environment. Zarathustra in 3500 B.C., for example, laid down the following precepts in the *Zend Avesta*:

> Do not pollute earth, air, and water.
>
> Do not cut trees nor destroy green vegetation but transform waste lands and deserts into gardens.

> Refrain from killing birds and animals. Treat them with love and affection and make use of them to improve the lot of mankind.
>
> Nature hates monopolies and knows no exception. It has always some levelling agency that puts the overbearing, the strong, the rich, the fortunate, substantially on the same ground with all others.[9]

In the Indian scripture the *Atharva Veda* (contemporaneous with the *Zend Avesta*) the following is stated:

> What of Thee I dig out,
> Let that quickly grow over,
> Let me not hit thy vitals,
> Or thy heart.[10]

If the *Atharva Veda* saying were to guide our relationship with the oceans, the loss of ecological integrity will be equivalent to hitting the vitals.

Buddha (560-480 BC) compared his teaching to the ocean. My doctrine, he stated, is like the ocean having the same eight wonderful qualities. He goes on to state:

(i) both the ocean and my doctrine become gradually deeper,

(ii) both preserve their identity under all changes,

(iii) both cast out dead bodies upon the dry land,

(iv) as the great rivers, when falling into the main, lose their names and are thenceforth reckoned as the great ocean, so all the castes, having renounced their lineage and entered the Sangha, become brethren and are reckoned as the sons of Shakyamuni,

(v) the ocean is the goal of all streams and of the rains from the clouds, yet it is never over-flowing and never emptied; so the *dharma* is embraced by many millions of people yet it neither increases nor decreases,

(vi) as the great ocean has only one taste, the taste of salt, so my doctrine has only one flavour, the flavour of emancipation,

(vii) both the ocean and the *dharma* are full of gems and pearls and jewels, and both afford a dwelling-place for mighty beings,

(viii) my doctrine is pure, and it makes no discrimination between noble and ignoble, rich and poor.[11]

The Eastern perspective, where the oceans have to be harmonised with, is akin to the Gaian thesis, whereby the Earth with all its living beings and inanimate matter forms one interrelated and "living" organism: the Earth requires to be treated like a living organism.

The Gaian hypothesis gives rise to many questions in the oceanic context. If, for example, the atmosphere is, among other things, a device for conveying raw materials to and from the oceans, it would be reasonable to assume the presence of carrier compounds for elements essential in all biological systems, for example, iodine and sulphur. Evidence has been found to the effect that both are conveyed from the oceans, where they are abundant, through the air to the land surface, where they are in short supply. The carrier compounds, methyl iodide and dimethyl sulphide respectively, are directly produced by marine life.

The oceans, those great expanses of deep blue sea, are vital parts of the global steam engine that transforms the energy from the sun into the motions of air and water which in turn distribute this energy all over the world. Collectively, the oceans form a reservoir of dissolved gases which helps to regulate the composition of the air we breathe and to provide a stable environment for marine life - about half of all living matter.[12]

The oceans are the cradle where life developed. The oceans today appear vast, covering more than two thirds of the earth's surface with waters up to ten kilometers deep. Yet, as Whitfield points out, if the earth were reduced in scale to a ball of rock a metre in diameter, the surface would just be moist to the touch. It is this thin film of moisture and the tenuous atmosphere that it helps to maintain that make the planet habitable.[13]

All the known chemical elements are to be found dissolved in sea water and there has been an intimate relationship between the composition of sea water and the evolution of life. The continued existence of life in the oceans is still critically dependent on the availability of nutrients for plant growth in the surface, sun-lit layers and on the effective control of the concentrations of potentially toxic elements.

Through photosynthesis by microscopic plants in the surface layers of the ocean, carbon dioxide is drawn from the atmosphere and oxygen released. The exchange of oxygen and carbon dioxide (and a range of other volatile compounds produced by the phytoplankton) has a profound effect on the suitability of the atmosphere for higher life forms. In addition, carbon dioxide and other trace gases influence the earth's climate by affecting the efficiency with which heat is trapped by the atmosphere.

Some of the carbon fixed by photosynthesis from the surface layer travels to the bottom either because the plants themselves die or because they are eaten by grazing animals which defaecate and their pellets fall down into the deep ocean. It is speculated that the main Gaian mechanism at work in the oceans may be driven by a steady rain of animal droppings.

The flow of material is impressive with approximately 400 million tons of carbon per year cascading into the deep ocean. The total mass of material is much greater than this since only 25 per cent by weight is organic material. The rest is made up of shell fragments (calcium carbonate or silica) produced in the surface layers (70 per cent by weight) or mineral debris introduced by the rivers or by wind-blown dust (5 per cent by weight).

Along with the carbon, essential elements such as nitrogen, phosphorus, iron and manganese are removed from the surface layers in the particulate material. Consequently, in productive areas the essential nutrients tend to be stripped out of the surface layers by the rain of particles. If all of this material was buried in the deep sea sediments the oceans would rapidly turn into a sterile desert fed only by the slow trickle of nutrients from the land. For life to continue to thrive in the oceans it is essential that the nutrients trapped in the particulate debris are recycled to the surface from the deeper layers of the ocean. The bulk of the material leaving the surface layers is indeed redissolved in the deep ocean - the organic matter through rapid decay via the action of bacteria and the shell material by the corrosive effects of the immense pressures exerted in the deeper layers. This process means only 0.1 per cent of the organic carbon which leaves the surface layers is permanently removed. The nutrients released in this way are recirculated to the surface by ocean currents.

The cycle of surface removal, deep ocean regeneration and circulation back to the surface distributes a wide range of elements in the ocean including biologically essential elements (such as carbon, phosphorus, zinc, copper, selenium, iodine), elements taken up by shell formation (calcium, strontium, silicon) and elements taken up by the growing phytoplankton because their chemistry is similar to that of essential elements (arsenic, cadmium, germanium). In addition the particles falling down from the ocean surface can remove trace metals from the ocean by geochemical scavenging reactions at the particle surface. Toxic elements such as beryllium and lead are removed in this way as are essential nutrient elements such as iron and manganese. All together, the biologically driven particle cycle dominates the distribution of more than three quarters of the elements dissolved in sea water.[14]

A further subtle link exists since phytoplankton growing in the open ocean also release a gas called dimethyl sulphide which is transformed into strong acids (sulphuric and methyl sulphuric acid) in the atmosphere. These acids provide cloud condensation nuclei and control the size of the cloud droplets and hence influence the clouds' ability to reflect the sun's radiation. This in turn influences the cooling effect of clouds on the earth's atmosphere and provides another biologically driven mechanism that affects the earth's climate.

The cycles of many elements are interlinked by their involvement in the biologically driven particulate cycle. Phosphorus is one such element. It is the nutrient whose availability controls plant growth. When particles containing phosphorus fall into the deep ocean, bacteria use oxygen to break down the organic matter and thereby release the phosphorus. When the input of phosphorus from the land to the ocean is increased the productivity in the surface layers rises and more particles fall into the seabed. This depletes the oxygen levels in the deep. As the oxygen levels fall the breakdown of particles become less efficient so that more phosphorus is absorbed by the sediments. Consequently the recirculation of phosphorus to the surface layers becomes progressively less. The feedback provided by the linking of the elemental cycles provides an active control mechanism.

Numerous other examples can be described but two more will suffice to make the point that there is feedback, involving living matter, within the oceans. The first example concerns the availability of tracemetals for phytoplankton growth. Careful research over the past decade has shown that the availability of such trace metals to phytoplankton can be strongly influenced by the presence of organic compounds in the water which react with the metals in solution. These organic compounds are in turn produced by biological processes. We therefore have a system which can be fine-tuned to regulate productivity by feedback since phytoplankton growth is controlled by trace metal availability which, in turn, is controlled by phytoplankton growth.

The second example concerns clearness of the water of the oceans. Continued photosynthesis depends on the transparency of sea water. Much of the organic matter produced in the oceans is designed to trap light and many of the condensation products produced after the death of the plankton give a yellowish tinge to the water. If such material were to accumulate in the oceans, the progressive deepening of the water colour would gradually reduce the useful depth for photosynthesis and hence restrict productivity. In fact a very complex but very effective pattern of light induced chemistry has evolved to remove such material and, incidentally, to release nutrient metals such as iron and manganese which are normally in short supply.

The question that arises is whether the biologically-controlled feedback systems are sufficiently powerful to control the environment. For if so, the pollution of the oceans would be handled by Gaian feedback and its self-regulating mechanism. In the past there have been major changes in the earth's climate associated with shifts in atmospheric carbon dioxide levels. The rapid changes in atmospheric composition involved argue strongly for the presence of effective positive and negative feedback mechanisms in the natural control systems. To some extent it is clear that these mechanisms are Gaian, that is, controlled by living organisms.

The connection between life and matter is very complex. In such a situation, it becomes necessary to be extremely cautious in discharging wastes into the oceans. Till more is known about the oceans, its resilience and carrying capacity it is not sustainable "development" that has to be thought of, and how to optimise it, but how to remain well behind the point where the oceanic system flips from its present state to another unknown, and undesirable, one. As pointed out by Whitfield:

> For instance, in the Baltic, aneoxic bacteria are doing very well and so far as production is concerned the overall changes may not be very great. But if

> you are worried about the availability, of fish or if you are worried about our requirements from the sea, then the effects have been catastrophic.[15]

The Gaian thesis would fit in very well with the Eastern perspective. It would bring out the fact that God's creation is not capable of being controlled, manipulated or managed since there are factors in it which man cannot possibly understand, and that the only way of dealing with Nature would be to fit into it and be harmonised with it.

In the context of sustainability of the oceans it would sem that the Eastern paradigm would be more suitable at present. The Western paradigm would become relevant only when enough data and information is available on the interlinkages between life and matter - whether internally in the oceans or externally with the atmosphere and the land.

Ocean: Economics and Wealth

Another important facet of the oceans is its value to humankind: in other words its wealth.

Ocean wealth and economics can be considered in the rubric of man-made, natural, human and social wealth, and economic values as values-in-use, values-in-exchange, values-in-threat and values-in-existence.

It is quite clear that by far the preponderant wealth of the oceans is its natural wealth and values-in-existence: its regulation of climate, its value as a Gaian self-regulating mechanism, the great biodiversity of marine life, and its future potential as a source of energy, space, minerals and protein.

No attempt has been made to quantify this, and perhaps no such effort can succeed. Attempts have, however, been made to look at values-in-exchange and man-made wealth as these are the only ones for which some data is available. But it needs to be noted that even this data is fragmentary for it only looks at ocean activities defined very narrowly and in a reductionist paradigm. For example, it looks at ocean transport but not at its essential systemic components: ports, harbours and the whole multi-modal transport system.

Weber and Gradwohl who have looked into ocean wealth have this to say:

> If economics is foreign territory for most people, the economics of marine and coastal resources is an even rarer venture. Not only is economics popularly considered a gloomy undertaking, but the economics of things marine is murky to boot. Conservationists are reluctant to throw in with analysts who see the world in terms of fungible assets, and economists are unsure of values such as biological diversity and beauty that are poorly represented in the marketplace.[16]

But the problem is much wider than that of getting economists and ecologists to understand and appreciate each other's points of view. The oceans are a planetary, global system but data from which to collate possible maritime wealth is available only on a national basis. Besides, the data is based on traditional economic thought: it is reductionist and based on categories having only limited relevance in today's world. It is also collected in a manner which enables only Gross National Product (GNP) to be measured, in other words it only measures values-in-exchange.

GNP, as many scholars have noted, has limited relevance. In a recent study, the World Bank has divided productive stock into: produced assets (machines, buildings infrastructure); human capital (education, knowledge and health); natural capital (soils, forests, water, minerals); and social capital (institutional and cultural bases of society).[17]

	Developed countries	*Developing countries*
Produced assets	16%	16%
Natural capital*	17%	32%
Human capital	67%	52%

* Most likely underestimated.

The World Bank study, which was not able to measure social capital, revealed the following picture.

Gross national product (GNP) by which economic growth is usually measured thus accounts for only 16% of a nation's capital stock.

Several years ago, James Broadus and his colleagues at the Woods Hole Oceanographic Institution analyzed available information on worldwide and U.S. economic activity in the marine area from 1978 through 1987 to establish "GNP" of the oceans. The Woods Hole group focused on expenditures associated with the four principle ocean-dependent activities: naval affairs, marine transportation, offshore oil and gas production, and commercial fishing. Taken together, the contribution of these activities to the world economy was estimated to be about 4 per cent.[18]

The above, even if we exclude activities not covered by Woods Hole, like marine-based tourism, hard minerals etc., only accounts for a small portion of oceanic wealth (16 percent if we extend the World Bank figures *pari passu* to the maritime field). It is quite obvious that in terms of natural resources, the oceans represent a far greater percentage of global wealth: it has 99 per cent of global water, a resource that from all accounts is, sooner rather than later, going to be in short supply; one-quarter to one-third of global oil supplies are estimated to be offshore; the ocean provides protein to about 2 billion people; it has the most productive ecosystems - coral reefs, mangroves, seagrass beds, wetlands. The oceans are also essential to life on earth: and that no amount of rational or economic calculation can account for.

In the Eastern and Gandhian paradigms the value of the oceans would not be a statistic: no figure can possibly evaluate the value of the provision of protein to 2 billion human beings. Besides the aesthetic and spiritual dimensions of the oceans cannot be covered only by the amounts spent on ocean-related tourism or the differential between property on the sea-front and elsewhere as routinely done by economists. For God's creation has to be rejoiced in and not subjected to an acountant's calculus.

Like science, which is searching for a new paradigm in understanding the oceans, there is need for a new economic paradigm to evaluate the wealth of the oceans. Some aspects of this new paradigm can be stated.

Firstly, the new ocean economics has to be concerned about *global* and *not national* measurements. It has to take note of the fact that in considering the oceans, it has not only to take note of activities that place on the oceans but also those that are *dependent* on the oceans. It has to go beyond the obvious - international trade, ports, fishing harbours, tourist resorts - to activities dependent on seawater either as an input or for waste disposal. The fact that more and more people (estimated from 60-70 per cent globally) are moving into the coastal zone shows how dependent 60-70 per cent of human activity is on the oceans.

Secondly, the new ocean economics has to concern itself with *potentials*. The oceans today have, potentially, over seventy per cent of global energy in the form of winds, currents, salinity gradients and an almost inexhaustible amount of resources: water, minerals, space. These resources only require humanity to acquire the knowledge and skills to sustainably utilise them.

Thirdly, the new ocean economics has to include "*deducted value*", as suggested by Giarini, into its calculations when dealing with destruction of ocean resources, whether by pollution or other use. Such a method would also link monetarised and non-monetarised activities.[19] Only through this method can the life-sustaining ocean be maintained at levels which are compatible with sustainability.

Fourthly, ocean economics needs to concern itself with *human capital*. This needs the placing of stress on human resources development, on the establishment of institutions for marine science and technology at national and regional levels (especially in the developing countries), on raising awareness of policy makers and others regarding the crucial importance to the oceans of the marine sector, and so on.

And, lastly, it needs to integrate all the above factors in a holistic, systems-analytic framework where the global interlinkages between the potential wealth of the oceans, the impact of pollution, utilization value (including "deducted value") and human resources in a global framework are made explicit.

Conclusion

The oceans as an ecosystem pose a problem to both science and economics. Their sustainability cannot be defined in pure scientific and/or economic terms. There is need to introduce value into the sustainability matrix, what the Brundtland Commission called the global "ethic". It is in this connection that the cultural values of the three Eastern religions could play a part - by modulating the dominant scientific - economic Western view thereby also taking it closer to the tenets of modern science.

There is, however, a point to be made here. The use of diverse cultural worldviews, while helping to achieve consensus at the cultural and/or societal levels, could make achieving a similar consensus at supranational (i.e., regional and international) levels that much more difficult. However if we go to deep-level spiritual values rather than the relatively superficial societal and/or cultural ones, the problem is not likely to be that acute. In fact, our study of three religions - Buddhism, Hinduism and Islam - suggest that the similarities between them are much more fundamental than their differences. As we shall see later, the tenets of Christianity, too, are complementary to the three Eastern religions. Spiritual ideals, based on an inter-religious discourse, therefore could be the catalyst that would actualise sustainable development of the oceans on a global basis.

References

1. E.M. Borgese, *The Future of the Oceans* (Montreal: Harvest House, 1986) p. 6.
2. Quoted in J.E. Lovelock, *The Ages of Gaia* (Oxford University Press, 1989) p. 84
3. Peter S. Thacher and N. Meith-Avcin, "The Oceans: Health and Prognosis", *Ocean Yearbook 1*, Borgese and Ginsburg eds., (Chicago University Press, 1978) p. 293.
4. K.E. Boulding, *Beyond Economics* (Ann Arbor: University of Michigan, 1968) p. 83.
5. E. Laszlo, *Systems Science and World Order* (New York: Pergamon, 1983) pp. 143-144.
6. See, for example, N. Myers, "Environmental Unknowns", *Science* 269 (1995): 358-60.
7. R.J. Bennett and R.J. Chorley, *Environment Systems* (London: Methuen, 1978) pp. 70-93.
8. Rajni Kothari, "Environment, Technology and Ethics" *Ethics of Environment and Development* (London: Belhoven Press, 1990), p. 27.
9. *Thus Spake Zarathustra*, compiled by B.S. Surti (Madras: Ramakrishna Math, 1993) pp. 20-21.
10. *Atharva Veda*, translated by W.D. Whitney, verse 12.1.35 (Delhi: Motilal Banarsidas, 1996).
11. Swami Suddhasatwananda, *Thus Spake the Buddha* (Madras: Ramakrishna Math, 1995) pp.39-41.
12. J.E. Lovelock, *Gaia: A New Look at Life on Earth* (New York: Oxford University Press, 1979) p.11.
13. Michael Whitfield, "Mechanisms or Machinations - Is the Ocean Self Regulating?" *Gaia, The Thesis, the Mechanisms and the Implications*, Peter Bunyard and Edward Goldsmith (eds.) (Cornwall U.K.: Quintell and Company, 1988) p.79.
14. Whitfield, ibid., pp. 82-83.
15. Ibid., p.88.

16. Michael Weber and Judith Gradwohl, *The Wealth of Oceans* (New York: W.W. Norton, 1995) p.96.
17. World Bank, *Monitoring Environment Progress* (Washington: The World Bank, 1995).
18. Weber and Gradwohl, note 13, p. 98.
19. Orio Giarini, *Dialogue on Wealth and Welfare* (Oxford: Pergamon, 1980) pp. 121 - 126.

9

Concluding Remarks

There is a general global consensus regarding poverty being at the root of deforestation, land degradation, and the destruction of coastal habitats. Hundreds of millions of the poor are forced to over-use their natural habitats in order to survive. The need to eradicate poverty is accepted globally: the question is how.

The dominant paradigm sees it in economic growth which would ultimately lead, through the "trickle down" effect, to the eradication of poverty. Others see it in a more caring, and spiritual, value system in which development would include patterns of production and distribution in the economic calculus.

In our view the two views are quite capable of being harmonised. This would have to be done through the mediation of modern science. In this concept, science has not to be pictured as driven by its own internal logic, developing according to its own laws in splendid isolation from the world around it. Many scientific hypotheses, theories, metaphors, and models (not to mention the choices made by scientists either to study or to ignore various problems) are shaped by economic, cultural, and political forces operating outside the laboratory. Lynn White also includes religion as one of the forces shaping science and argues that 'every culture, whether it is overtly religious or not, is shaped by its religion', and specifically that 'not only modern technology but also the unhesitatingly exploitative approach to nature that has characterised our culture are largely reflectious of value structures emerging from the matrix of Latin Christianity'.[1]

This is not to suggest too neat a parallel between the nature of society and culture and the reigning scientific world view or paradigm. But science is not an "independent variable." It is an open system embedded in society and linked to it by very dense feedback loops. It is powerfully influenced by its external environment, and, in a general way, its development is shaped by cultural receptivity to its dominant ideas.

For example, consider the body of ideas that came together in the seventeenth and eighteenth centuries under the heading of "classical science" or "Newtonianism." They pictured a world in which every event was determined by initial conditions that were, at least in principle, determinable with precision. It was a world in which chance played no part, in which all the pieces came together like cogs in a cosmic clock-like mechanism.

The acceptance of this mechanistic view coincided with the rise of factory civilization and the introduction of machines on a large scale. The Age of the Machine enthusiastically embraced scientific theories that pictured the entire universe as a machine.

With the transition from an industrial society based on heavy inputs of energy, capital, and labour to a high-technology society in which information and innovation are the critical resources, it is not surprising that new scientific views of the world, based on the work of Prigogine and others, should appear.

In Prigoginian terms, all systems contain subsystems, which are continually "fluctuating." At times, a single fluctuation or a combination of them may become so powerful, as a result of positive feedback, that it shatters the pre-existing organization. At this revolutionary moment - Prigogine calls it a "singular moment" or a "bifurcation point" - it is inherently impossible to determine in advance which direction change will take: whether the system will disintegrate into "chaos" or leap to a new, more differentiated, higher level of "order" or organization, which he calls a "dissipative structure."[2]

The work of Prigogine, and many others, has led to the emergence of a theory of the dynamics of evolution whose central characteristic is not adaptation but creativity. Based on systems analysis and a multi-disciplinary approach it draws upon contributions from chemistry (Prigogine and Eigen), biology (Waddington and Weiss), anthropology (Bateson), and systems theory (Jantsch and Laszlo) to focus on the dynamics of self-transcendence. A comprehensive synthesis of the theory has been published by Jantsch, who regards evolution as an essential aspect of the dynamics of self-organisation. His book throws new light on biological, social, cultural, and cosmic evolution in terms of similar patterns of system dynamics, even though different mechanisms are involved. A basic complementarity is manifest throughout his theory, examples being the interplay between adaptation and creation, the simultaneous operation of chance and necessity, and the interlocking of macro and micro-evolution.[3]

Another model of the self-regulating type that has developed in recent times is the Gaian model. Developments in space technology and space travel have profoundly modified humanity's ideas of itself and its place in the universal scheme of things. As we looked at the Earth from space and saw from the outside our azure-green planet in all its global beauty, a whole set of questions arose. One question which interested Lovelock was the interactions between the living and inorganic elements of Earth and how it made the Earth, unlike Mars and other planets, a fit place for life. Out of this interest has grown the Gaia hypothesis in "which the Earth's living matter, air, oceans and land surface form a complex system which can be seen as a single organism and which has the capacity to keep our planet a fit place for life."[4]

We have seen how the interaction of recent developments in scientific thought with economics have impacted on the latter in various ways: made it more holistic and dynamic; introduced nonlinearity into economic models; made economics a subsystem of the overall system by including non-economic forces in the models; made it an evolving and adaptive system; and so on.

The global economy was also seen to be an *adaptive nonlinear network* (ANN). ANNs provide for a substantial extension of traditional economics. The building blocks of traditional economics are fixed rational agents that operate in a linear, static, statistically predictable environment. In contrast ANNs allow for intensive nonlinear interactions among large numbers of agents. These interactions are characterised by limited rationality, adaptation (learning), and increasing returns.

The mathematical tools used in linear models prove inadequate to understanding ANNs. Deeper understanding requires a mathematics that puts more emphasis on combinatorics coordinated with computer modeling. In particular, the understanding of ANNs require mathematical and modeling techniques that emphasise the emergence of structure through the combination and interaction of various units.

We have noted how ANNs are akin to the Buddhist system. Other aspects of the three religions, Buddhism, Hinduism and Islam, are also compatible with the views of modern science. The emphasis on the essential unity of creation echoes the Gaia thesis. The stress on considering human beings and society as one indivisible whole is in line with the stress on considering everything in an ecosystem as interrelated. The placing of living beings at the centre also has its parallels in post-modern thought which is in favour of harmonising science and spirituality.

The views articulated by the religions studied have similarities with Christian thought. Long before the publication of the report of the Brundtland Commission, Barbara Ward and her colleagues had begun warning of the catastrophic consequences of the extant philosophical, theological, and technological perspectives on nature. They saw nothing short of a collapse of the planet in the face of the continuing battering to which humankind was subjecting it. Barbara Ward, in particular, challenged her fellow Christians to re-examine their theologies and practices in the light of global environmental degradation and literally to reread their scriptures with fresh eyes:

> When we confront the ethical and the natural context of our daily living, are we not brought back to what is absolutely basic in our religious faith? On the one hand, we are faced with the stewardship of this beautiful, subtle, incredibly delicate, and fragile planet. On the other, we confront the destiny of our fellow man, our brothers. How can we say that we are followers of Christ if this dual responsibility does not seem to us the essence and heart of our religion?[5]

Barbara Ward was trying to move Christian thought to an ecological basis and away from the domination of nature started by Francis Bacon with his statement,

> 'I am come in very truth leading you to Nature with all her children to bind her to your service and make her your slave.'[6]

Bacon's statement epitomizes an attitude and a set of assumptions that became the common stock in trade of the Western scientific and industrial culture. Those who required scriptural support for those assumptions thought they found it conveniently and succinctly expressed in the Bible in the statement: 'Be fruitful and multiply, and fill the earth and subdue it; and have dominion over the fish of the sea and over the birds of the air and over every living thing that moves upon the face of the earth.'[7] That certainly sounded like a charter for imperialistic human behaviour - a divinely granted mandate for humanity to do as it pleased with nature. Furthermore, a previous biblical verse had said that we were made in the image of God.[8] Did this not mean that our, admittedly finite, sovereignty over nature on this planet mirrored God's transcendent sovereignty over the cosmos?

The earlier belief of humanity's sovereignty and domination over nature is being challenged by thelogians today. This is due to the ecological crisis brought about by the scientific and technological civilization, and by the exhaustion of nature through the actions of human beings. The feeling is that unless there is radical reversal in the fundamental orientation of human society, and unless an alternative way of living and dealing with other living things and with nature, is found, the result would be disastrous. According to Moltmann, this crisis is going to end in a wholesale catastrophe:

> The ecological crisis of the modern world has its starting point in the modern industrial countries. These grew up in the midst of civilizations which had been shaped by Christianity. We cannot ignore the historical effects of the Christian belief in creation. Those effects throw a light of their own on the belief itself, and today require us to criticize the developments which we know have gone wrong and to interpret belief in creation in a new way, in the light of its true beginnings.[9]

Under the threat of ecological catastrophe, Christian theology is rediscovering the Holy Spirit. The third Person of the Trinity, the Giver of gifts, is not only responsible for the creative genius of humankind, but is also the Spirit of the universe. He interpenetrates the creation. It is his abode, the place of his indwelling. This point is well articulated by Moltmann:

> Through the powers and potentialities of the Spirit, the Creator indwells the creatures he has made, animates them, holds them in life, leads them into the future of his Kingdom. In this sense the history of creation is the history of the efficacy of the divine Spirit. So even when we consider the original biblical traditions, it is one-sided to view creation only as the work of 'God's hands' and, as his 'work', something that has simply and solely to be distinguished from God himself. Creation is also the differentiated presence of God the Spirit, the presence of the One *in* the many.[10]

Indeed, in Moltmann's reconception, the Holy Spirit is the power that not only sustains the creation but has propelled the evolutionary process through the billions of years it has taken to move our planet from a molten star to the intricate ecosystem that now constitutes its being. From the time when the first amoeba-like animal moved about the waters until the time when humankind eventually emerged, it was the Holy Spirit that directed the process. God, in short, is immanent as well as transcendent.[11]

The Bible grew up in the Semitic world of the Middle East which is very different from the world of ancient India. Its mythology, at least on the surface, differs from the Hindu (and Buddhist) though, as we shall see, it reaches very similar conclusions. The Bible is often described as the word of God, but it is the word of God expressed through the words of men with the inevitable limitation of all human words. Only by faith, that is by an intuitive understanding, which goes beyond the letter to the spirit, which enables us to share in the experience of the prophets and sages, can we learn something of that truth, of that reality, to which they sought to bear witness.

Bede Griffiths regards the Bible as a work of supreme imagination. There is history and morality, and some philosophy and theology in the Bible, but essentially it is a work of imaginative genius in the deep sense of being an insight into ultimate reality, or as Blake put it in more poetic language 'the divine body of the Lord Jesus, who is blessed forever'. Being a work of imaginative genius, we have to approach the biblical revelation as a mythology.[12]

The myth of the Garden of Eden starts, after 'man's body has been created from the dust of the earth and God has breathed into it the breath of life',[13] with the words, The Lord God planted a garden in Eden, to the east.[14]

To Bede Griffiths the myth of the Garden of Eden is one of the most significant in the Bible.[15] It has all the elements of an archetypal myth, the garden and the tree, the serpent, the man and the woman. The significance of this myth is inexhaustible, but he suggests some of its meaning for man today. There is first of all the garden, symbol of the original harmony of man's environment. Man was originally a child of nature. He was formed 'of the dust of the ground', the same ground from which 'the Lord God made to grow every tree that is pleasant to the sight and good for food.'[16] Man is thus part of this world of nature and has an intrinsic bond with it.

Man was allowed to eat of all the fruits of the trees in the garden, but of the fruit of the tree of knowledge of good and evil, he could not eat. The tree of knowledge of good and evil is the tree of wisdom, and it stands close to the tree of life, which is the tree of immortality. Wisdom and immortality were the two gifts offered by God to man, but they had to be received as a gift; the moment man sought to *seize* them for himself, he was doomed to die. This is the drama of human existence. Man has a body formed from the 'dust of the ground' and a soul which he received from God. 'The Lord God breathed into his nostrils the breath of life; and man became a living person.'[17] The soul of man is a 'breath' or 'spirit' from God. By it man is raised above the animal world and is able to partake of the Spirit of God. But he has to receive this spirit, this life, as a gift. It is not under his control. The other faculties of the soul, the senses, the feelings, the imagination are under his control and he can eat of their fruit, but the Spirit is from God and he cannot appropriate it to himself.

The symbolism of the garden reappears in the New Testament stories of the crucifixion and the resurrection. The last hours that Jesus spends in prayer before going to his trial are spent in a garden - Gethsemane. The crucifixion stands in stark contrast to that lovely garden. A dead man on a dead tree symbolizes, in the most shocking and ultimate way, the effect of evil on God, on humankind, and on nature. But we return to a garden on the morning of the resurrection. This is one of the most overlooked but genuinely revealing symbols in the New Testament. And according to the Gospel of John, when Mary Magdalene sees the risen Lord, she instantly assumes that he is the gardener. On a superficial level, Mary made a mistake; but on a deeper level, she had a profound recognition of the nature of him who once said: 'Consider the lilies of the field, how they grow; they toil not, but neither do they spin; but Solomon in all his glory was not arrayed like one of these'.[18]

As they come to a more profound understanding of creation and of the place of human beings in it, Christians are beginning to feel empowered to approach the ecological crisis with theologies and methodologies relevant to the task in hand. But they have also learned that they must cooperate with the people of other religions to save the planet. Many Christians are willing to acknowledge the debt they owe to other religions in helping them to rediscover a genuinely biblical doctrine of creation and the significance of the prophets. They have lived by rather inadequate interpretations of both for some centuries now.[19]

There is also the stress on equitable distribution in the Bible. In the parable of the last judgement, Christ praises those who fed him when he was hungry, gave him water when he was thirsty, invited him to their homes as a guest, clothed him when he was naked, and visited him when he was sick and in prison. In answer to their question as to when they had fed, clothed him etc., Christ gave the deeply moving and morally uplifting reply that "you did it for me when you did it for your brothers".[20] Here we have the clearest indication of the importance that Christ laid on tackling poverty and helping our more unfortunate brethren in all ways if we want to be exalted in Heaven.

The need for distributing wealth and giving to the poor and needy is stressed in the New Testament a number of times - Christ's advice to the young man who kept all the commandments that this was not enough but that he should distribute his riches to the poor if he wanted to be perfect and become a follower of Christ;[21] the commandment not to store up treasures on earth but to store them in heaven (by serving God);[22] the story of the rich man and Lazarus, of how the rich man went to hell because he didn't look after Lazarus - all these point to the stress Christianity places on distribution of wealth.

The conclusions of Christian thought, as being interpreted today, are very much in line with the Eastern paradigm developed earlier: the stress on unity of all life and nature; there being no absolute right to property but only to its unsufruct as the trustee, vice-regent or steward; there being no hoarding of wealth but distributing it to the least privileged members of society; recognising the right of eveyone to a full life of self-fulfillment and happiness.

To adequately tackle the present ecological crisis, a radical change of outlook, approach and behaviour is imperative. Only by a comprehensive assessment of the ensemble of human needs and demands over a long-period - well beyond our generation - will it be possible to ensure the intelligent combination, use and conservation of whatever resources are available. It is manifestly evident that, without proper management of resources globally, the needs of an ever more demanding multi-billion society can never be satisfied.

The natural environment has to be understood in the context of the cultural and religious environment. The processes which intervene destructively in the natural environment originate in the economic and the social system. So if the destruction of nature is to be halted, the norms driving the economic and social forces of society must be changed - norms which derive from its religio-cultural traditions. These traditions have emerged from the interplay between the meaning of life as the society see it, and the social and economic form of that life. Over a long period of history, systems of value and meaning have become very deeply rooted in the societal subconscious. There are differences between West and East in this regard. Modern science can form a bridge between the "spiritual" East and the "material" West. An inter-religious dialogue between East and West, and the integrating into it of modern science, could led to a truly global ethic of sustainable development. The integration of science with spirituality, of materialism with morality, are the necessary preconditions if the oceans and other planetary ecosystems are to be sustainably managed and life on Earth preserved.

References

1. Lynn White, Jr., "Continuing the Conversation" *Western Man and Environmental Ethics*, Ian Barbour (ed.) (Reading, Mass.: Addison-Wesley, 1973) p.60.

2. Ilya Prigogine and G. Nicolis, *Self-Organisation in Non-Equilibrium Systems: From Dissipative Structures to Order through Fluctuations* (New York: Wiley Interscience, 1977).
3. Eric Jantsch, *The Self-Organising Universe* (New York: Pergamon, 1980).
4. J.E. Lovelock, *Gaia: A new look at life on Earth* (Oxford University Press, 1979) p.1.
5. Barbara Ward, "Justice in a Human Environment", *IDOC International / North American Edition 53* (1973) p. 36.
6. Quoted in William Leiss, *The Domination of Nature* (New York: Braziller, 1972) p.55.
7. Genesis, 1:28.
8. Genesis, 1:26.
9. Jurgen Moltmann, *God in Creation* (London: Harper Row, 1985) p. 20.
10. *Ibid.*, p. 14.
11. In this sense the Christian conceptual framework moves closer to the Buddhist and Hindu conceptions where the One is said to be simultaneously both immanent and transcendent.
12. Bede Griffiths, *The Marriage of East and West* (London: Fount, Harper Collins, 1983) pp. 102-103.
13. Genesis, 2:7.
14. Genesis, 2:8.
15. Bede Griffiths, note 11, pp. 117-123.
16. Genesis, 2:9.
17. Genesis, 2:7.
18. Matthew, 6:28.
19. Robert J. Moore, "A new Christian reformation" *Ethics of Environment and Development*, J.R. Engel and J.G. Engel (eds.) (London: Belhaven, 1991) pp. 106-107.
20. Matthew, 26:31-40.
21. Matthew, 19:21, Mark 10:21.
22. Matthew, 6:19-21.

Bibliography

Ahmad, S.M., 1974, *Economics of Islam*, Lahore: S.M. Ashraf

Ali, A. Yusuf, 1938, *The Holy Quran*, Lahore: S.M. Ashraf.

Anderson, Philip W., Kenneth J. Arrow and David Pines (eds.), 1988, *The Economy as an Evolving Complex System*, Reading, Mass.: Addison-Wesley.

Anderson, Philip W., 1988, "A Physicist Looks at Economics: An Overview of the Workshop", Anderson et. al. eds., *Economy as an Evolving Complex System*, Reading, Mass.: Addison Wesley.

Anguttara Nikaya, Pali Text Society, London.

Arnold, Edwin, 1885, *The Light of Asia*, London: Trubner.

Arrow, Kenneth J., 1988, "Workshop on the Economy as an Evolving Complex System: Summary", Philip W. Anderson, K.J. Arrow and David Pines, eds., *Economy as an Evolving Complex System*, Reading, Mass.: Addison Wesley.

Atharva Veda, 1996, translated by W.D. Whitney, Delhi: Motilal Banarsidas.

Batchelor, Martine and Kerry Brown, (eds.), 1994, *Buddhism and Ecology*, New Delhi: Motilal Banarsidas.

Bell, Daniel and Irving Kristoff (eds.), 1981, *The Crisis in Economic Theory,* New York: Basic Books.

Bennett, R.J. and R.J. Chorley, 1978, *Environmental Systems*, London: Methuen.

Berry, A., 1974, *The Next Ten Thousand Years*, New York: Saturday Review Press.

Blackmore, Christine, 1989, *Taking Responsibility: Science and Technology*, London: Pluto Press.

Bondurant, J.V., 1965, *Conquest of Violence*, Berkeley: University of California Press.

Boon, Mieke and Joop Doorman, 1996, "Virtues and values of science", *The Transformation to a Sustainable Future*, Zeist: CLTM, Kerkebosch.

Borgese, E.M., 1986, *The Future of the Oceans*, Montreal: Harvest House.

Borgese, E.M., 1995, *Ocean Governance and the United Nations,* Halifax: Centre for Foreign Policy Studies, Dalhousie University.

Bose, N.K., 1948, *Selections from Gandhi*, Ahmedabad: Navjivan Printing Press.

Boulding, K.E., 1968, *Beyond Economics*, Ann Arbor: University of Michigan.

Bowonder, B. and T. Miyake, 1992, "A model of corporate innovation management: some recent high tech innovations in Japan", *R & D Management*, 22(4).

Buhler, G., 1886, *Laws of Manu*, reprinted 1982, Delhi: Motilal Banarsidas.

Capra, Frijof, 1976, *The Tao of Physics*, New York: Fontana Books.

Capra, Fritjof, 1982, *The Turning Point: Science, Society and the Rising Culture*, New York: Flamingo, Harper Collins.

Chander, J.P. (ed.), 1945, *Teachings of Mahatma Gandhi*, Lahore: The Indian Printing Works.

Cicin-Sain, Biliana, 1993, "Sustainable Development and Integrated Coastal Management," *Ocean and Coastal Management*, 21(1-3).

Cole, H.S.D., et.al., 1971, *Models of Doom: A Critique of the Limits to Growth*, New York: Universe Publishing.

Constanza, Robert, 1991, "The ecological economics of sustainability: Investing in natural capital", *Environmentally Sustainable Economic Development: Building on Brundtland,* UNESCO: 1991.

Coughanowr, C. and G. Kullenberg, 1993, "On the need for scientific input on an international scale", *Coastal and Ocean Management*, 21(1-3).

Couper, Alistair D., 1992, "History of Ocean Management," Paolo Fabri (ed.), *Management in Global Change*, London: Elsevier.

Dag Hammarskjold Foundation, 1975, "What Now: Another Development?" *Development Dialogues*, Nos. 1, 2.

Daly, H., 1977, *Steady-State Economics*, San Fransisco: W.H. Freeman.

Daly, H., 1987, "The economic growth debate", *Journal of Environmental Economic Management*.

Das, Amritananda, 1979, *Foundation of Gandhian Economics*, New York: St. Martins Press.

Dasgupta, Partha, 1990, "The Environment as a Commodity" *Oxford Review of Economic Policy*, Vol. 6, No. 1.

Denison, E.F., 1967, *Why Growth Rates Differ*, Washington D.C.: Brookings.

Desai, Mahadev, 1946, *The Gospel of Selfless Action or the Gita According to Gandhi*, Ahmedabad: Navjivan Press.

Despagnat, B., 1976, *Conceptual Foundations of Quantum Mechanics*, New York: Benjamin Inc.

Diwan, Romesh, 1985, "Economics of Love", Romesh Diwan and Mark Lutz (eds.), *Essays in Gandhian Economics*, New Delhi: Gandhi Peace Foundation.

Diwan, Romesh and Sushila Gidwani, 1985, "Elements in Gandhian Economics", Romesh Diwan and Mark Lutz (eds.), *Essays in Gandhian Economics*, New Delhi: Gandhi Peace Foundation.

Diwan, Romesh and Dennis Livingston, 1979, *Alternative Development Strategies and Appropriate Technology*, New York: Pergamon.

Diwan, Romesh and Mark Lutz, (eds.), 1985, *Essays in Gandhian Economics*, New Delhi: Gandhi Peace Foundation.

Dopfer, Kurt, 1976, "Towards a New Paradigm", Kurt Dopfer (ed.), *Economics in the Future*, London: Macmillan.

Dopfer, Kurt, 1990, "Introduction: Sik's Third Way of Economic Evolution," Dopfer and Raible (eds.), *The Evolution of Economic Systems*, London: Macmillan.

Drucker, Peter, 1981, *Toward the Next Economics and Other Essays*, London: Walter Heinemann.

Drucker, Peter, 1992, *Managing the Future*, London: Butterworth -Heinemann.

Ehrlich, P. and A. Ehrlich, 1972, *Population, Resources and Environment: Issues in Human Ecology*, San Fransisco: W.H. Freeman.

Fisher, Louis (ed.), 1962, *The Essential Gandhi*, New York: Vintage Books.

Forrester, J.W., 1971, *World Dynamics*, Cambridge, Mass.: Wright Allen Press.

Frawley, David, 1991, *Gods, Sages and Kings*, Delhi: Motilal Banarsidas.

Freeman, C., and J. Hagedoorn, 1992, "Convergence and divergence in the internationalisation of technology", *MERIT Conference*, 10-12 December, Maastricht.

Galbraith, J.K., 1956, *The Affluent Society*, Boston: Houghton - Mifflin.

Gandhi, M.K., 1958, *The Collected Works of Mahatma Gandhi*, Ahmedabad: Navjivan.

Gandhi, M.K., 1972, *Non-Violent Resistance (Satyagraha)*, 7th Edition, New York: Schocken Books.

Gandhi, M.K., 1966, *Socialism of My Conception*, Bombay: Bharatiya Vidya Bhawan.

Gandhi, M.K., 1947, *India of My Dreams*, edited by R.K. Prabhu, Bombay.

Giarini, Orio and Henri Louberge, 1978, *The Diminishing Returns of Technology*, New York: Pergamon.

Giarini, Orio, 1980, *Dialogue on Wealth and Welfare*, Oxford: Pergamon Press.

Giarini, Orio and Walter Stahel, 1989, *The Limits to Certainty*, New York: Pergamon Press.

Glasenapp, Helmuth von, 1977, *Buddhism: a non-theistic religion*, London: Allen Unwin.

Goulet, Denis, 1989, "Ethics in Development Theory and Practice", Sanders and Matsuoka, eds., *Peace and Development: An Interdisciplinary Perspectives*, University of Hawaii, School of Social Work.

Griffiths, Bede, 1983, *The Marriage of East and West*, London: Fount, Harper Collins.

Griffith, Bede, 1987, *River of Compassion: A Christian commentary on the Bhagavad Gita*, Warwick, New York: Amity House.

Handa, Madan, 1980, *Manifesto for a Peaceful World Order: A Gandhian Perspective*, New Delhi: Gandhi Bhavan.

Hayek, Friedrich A., 1978, *New Studies in Philosophy, Politics, Economics and the History of Ideas*, Chicago: University of Chicago Press.

Heaton, G., R. Repetto and R. Sobin, 1992, *Backs to the Future*, World Resources Institute.

Hodgson, G.M. and E. Screpanti (eds.), 1991, *Rethinking Economics: Markets, Technology and Economic Evolution*, Aldershot, Hampsire, U.K.: Edward Elgar.

Holland, J.H., "The Global Economy as an Adaptive Process", Philip W. Anderson, Kenneth J. Arrow, David Pines, eds., *The Economy as an Evolving Complex System*, Reading, Massachusetts: Addison Wesley.

Hook, Sidney (ed.), 1967, *Human Values and Economic Policy*, New York: New York University Press.

Humphreys, Christmas, 1969, *The Buddhist Way of Life*, London: Allen Unwin.

Huq, A.M., 1985, "Welfare Criteria in Gandhian Economics", *Essays on Gandhian Economics*, Diwan and Lutz (eds.), Delhi: Gandhi Peace Foundation.

Huq A.M., 1985, "The Doctrine of International Trade: A Gandhian Perspective, "*Essays in Gandhian Economics*, Diwan and Lutz (eds.), Delhi: Gandhi Peace Foundation.

Independent Commission on International Development Issues, 1980, *North-South: A Programme for Survival*, London: Pan.

IUCN/UNEP/WWF, 1991, *Caring for the World*, Switzerland: Gland.

Iyer, Raghavan, 1973, *The Moral and Political Thought of Mahatma Gandhi*, New York: Oxford University Press.

Jansen, Leo, 1996, "Towards a sustainable future enroute with technology", *The Transformation to a Sustainable Future*, Zeist: CLTM, Kerkebosch.

Jantsch, Erich, 1980, *The Self-Organising Universe*, New York: Pergamon.

Jevons, W.S., 1879, *The Theory of Political Economy*, 2nd. ed., London: Macmillan.

Jorgenson, D., 1990, "Investing in Productivity Growth" *National Academy of Engineering Symposium*, Washington D.C.

Joshi, Kireet, 1992, *The Veda and Indian Culture*, New Delhi: Motilal Banarsidas.

Kahn, H., et.al., 1976, *The Next Two Hundred Years*, New York: Morrow.

Kangle, R.P., 1992, *The Kautilya Arthashastra*, Vols. I-III, Delhi: Motilal Banarsidas.

Kapp, K.W., 1976, "The Open-System Character of the Economy and its implications", Kurt Dopfer, ed., *Economics in the Future*, London: Macmillan.

Katha Upanishad, trans: Swami Sarvananda, Madras: Ramakrishna Math, 1973.

Kenneth Arrow, Bert Bolin, Robert Constanza, Partha Dasgupta, Carl Folke, C.S. Holling, Bengt-Owe Jansson, Simon Levin, Karl-Goran Maler, Charles Perrings, David Pimentel, 1995, "Economic Growth, Carrying Capacity, and the Environment", *Science*, Vol. 268.

Khalid and O'Brien, eds., 1992, *Islam and Ecology*, London: Cassel.

Kluckhon, Clyde, 1962, *Culture and Behaviour*, New York: Free Press of Glenco.

Kothari, Rajni, 1990, "Environment, Technology and Ethics", J.R. Engel and J.G. Engel, eds., *Ethics of Environment and Development*, London: Belhoven Press.

Kullenberg, Gunnar and Augustine Ayala-Castanares, 1994 "Regional cooperation in marine sciences", Peter Payoyo (ed.), *Ocean Governance: Sustainable development of the seas*, Tokyo: United Nations University Press.

Laszlo, Ervin, 1983, *Systems Science and World Order*, New York: Pergamon.

Leiss, William, 1972, *The Domination of Nature*, New York: Braziller.

Lewis, C.S., 1978, *The Abolition of Man*, London: Fount Paperbacks.

Litterer, J.A., 1973, *The Analysis of Organisations*, 2d ed., New York: Wiley.

Lohia, R.M., 1963, *Marx, Gandhi and Socialism*, Hyderabad: Navahind Publications.

Lovelock, J.E., 1979, *Gaia: A new look at life on Earth*, New York: Oxford University Press.

Lutz, Mark, 1985, "Human Nature in Gandhian Economics", Romesh Diwan and Mark Lutz (eds.), *Essays in Gandhian Economics*, New Delhi: Gandhi Peace Foundation.

MacNeill, J., P. Winsmius and T. Yakushiji, 1991, *Beyond Interdependence*, London: Oxford University Press.

Macy, Joanna, 1985: *Dharma and Development*, West Hartford CT: Kumarian Press.

Madan, G.R., 1966, *Economic Thinking in India*, Bombay: S. Chand & Co.

Malpas, Robert and Simon Watson, 1992, "Technology and Wealth Creation", James Ball (ed.), *The Economics of Wealth Creation*, Aldershot, Hampshire, U.K.: Edward Elgar.

Marshal, Alfred and Mary Marshal, 1879, *The Economics of Industry*, London: Macmillan.

Marshal, Alfred, 1920, *The Principles of Economics*, 8th ed. London: Macmillan.

Maslow, Abraham, 1970, *Motivation and Personality*, New York: Harper and Row.

Maslow, Abraham, 1982, *The Further Reaches of Human Nature*, New York: Penguin Books.

Maududi, S.A., 1983, *Islamic Law and Constitution*, translator and editor Khurshid Ahmed, Lahore: Islamic Publications.

Mazumdar, H.T., 1952, *Mahatma Gandhi: Peaceful Revolutionary*, New York: Charles Scribner and Sons.

Meadows, D. et. al., 1972, *The Limits of Growth*, New York: Potomac Associates.

Moltmann, Jurgen, 1985, *God in Creation*, London: Harper Row.

Moore, Robert J., 1991, "A new Christian reformation", J.R. Engel and J.G. Engel (eds.), *Ethics of Environment and Development*, London: Belhaven.

Muhajir, A.M.R., 1974, *Islam in Practical Life*, Lahore: S.M. Ashraf.

Munn, R.E., 1990, "Towards Sustainable Development," *Proceedings of a Symposium on Managing Environmental Stress*, Australia: University of New South Wales.

Myers, N., 1995, "Environmental Unkowns", *Science* 269.

Naqvi, S.N.H., 1994, *Islam, Economics and Society*, New York: Kegan Paul.

Narayan, S. (ed.), 1988, *The Selected Works of Mahatma Gandhi*, Ahmedabad: Navjivan Publishing House.

Nasr, S.H., 1985, *Ideals and Realities of Islam*, London: Allen & Unwin.

Nelson, W.S., 1967, "The tradition of non-violence and its underlying forces", in G. Ramachandran et al., (eds.) *Gandhi: His Relevance for Our Times*, Berkeley: World Without War Council.

Paige, Glenn D., Chaiwat Satha-Anand and Sarah Gilliat (eds.), 1993, *Islam and Nonviolence*, Honolulu, University of Hawaii.

Pearce and Turner, 1980, *Economics of Natural Resources and the Environment*, New York: Harvester Wheatsheaf.

Peet, Gerard, 1992, "Ocean Management in Practice", Paolo Fabri, ed., *Management in Global Change*, London: Elsevier.

Peter Bunyard and Edward Goldsmith (eds.), 1988, *Gaia, the Thesis, the Mechanisms and the Implications*, Cornwall, U.K.: Quintell and Company.

Prabhavananda and Manchester, (eds.), 1957, *Upanishads*, New York: Mentor.

Prabhu, R.K. and V.R. Rao, 1967, *The Mind of Mahatma Gandhi*, Ahmedabad: Navjivan Publishing House.

Prigogine, Ilya and G. Nicolis, 1977, *Self-Organisation in Non-Equilibrium Systems: From Dissipative Structures to Order through Fluctuations*, New York: Wiley Interscience.

Prigogine, Ilya and Isabelle Stengers, 1984, *Order Out of Chaos*, 4th edition, New York: Bantam.

Prime, Ranchor, 1992, *Hinduism and Ecology*, London: Cassel.

Radhakrishan, S., 1948, *Bhagvadgita*, London: Allen and Unwin.

Radhakrishan, S., 1939, *Eastern Religions and Western Thought*, Delhi: Oxford University Press, reprinted 1991.

Ramachandran, G. and T.K. Mahadevan, 1967, *Gandhi-His Relevance to Our Times*, New Delhi: Gandhi Peace Foundation.

Ramesh Diwan, 1985, "Economics of Bread Labour", Romesh Diwan and Mark Lutz (eds.), *Essays in Gandhian Economics*, New Delhi: Gandhi Peace Foundation.

Rifkin, J., 1989, *Entropy: Into the Greenhouse World*, New York: Bantam.

Rifkin, Jeremy, 1995, *End of Work*, New York: Putnam Books.

Rig Veda, translated by R. Griffith, Delhi: Motilal Banarsidas reprinted 1976.

Rig Veda, 1994, translated by Wendy O'Flaherty, New York: Penguin.

Ritchie-Calder, 1978, "Perspectives on the sciences of the sea", *Ocean Yearbook 1*, Borgese and Ginsburg (eds.), Chicago University Press.

Rodinson, Maxine, 1974, *Islam and Capitalism*, tr. by Brian Pearce, London: Penguin.

Ruskin, John, 1866, *Unto This Last: Four Essays on the First Principles of Political Economy*, New York: John Wiley.

Sachs, Ignacy, 1992, "Transition Strategies for the 21st Century", *Nature and Resources*, 28(1), 1992.

Sachs, Ignacy, 1994, "The Environmental Challenge", *The Uncertain Quest: Science, Technology and Development*, Tokyo: United Nations University.

Saigal, Krishan, 1994, "Regional centres for marine science and technology," Peter Payoyo, ed., *Ocean Governance*, Tokyo: United Nations University.

Samyutta Nikaya, London: Pali Society.

Schumacher, E.F., 1973, *Small is Beautiful*, New York: Harper and Row.

Sen, Amartya, 1977 "Rational Fools: A Critique of the Behavioural Foundation of Economic Theory, "*Philosophy and Public Affairs*", Summer.

Sethi, J.D., 1978, *Gandhi Today*, Durham: North Carolina University Press.

Sethi, J.D., "Foreword", 1985, Romesh Diwan and Mark Lutz, eds., *Essays in Gandhian Economics*, New Delhi: Gandhi Peace Foundation.

Sethi, J.D., 1985, "Poverty, Alienation, and the Gandhian Way Out", Romesh Diwan and Mark Lutz (eds.), *Essays in Gandhian Economics*, New Delhi: Gandhi Peace Foundation.

Sharma, Arvind, 1986, *The Hindu Gita*, London: Gerald Duckworth.

Shriman Narayan, 1970, *Relevance of Gandhian Economics*, Ahmedabad: Navjivan.

Sivaraman, K. (ed.), 1995, *Hindu Spirituality*, Delhi: Motilal Banarsidas.

Skolimowski, Henryk, 1991, "Reverence for life", J.R. Engel and J.G. Engel, eds., *Ethics of Environment and Development*, London: Belhoven.

Snelling, John, 1990, *The Elements of Buddhism*, Shaftesbury, Dorset: Element Books Limited.

Solow, R.M., 1957, "Technical Change and the Aggregate Production Function," *Review of Economics and Statistics*, 39.

Speth, J.G., 1989, "Can the world be saved?" *Ecological Economics*, Vol. 1.

Sri Aurobindo, 1971, *The Secret of the Veda*, Pondicherry: Aurobindo Ashram.

Sri Aurobindo, 1986, *The Upanishads: Texts, Translations, and Commentaries*, Pondicherry: Sri Aurobindo Ashram.

Sri Aurobindo, 1989, *Essays on the Gita*, Pondicherry: Sri Aurobindo Ashram.

Starik, Mark and Gordon P. Rands, 1995, "Weaving an Integrated Web: Multilevel and Multisystem Perspectives of Ecologically Sustainable Organisations," *Academy of Management Review* 20, no. 4.

Sustainable Development, Science and Policy - The Conference Report, The Norwegian Research Council for Science and the Humanities, Oslo, August, 1990.

Swami Sarvananda, 1973, *Katha Upanishad*, Madras: Ramakrishna Math.

Swami Ranganathananda, 1971, *External Values for a Changing Society*, Bombay: Bharatiya Vidya Bhavan.

Swamy, N.V.C., 1996, "Values in Science and Technology", Swami Tyaganand (ed.), *Values*, Madras: Ramakrishna Math.

Tawney, R.H., 1921, *The Acquisitive Society*, New York: Harcourt Brace.

Tendulkar, D.G., 1960, *Mahatma: Life of Mohandas Karamchand Gandhi*, Delhi: Publications Division.

Teveodjre, Albert, 1978, *Poverty: Wealth of Mankind*, New York: Pergamon Press.

Thacher, Peter S. and N. Meith-Avcin, 1978, "The Oceans: Health and Prognosis", *Ocean Yearbook 1*, Chicago University Press.

The Commission on Global Governance, 1995, *Our Global Neighbourhood*, Oxford University Press.

The Dhammapada, 1987, translated by Juan Mascaro, London: Penguin.

Thorner, Daniel, 1955, "Long-Term Trends in Output in India", S. Kuznets ed., *Economic Growth: Brazil, India, Japan*, Durham N.C.: North Carolina Press.

Thus Spake Zarathustra, compiled by B.S. Surti, Madras: Ramakrishna Math.

UNCED, Agenda 21, paragraphs 34.1, 34.2 and 34.3 (*UNCED Doc. A/CONF.151/26 (Vol.III)*, 1992) p.49.

Underdahl, Arild, 1980, "Integrated Marine Policy," *Marine Policy*.

UNEP, 1992, *The World Environment 1972-92*, London: Chapman & Hall.

Vannucci, M., 1994, *Ecological Readings in the Veda*, Delhi: D.K. Printworld.

Varma, V.P., 1965, *The Political Philosophy of Mahatma Gandhi and Sarvodaya*, Agra: Lakshmi Narain Agrawal.

Vogel, Erza F., 1979, *Japan as Number 1*, Cambridge Mass.: Harvard University Press.

Ward, Barbara, 1973, "Justice in a Human Environment" *IDOC International/North American Edition 53*.

Weber, Michael and Judith Gradwohl, 1995, *The Wealth of Oceans*, New York: W.W. Norton.

Weisskopf, W.A., 1971, *Alienation and Economics*, New York: Dutton.

White, Lynn Jr., 1973, "Continuing the Conversation" Ian Barbour (ed.), *Western Man and Environmental Ethics*, Reading, Mass.: Addison-Wesley.

Whitfield, Michael, 1988, "Mechanisms or Machinations - Is the Ocean Self Regulating?" Peter Bunyard and Edward Goldsmith (eds.), *Gaia, The Thesis, the Mechanisms and the Implications*, Cornwall U.K.: Quintell and Company.

Woods, John, 1991, "New technology for ocean sciences", *The Second Mike Adye Memorial Lecture*, The Marine Technology Directorate Ltd., London.

World Commission on Environment and Development, 1987, *Our Common Future*, New York: Oxford University Press.

World Bank, 1995, *Monitoring Environment Progress*.

Yusuf, S.M., 1971, *Economic Justice in Islam*, London: S.M. Ashraf.

Zaehner, R.C., 1995, *Hindu Scriptures*, Delhi: Rupa & Co.

Index

A

Acquisitive societies (modern)
-nature, 230
Activities/trade that harm
society, 153
Adaptive Non-Linear Network
(ANN), 66
Features, 66-67, 274
Environment, 67
Affluence and poverty, 73
Agriculture and economic
growth, 69
Ahimsa, 208-209, 242
Air-Quran on, 185
Air-Sea interface, 253
Ancient man, 90
Anderson Philip, 64
Animal/Birds-Quran on, 185
Artha, 97, 109, 116-17, 124
Asian/eastern paradigm, 42
Atharva Veda on Oceans/
environment, 257
Attitudes, values, 38
Aurobindo, Sri on mine and
thine, 113-14
Austerity, 229
Authority exercising, 189-90

B

Bacon, Francis, 275
Bennett and Chorley on
environmental ecosystems,
252
Bentham's Concept and Gandhi,
210
Bhagavad Gita on the qualities
of each class, 106
Bibles, 278
Biology and development, 65
Brahmins, 100
Concept of, 104
Brandt, Willy, 27-28
Report, 29-30
Brundtland Commission, 11, 27,
29
Concepts of sustainable
developments, 11-12, 33
Report, 29
Definition of S.D., 32
Brundtland Report, 40, 58

Buddha, 131
  Doctrine, 131
Buddhist
  System, 131-32, 153
  Sects, 132
  Scriptures, 133
  Path, 164
  And sustainable Development, 144
  Society, 148
  Teachings, 155
    -misconception, 152, 162
  Tenets, 153
  Goal-achieving, 153
  Economics, 154
  Goal, 156
  And neo classical-differences, 155
Buddhist economy, 158-59
  Features, 158
  Critique, 161
Buddha
  On oceans, 257

C

Capital accumulation, 220
Carrying capacity, 54
Caste system-features, 106
Chakras, 102
Chaos theory, 59
Christian
  Theologies-reexamining, 275
  Approach to ecological crisis, 279
Classical science/system, 56-57
Classes (four) in Vedas, 99
Commercial Practices Islam, 198
Communitarian economy, 126
Competition, 163
Complementarity of capital, 32
Concept of Balance, Islam, 173-74
Confidence, 137
Consciousness, 93, 102
Constanza
  On sustainability, 31
  - Conditions, 32
On natural capital, 31
Contentment, 137, 147
Core set of values, 41
Cosmological view of time and space, 154
Covetousness-Islam, 198
Creative-myth of, 91
Creation process-factors, 92
Crisis in Economic Theory, 59
Cultural sustainability, 43
Cyclic view of time, 16

D

Daly's distinction between growth and development, 51
Danda, 119

Darkness-power of, 90
Death, 91
Debt
Rising of, 28
Interests, 28
Deep ocean regeneration, 260
Deforestation and Poverty, 271
De-industrialization of rich countries, 50
Delusion, 138-39
Denison on macro-economics system, 68
Desire, 138, 140
Development thinking, 33
Criteria, 34
Dhammapada, 137
Dharma, 96, 123-24
Meaning, 134
Aim of, 99
Karma and Rebirth, 133, 135
Artha, *kama*, 97, 109, 116
Dialogue on wealth and welfare, 79
Dissipative structure, 58
Distribution, 227
Divine law, 175-76
Diwan on *Swadeshi*, 232
Dopfer on neoclassical theory, 71
Drucker on economics, 67
Dukkha/*Sukkha*, 136
Durability of products, 36
Duty towards fellow beings, 149

E

Earning one's livelihood, 151
Eastern paradigm
Of sustainable development, 45
Value system, 45
Eastern perspective of oceans, 256, 258
Ecological
Crisis, 38, 276
- Tackling, 280
Integrity, 49
Sustainability, 43, 67-68, 144
Ecology and Quran, 179, 187
Ecosystem, 61
Management, 42
Economics, 43
Goal of, 123
And Biology, 64
And Gandhi, 215
Defining, 60
Economic
Abundance-Gandhi on, 212
Equality, 234
Liberalization and economic policies, 52
Development, 34
-dimensions, 42
Education
Aim, 108, 148
And economics, 148
In Buddhism, 160

Efficiency, 70
Effort, 143-44
Eightfold Path, 136, 141
Einstein, 57
Einsteinian-Heisenbergian
    -Prigoginian world, 55
Elasticity of production, 236
Entropy, 54, 74
Environmental
    Capacity, 70
    Crisis early, 1970, 49
    Economics, 53
    Issues, 25
Environmentally sound
    technologies, 36
Equality-Gandhi on, 236
Ethics, 75, 110
    Role of, 12, 45
    And morality, 122
Ethical Issues in Development-
    Seminar, 43
Euclidean points, 18
Exchange values/pricing, 69
Exploitation of resources,-Quran,
    183, 193
Externalities of production and
    economic growth, 52

F

Fish catch, 31
Four-fold scheme of classes, 104
Freedom
    Definition in Quran, 171,
        174-75
    Of individuals, 123
Frugality and prevention of
    waste, 147
Full employment-Gandhi on,
    233
Full-life paradigm, 44

G

Gaian
    Thesis 20-21
    Model, 58, 273
    Hypothesis, 59
    - on oceans, 258
Gandhi
    Views on poverty, 18
    Vews on man, 18
    And religion, 20
    And sustainable
        Development, 205
    Early life, 206
    Principles, 206
    And village industry, 207
    Cultures influencing, 207
Gandhian
    Principles (7), 216
    Model/relevance, 228
    Model-critique, 237
Gandhian socio-economics, 211
    Foundation, 214
    Parameters, 214
Garden of Eden myth, 278-79
Genetic algorithm-Buddhism,
    159

Generosity, 114-15
Giarini
On economic growth, 69
On values, 78
Globalization impact on society, 160
GNP-World Bank on, 264
Good/Bad distinguishing, 111
Griffiths, Bede, 278
Gro Brundtland, 27, 30, 40

H

Happiness, 110-11
Healing Process, 140
Hegemonies, 65
Hierarchy-Gandhi on, 236
High Standard of Living and Environment, 50
Hinayana Buddhism, 132
Hindu and Buddhist
Myths, 16
View of the universe, 17
Hinduism
And nature, 89
Study, 86
Hindu
Societal system, 94
Socio-economic system, 109, 117, 123
Economy, 121
Hoarding, 147, 201
Hodgson and Screpanti, 59
Holistic nature of sustainable development, 13, 46
Holland's Prof-adaptive
Non-linear network, 65
Holy words, 151
Householder, 108
Human
Welfare approach, 71, 125
Unity, 85
Life, 153
Species-Quran, 186
Authority-Quran, 189
Labour-Gandhi, 221

I

Ideal and reality-space between, 170
Ideal state, 161
Immanent One, 92
Income
Differentials, 235
Redistribution in Quran, 194
Inequalities, 234
Inner goal of life, 103
Integrity of eco-systems, 255
International Trade
Gandhi on, 239-40
Distinctive features, 240
Islamic
Concept/Philosophy, 168-69
Ethics, 169-70
Social classes, 195
Economics-principles, 199-200

System-parameters, 202

J

Jansen, 71
Jantsch, Eric, 74
Jati system, 106
Jorgenson, Dale
On productivity growth, 68
Joyous, 137
Justice in Islam, 197-98

K

Kama, 97-98, 124
Kapp on shift in agriculture, 69
Karma-law of, 134
Kautilya's *Arthashastra*, 101, 117
Kenneth Arrow, 62
Kothari, Rajnish
On ethical imperative, 44
Kothari's formulations, 13
Krishna on sacrifice, 125
Kshatriya, 100, 105

L

Labour, 102
Component, 18-19
Gandhi on, 221
Laplace's claim, 56
Laying off of workers, 156
Least cost solution, 52
Leisure, 72
Gandhi on, 221
Liberation-attainment, 95-96, 103
Liberty of individual, 123
Life stages, (4), 107
Linear cause-and effect relationships, 61
Localization of production, 19
London-problems, 25
Long distance transportation of materials, 34
Luxury and showing-off-Quran on, 194

M

Mahayana Buddhism, 133
Man and Psycho-ethical nature, 100
Man as trustee, 192
Mankind in Quran, 192
Mann on levying taxes, 119-20
Marine
sciences, 249
Economic activities, 265
Maslow's hierarchy of needs, 71
Material consumption, 155
Regulation, 121
And Gandhi, 212
Miserliness, 147
Moltmann's interpretation, 277
Moral plight/ideas, 14-15
Moral growth, 16

Morality
- Impacts on nature, 146
- Of Buddhists, 149

Myth, 90
- Meaning of, 15-16
- Hindu/Buddhist, 16
- Of creation, 91

N

Nachiketas
- Story of, 112

Nature
- Harmony with, 126
- And Buddhism, 145
- View of , 56

Natural Capital, 31
- Examples, 31
- Stock, 31

Natural Resources
- Use in Quran, 181-82

Needs and wants, 122, 139, 156

Neoclassical
- Value premise, 121
- Theory, 71, 157
- Economics, 73
- System, 121, 154
- And Gandhi, 222, 225
- Gandhian system-
  - Differences, 223

Newtonianism, 56

Newtonian model, 57, 272
- Of world, 16

New Economics, 55

New Ocean Economics, 266

New Testament
- On distributing wealth, 280

Nirvana, 137, 142, 148-49, 154, 161

Noble Truths (Four), 135

Non charging of interest, 201

Non-European Civilizations, 86

Non-homogenuity, 157

Non-linear nature, 61

Non-market valuation methods, 52

Non-possession, 230

Non-violence, 151, 214, 216-18, 229, 241
- Concept, 206

Non-western religious study, 15, 17

North-south perceptual confrontation, 38

O

Object of life (man's), 94, 108-109

Oceans, 20, 46, 247
- Wealth, 22, 23, 263, 266
- Poetic/spiritual dimension, 22
- Churning of, 23
- Values, 265

Ocean water
- Clearness, 262
- Pollution handling, 262

Oceanic ecosystem, 248
- Sustainable management of, 252, 263, 267

Important aspect, 253
Management, 256
One (the), 91
Ways to, 152
Optimizing values, 78
Order out of chaos, 57
Order of society, 94
Outer goals of life, 103
Oxygen level in ocean, 26

P

Panch Shila of Buddhism, 145
Paradigm shift in science, 13
Particulate cycle, 261
Pearson Commission, 26-27
Peaceful coexistence, 150
Per capita income and environmental quality, 49
Phosphorus levels in oceans, 261
Phytoplankton growth, 260-61
Planetary sciences-advances in, 248
Pleasure, 110-11
Pluralistics, 94
Political economy, 59
Pollution/pollutants, 250
Population increase, 180, 220
Positive feedback, 62
Post-war economic boom, 26
Environmental impact, 26
Poverty and alienation-Gandhi, 18
Deforestation, 271
Christon, 280
Poverty
Eradication, 74
Reasons, 77
Prigogine
Theories, 55, 57
Model, 272-73
Principle of trusteeship, 19
Privileges in Quran, 189
Production
In Gandhian system, 224
Structure, 236
Categories, 74, 77
System, 122, 156
And distribution differences in Neo classical and Gandhian system, 226
Productive stock
World Bank on, 264
Prohibitions in Islam, 198-99
Prosperity, 116
Protection, 119
Puranic story of Devas and Asuras churning the ocean, 23
Purusha, 93, 99
Purusharthas-types, 98
Purusha Sukta and the four classes, 99

Q

Quran's
Message, 16
View of time, 16

Quran, 167
On righteousness, 167
And scientific theories, 180

R

Radha Krishnan, 104
On four fold scheme, 104-105
Rationality, 77
Rational mind, 90
Relativity, 55
Religion and science, 271
Rememberance (right),144
Renunciation and Buddhism, 152
Renunciation of desire, 113
Resource economics, 51
Resource conservation through demand management, 34
Responsibility- Islamic concept, 176-77
Reversible/non-reversible processes, 56
Reward for deeds, 168
Riba, 199
Rig Veda, 92
Right and wrong/Righteousness, 141, 150
In Quran, 167
Right
Words, 143
Effort, 143
Living, 150
Vision, 154
Means of supporting ones life, 143

S

Sachs model, 43, 164
Of economic development, 242
Sacchidananda, 109
Sacrifice, 125
Sagara manthan, 22
Puranic story, 23
Sannyasin, 108
Sarvodaya, 210
Satyagraha, 208
Scale factor
Gandhian, 240
Scarcity, 76
Science
And value system, 41
Nature of, 272
Scientific world view, 55
Scriptures, 88
Self/selfishness, 114, 148
Self Control, 115, 121, 155, 230
Self
Of man, 140
Regulation, 117
Sacrifice-Gandhi, 210-11
Separate selves/world, 138
Service, 235
Sex, 108, 138
Shreyas / *Preyas*, 111

Shudra, 105
Social and economic systems
- rules of management, 61
Societal needs/aspirations, 35
Social
Choices, 61
Structures, 95
States-Buddhism, 161
Ideal of Islam, 175
Solow, Robert-on economic growth, 68
Sorrow (end of), 136
Sovereignity and Quran, 187
Space Technology
Development, 273
And Travel technology, 58
Spatial sustainability, 43
Spending-Islam, 201
Speth approach, 70
Spiritual
/Moral ideas, 12
Life, 97
Meaning of life, 146
Stages of life, 95
Stockholm UN
Conference on environment 1972, 26
Focus, 26
Submission to God, 172
Sukkha-Dukkha, 110
Sustainable development, 30
Dimensions, 46
Meaning, 30, 32, 37, 44-45
Models, 42
Elements inducing, 31
And Buddhism, 144
Systems analysis-use of, 14
Systems view, 13
Of economy, 70
Systems
Meaning, 251
Theory, 251
Swadeshi, 213
Concepts, 231, 235

T

Taittriya
Upanishad, 116
Technology
And sustainable development, 12
As harmonizing factor, 35-36
And economic growth, 67-69, 224
In Gandhi system, 225, 237
Techno-economic basis of sustainable development, 12
Theory of Model Building, 251
Timber, 31
Traditional sector and Gandhi, 219
Trayidharma, 119
Trivarga, 116
Trusteeship
Aspects, 19, 232-33

Gandhian Principles, 233
Truth, 150, 208, 214

U

UNCED-Brazil
Global work plan, 11
Unity in Quran, 171, 188, 197
Unity of God Concept, 187
Universe/world
View of classical western science, 16
Newtonian, 16
Hindu/Buddhist view, 17
Upsetting of nature's balance-Quran, 182
Up-to-date technologies, 36
Utility
Role in economics, 67
Of consumer, 77

V

Vaishyas, 101
Vajrayana, 133
Values,
Premise in Hinduism, 121
In economics, 158
System, 40, 75
Role of inhuman Activity, 12, 35
Meaning, 38-39
Divergent, 40
In economics, 75
In use and exchange, 76, 158
In threat, 77
Varna system, 106
Vedas, 89-90
Vice regent and trustee concept, 191
Village communities
Linking with international community, 238
Virtues of Buddhism (4), 142

W

Walter Weisskopf, 76
Ward, Barbara, 275
Waste, 147
Discharge, 249
Water-Quran on, 184
WCED (World Commission on Environment and Development), 27, 51
Report, 27
1987, 30
Wealth, 14
And material well being, 97, 155
Earning of, 115, 122, 124, 147
Sharing in Quran, 193, 195
Piling –Quran, 197
Of Oceans, 263-64
Distribution, 280
Weapons, 78
Web's effect on macro-economics, 65

Western paradigm, 13, 42
  Of oceanic system, 255
Woods Hole Oceanographic
  Institution
  On marine economics
    activities, 264
Work-notion of, 222, 234
Workshop held at Santa Fe, 62
World Bank
  Study, 265
  Assessment of productive
    stock, 162-63

Y

Yama to Nachiketa, 112
Yoga, 118
Yogic interpretation of Vedas,
  112

Z

Zend Avesta
  On nature and environment,
    256
Zero rate of growth, 50